Lead with a Story

A Guide to Crafting Business Narratives That Captivate, Convince, and Inspire

Paul Smith

AMACOM

American Management Association
New York • Atlanta • Brussels • Chicago • Mexico City • San Francisco
Shanghai • Tokyo • Toronto • Washington, D.C.

Bulk discounts available. For details visit:
www.amacombooks.org/go/specialsales
Or contact special sales:
Phone: 800-250-5308
E-mail: specialsls@amanet.org
View all the AMACOM titles at: www.amacombooks.org

This publication is designed to provide accurate and authoritative information in regard to the subject matter covered. It is sold with the understanding that the publisher is not engaged in rendering legal, accounting, or other professional service. If legal advice or other expert assistance is required, the services of a competent professional person should be sought.

The story "Special Olympics" in chapter 18 is from *The Imagineering Way* © 2003 by The Imagineers of Disney. Reprinted by Permission of Disney.Hyperion, an imprint of Disney Book Group LLC. All Rights Reserved.

Library of Congress Cataloging-in-Publication Data
Smith, Paul, 1967 July 3–
    Lead with a story : a guide to crafting business narratives that captivate, convince, and inspire / Paul Smith.
        p. cm.
    Includes index.
    ISBN 978-0-8144-2030-0 (hbk.)
        1. Communication in management. 2. Storytelling. 3. Leadership.
4. Organizational behavior. I. Title.
    HD30.3.S5774 2012
    658.4'5—dc23   2012005591

About AMA
American Management Association (www.amanet.org) is a world leader in talent development, advancing the skills of individuals to drive business success. Our mission is to support the goals of individuals and organizations through a complete range of products and services, including classroom and virtual seminars, webcasts, webinars, podcasts, conferences, corporate and government solutions, business books, and research. AMA's approach to improving performance combines experiential learning—learning through doing—with opportunities for ongoing professional growth at every step of one's career journey.

Dedicated to **David M. Armstrong (1957–2010)**
for starting this revolution.

Contents

v

Acknowledgments

FIRST AND FOREMOST, I'd like to thank the people whose names and stories grace the pages of this book. For some, it was your noble actions that inspired me to write a story. Others were generous enough to share your stories with me. Either way, I am grateful to over 100 of you for contributing to this effort.

For most, your names are already included elsewhere in the book, so I won't repeat them here. But I am just as humbled by those who contributed to these stories in some way without showing up as a character. You include Shaun Adamec, Kelly Anchrum, Amy Anthony, John Burchnall, Ann Calcara, David Casterline, Steve Cooper, Mary Lynn Ferguson-McHugh, Kim Fullerton, Tony Gardner, Kyle Garner, Dan Geeding, Chuck Gentes, Tom Glenn, Anand Jayaraman, Greg Kurkjian, Tim McKenna, Surya Menon, Prabhath Nanisetty, Lenora Polonsky, Ed Rider, George Sine, Lisa Smith, Shawn Spradling, Jim Stengel, and Mariela Vargas.

I am also indebted to the many authors on storytelling who came before me, most notably David M. Armstrong, Annette Simmons, Margaret Parkin, Evelyn Clark, Peg C. Neuhauser, Stephen Denning, Lori Silverman, Mary Wacker, Richard Maxwell, Robert Dickman, Craig Wortmann, Doug Stevenson, Doug Lipman, Jack Maguire, Ryan Mathews, Watts Wacker, T. Scott Gross, Michael B. Druxman, Robert Shook, Tom Sant, Grady Jim Robinson, and Peter Guber, among many others too numerous to mention. You blazed the trail I now follow. I've been influenced by each of you and hope I've contributed in some small way to what you started.

Special thanks to my editors, Christina Parisi and Erika Spelman, and my "secret agent," Maryann Karinch, for leading me through the publishing process. And a very special thanks to Chip Heath and Dan Heath for their invaluable support and advice along the way, and to Steve

vii

Blair for the many conversations that inspired me to begin this journey in the first place.

Lastly, I'd like to thank the brilliant and creative people at Procter & Gamble I've had the privilege of working with for the past 19 years. Thank you for putting up with my awkward stumbling toward an understanding and practice of leadership, one story at a time.

Introduction

"*Long before the first formal business was established . . . the six most powerful words in any language were* Let me tell you a story."[1]
—MATHEWS & WACKER, *What's Your Story*

WHEN JAYSON ZOLLER WAS A COLLEGE STUDENT, one of his favorite professors told the class a story so compelling Jayson is still retelling it two decades later. Apparently the professor's students from a previous class had an unusual project working for a local district judge. The assignment: Investigate the jury deliberation process and determine how to improve it. As young, idealistic college students, his young team was excited to tackle such a noble mission.

The students interviewed dozens of judges, attorneys, former jurors, and other court officials around the district. They asked all the questions you would think a smart group of would-be consultants should ask. How many men were in the jury versus women? What was the mix of ethnic backgrounds? How many older jurors were there versus younger ones? Were there differences in the instructions given the jurors, or what kind of information they were allowed to have in the jury room? Did the trials last days, weeks, or months? They even asked how late the jurors were made to work into the evening and what kind of food they were fed.

To their surprise, none of those things seemed to matter much. What did matter, it turned out, was the shape of the table in the jury room! In courtrooms where there was a rectangular table, the juror sitting at the head of the table (even if that person wasn't the jury foreman) tended to dominate the conversation. This kept some jurors from sharing their points of view as openly. But in jury rooms that had a round or oval table, the jurors tended to be more egalitarian and their debate of the facts was

1

more thorough and robust. The team concluded it was those juries with round tables that came to the most accurate and just verdicts.

The students were excited about this finding for two reasons. First, they felt like they had really nailed the key to improving the jury deliberation process. And second, it was such an easy thing to change. Imagine, instead, if their conclusion had been that the jury needed to be seated with more intelligent, open-minded, better-educated jurists. That's much harder to do.

They were proud of their success as they presented the results to the chief judge. He was just as excited as they were, and for exactly the same two reasons. The judge immediately issued a decree to all the courthouses in his jurisdiction. Effective immediately, "All jury rooms that have round and oval tables are to have the tables removed. Replace them with rectangular tables."

Read those last two sentences again. That wasn't a typo. In direct contradiction to their recommendation, the judge removed all the round and oval tables and put in rectangular tables. Why? Because the judge's objective in improving the jury deliberation process wasn't to make it more robust, fair, or even accurate. It was to make it faster. He wanted to reduce the backlog of cases clogging up his court docket.

The students were mortified. They thought they were single-handedly fixing the sometimes-brutal consequences of an imperfect judicial system. Instead, they were unwittingly responsible for making it, in their eyes, a little bit less perfect. They may have finished the year with an A on their report card, but they felt completely defeated.

Twenty years later, Jayson is now a professional market researcher. He tells this story to new researchers to teach them the importance of being clear on objectives before they embark on a research project. Instead, he could simply tell them, "Experience suggests it is very important to be clear on your objectives before you start your research project." But that wouldn't be nearly as effective, would it? By telling a story, Jayson lets his audience learn a lesson almost firsthand and experience what it would feel like to *not* be clear on objectives up front—and suffer the consequences.

Experience is the best teacher. A compelling story is a close second.

This account illustrates the power of storytelling in business. But until recently, storytelling was about as welcome in the workplace as a crayon doodle on a napkin. It was considered too imprecise and trite for professional dialogue. Not so anymore. Like the personal computer—once considered a toy and unworthy of a place on any serious leader's desk[2]—storytelling has come of age.

Today, many of the most successful organizations on the planet intentionally use storytelling as a key leadership tool: Microsoft, Nike, Motorola, 3M, Saatchi & Saatchi, Berkshire Hathaway, Eastman Kodak, Disney, Costco, Bristol-Myers Squibb, Southwest Airlines, FedEx, Procter & Gamble, Armstrong International, Mary Kay Cosmetics, Kimberly-Clark, The Container Store, REI, Northwestern Mutual, NASA, and The World Bank.[3]

Many of these companies have assigned a high-level "corporate storyteller" to capture and share their most important stories. At Nike, *all* the senior executives are designated "corporate storytellers."[4] Several companies actively teach storytelling skills to their leaders. Kimberly-Clark, for example, has held two-day seminars to teach its 13-step program for crafting a story and structuring presentations using them.[5] 3M banned bullet points years ago and replaced them with a process of writing "strategic narratives."[6] Procter & Gamble has hired Hollywood movie directors to teach its senior executives storytelling techniques. And some storytellers at Motorola participate in outside theater and improvisational groups to hone their story skills.[7]

Some forward-thinking business schools like at Notre Dame and DePaul University have even added storytelling courses to their management curriculum.[8]

So how did we get here? How did storytelling go from an office obscurity to a defining characteristic of leadership? The short answer is that it was simply returning to the natural order of things. The better question might be, "Why did it take a temporary hiatus to begin with?"

To answer that question, consider the role of storytelling before the printing press—a time noted by professional storyteller Jack Maguire when communication among people almost always went directly from mouth to ear. Back then, telling stories was a major means of conducting day-to-day business. After all, when human beings themselves are the medium, even work-related messages tend to be narrative in style and experiential in content.[9] Actually, for most of man's history on the earth, storytelling was a natural part of leadership.

Training coach and bestselling author Margaret Parkin points out that before the printed word, storytelling existed in every nation, each with its own traditions: The Celtic culture had its bards and Druids, the Norsemen of the Scandinavian countries told sagas, the Islamic countries listened to teaching from Sufi masters and dervishes, the people of Mongolia and Siberia were influenced by the tales and medicine of the shamans,[10] and the Ute tribes of Native Americans made their best storytellers their tribal leaders.[11]

Storytelling was popular because before writing was developed, the success of communication was measured largely by how much of it was remembered by the audience. They couldn't just go write it down. So a high value was placed on techniques that helped people remember things, like the rhythm of song, the rhyme of a poem, or the engagingness of a story.[12]

Eventually, after several millennia of success, storytelling in business began a gradual decline. The advent of writing, the printing press, and organized business practices made business communication far more technical in style and databased in content than it used to be.[13] Storytelling slowly gave way to formal reports, memos, and policy manuals. The professionalization of business in the early 1900s accelerated this trend. Business schools churned out thousands of bright, analytical management professionals trained to look at a business like a machine that needed to be finely tuned. Telling stories would have identified someone as old school—certainly not a member of the new avant-garde of business leaders.

That explains storytelling's originally lofty status, and its eventual fall from grace. But when did it start its comeback? According to professional storyteller Doug Lipman, that began in the 1960s and 1970s, when people around the world started to rediscover storytelling.[14] Then, in 1973, the movement gained national attention when the first National Storytelling festival was held in Tennessee.[15]

But it wasn't until the early 1990s that storytelling moved back into the realm of business in any serious way. This was fostered by three concurrent forces:

1. Several academic studies reported the effectiveness of storytelling in the workplace (like those by David M. Boje).[16]

2. A number of successful trade books explored the topic (the earliest being *Management by Storying Around*, by David Armstrong, and *Corporate Legends & Lore*, by Peg C. Neuhauser).

3. Leading storytelling practitioners emerged in the corporate world, such as Stephen Denning at The World Bank.

That's the short history. Over the last 20 years, and especially the last decade, storytelling has retaken its rightful place in management's bag of leadership and influencing tools.

What this book adds to the growing body of literature consists of two things. First, it extends the usefulness of storytelling to a much wider range of leadership challenges. Instead of only six or seven of the most common situations a leader faces, this book covers 21 of the toughest leadership challenges, with a handful of insightful and inspiring stories to help you navigate each with success. There are over 100 stories in total. A matrix in the appendix will help you locate exactly the right story at the right time.

Second, it offers more thorough and practical advice for how to craft your own stories for any leadership challenge. That starts with a simple structure for a good business story. But it also includes advice on six other key elements you'll need to turn that good story into a great one: metaphors, emotion, realism, surprise, style, and how to put your audience into your story.

There are two kinds of stories in this book. Some are ready-to-tell stories that can be retold, as they are written, by anyone when the situation calls for it. Others are intended as a springboard to provide inspiration for creating your own similar stories. Many can serve both purposes. All the stories, however, teach critical lessons in leadership worthy of learning. That can be beneficial for your own leadership skills, or for teaching others how to be better leaders.

In addition to learning from them, I hope you enjoy the stories. Some will make you laugh, some might make you cry, most will make you think. More important, I hope this book makes you *do* something—start crafting, collecting, and telling stories today.

* * *

How should you read this book? Many will want to read straight through, chapter by chapter. And that's what I recommend. Some of the later chapters refer to stories earlier in the book to illustrate a point. But it's not crucial that you read in that order. The "how-to" chapters are interspersed throughout the book. If you're eager to learn how, you can read those chapters first. If you're already an accomplished storyteller and are mostly looking for stories to add to your collection, start with the "leadership challenges" chapters. And of course, anytime you find yourself in one of these tough challenges, refer back to the appropriate chapter.

Chapters are grouped in five leadership themes: Envision success, create an Environment for winning, Energize the team, Educate people, and Empower others. Even the how-to chapters are included in the same groups, based on the role they play in creating the story. Story structure is how you should see your story in your mind's eye before you create it (Envision). Realism and appropriate writing style should be pervasive throughout your entire story (Environment). Emotion and surprise punctuate your stories with excitement and interest (Energize). Metaphors are the most efficient literary device to teach lessons in stories (Educate). And recasting your audience into your stories, instead of just telling them stories, takes the power of storytelling to a completely new level (Empower).

There's something about leadership that lends itself to the letter e. Jack Welch at GE espoused the four E's of leadership (energy, energize, edge, execute). Procter & Gamble teaches five E's of leadership (envision, engage, energize, enable, execute). Many others have their own similar multi-E leadership philosophy. I don't claim any superiority of my five-E structure over the others. In fact, I don't intend to create a new leadership philosophy at all, I've only chosen five logical groups of the 21 leadership challenges I believe storytelling is required to navigate. And they happen to be nicely described in five words starting with the letter e.

Most chapters have a brief summary and exercises to help you leverage the stories and begin to develop your own. Use them. You'll get much more out of this book if you do. There are also two templates in the appendix to help you when crafting your own stories. Use them every time you need to develop a new story or improve an existing one. Make as many copies as you need. I give you permission.

Let's get started.

Notes

1. Ryan Mathews and Watts Wacker, *What's Your Story? Storytelling to Move Markets, Audiences, People, and Brands* (Upper Saddle River, NJ: FT Press, 2008).

2. Craig Wortmann, *What's Your Story: Using Stories to Ignite Performance and Be More Successful* (New York: Kaplan Publishing, 2006), p. 27.

3. Evelyn Clark, A *round the Corporate Campfire: How Great Leaders Use Stories to Inspire Success* (Sevierville, TN: Insight Publishing, 2004); and Lori Silverman, *Wake Me Up When the Data Is Over: How Organizations Use Storytelling to Drive Results* (San Francisco: Jossey-Bass, 2006).

4. Clark.

5. Silverman, p. 165.

6. Margaret Parkin, *Tales for Change: Using Storytelling to Develop People and Organizations* (London: Kogan Page, 2004), p. 65.

7. Silverman, p. 19.

8. Clark, p. 189.

9. Jack Maguire, *The Power of Personal Storytelling: Spinning Tales to Connect with Others* (New York: Tarcher/Putnam, 1998), p. 201.

10. Parkin, pp. 8–9.

11. David M. Boje, "Learning Storytelling: Storytelling to Learn Management Skills," *Journal of Management Education* 15, no. 3 (1991): 279–294.

12. Parkin, p. 13.

13. Maguire, p. 201.

14. Doug Lipman, *The Storytelling Coach: How to Listen, Praise, and Bring Out People's Best* (Atlanta: August House, 1995), p. 24.

15. National Storytelling Network, www.storynet.org.

16. Boje, pp. 279–294.

CHAPTER 1

Why tell stories?

"Every great leader is a great storyteller."[1]
—HOWARD GARDNER, Harvard psychologist

I'VE HAD THE OPPORTUNITY to deliver a presentation to Procter & Gamble's then-CEO A. G. Lafley four or five times in the decade he held that position. The first time was unforgettable. That day I learned a valuable lesson—the hard way—about how *not* to present to the CEO.

I'd been given 20 minutes on the agenda of the Executive Global Leadership Council meeting. This group included the CEO and a dozen or so of the top officials in the company. They met weekly in a special room on P&G's executive floor designed just for this group. It's a perfectly round room with modern features, centered on a perfectly round table. Even the doors are curved so as not to stray from the round motif. My presentation was the first item on the agenda that day, so I arrived 30 minutes early to set up my computer and make sure all of the audiovisual equipment worked properly. I was, after all, making my first presentation to the CEO. I wanted to make sure everything went smoothly.

The executives began filing into the room at the appointed time and taking up seats around the table. After half of them had arrived, the CEO, Mr. Lafley, entered the room. He walked almost completely around the table, saying hello to each of his team members, and—to my horror—sat down in the seat immediately underneath the projection screen—with his back to it!

8

This was not good. "He'll be constantly turning around in his seat to see the presentation," I thought, "and probably hurt his neck. Then he'll be in a bad mood, and might not agree to my recommendation." But I wasn't going to tell the boss where to sit, so I started my presentation.

About five minutes in, I realized Mr. Lafley hadn't turned around even once to see the slides. I stopped being worried about his neck and started worrying that he wasn't going to understand my presentation. And if he didn't understand it, he certainly wouldn't agree to my recommendation. But again, I wasn't going to tell the CEO what to do. So I just kept going.

At 10 minutes into the presentation—halfway through my allotted time—I noticed he still hadn't turned around once to look at my slides. At that point, I stopped being worried and just got confused. He was looking right at me and was clearly engaged in the conversation. So why wasn't he looking at my slides?

When 20 minutes had expired, I was done with my presentation, and the CEO hadn't ever bothered to look at my slides. But he did agree to my recommendation. Despite that success, as I was walking back to my office, I couldn't help but feel like I'd failed somehow. I debriefed the whole event in my head, wondering what I had done wrong. Was I boring? Did I not make my points very clear? Was he distracted with some billion-dollar decision far more important than whatever I was talking about?

But then it occurred to me. He wasn't looking at my slides because he knew something that I didn't know until that moment. He knew if I had anything important to say, I would say it. It would come out of my mouth, not from that screen. He knew those slides were there more for my benefit than for his.

As CEO, Mr. Lafley probably spent most of his day reading dry memos and financial reports with detailed charts and graphs. He was probably looking forward to that meeting as a break from that tedium, and as an opportunity to engage someone in dialogue—to have someone tell him what was happening on the front lines of the business, to share a brilliant idea, and to ask for his help. In short, for someone to tell him a story. Someone like me. That was my job during those 20 minutes. I just didn't know it yet.

Looking back, I realize it was probably no accident Mr. Lafley chose the seat he did. There were certainly others he could have chosen. He sat there for a reason. That position kept him from being distracted by the words on the screen and allowed him to focus on the presenter and on the discussion.

Mr. Lafley taught me a valuable lesson that day, and probably didn't even know it. My next such opportunities involved fewer slides, used more stories, and were far more effective.

In fact, storytelling has become so impactful at P&G that for many years we had a person whose job title was "corporate storyteller." The history of that role is a story in itself.

Forty years ago, a young mathematician named Jim Bangel was hired by P&G in the research & development department. Like all R&D employees, Jim wrote a monthly memo to his boss detailing the results of his research over the past 30 days. These memos are usually dry and detailed and filled with the kind of language only a fellow chemist or engineer would appreciate or even understand.

After many years of writing the same type of memo as all of his colleagues, Jim decided to do something different. He decided to write a story. He named his main character Earnest Engineer. In the story, readers got to see and follow along as Earnest learned something. It included dialogue between Earnest and his boss and peers. And it always concluded with the lesson learned. The lesson was the same as the conclusion Jim would have written about in the more traditional memo. But the story was much more compelling—and certainly more readable. As a result, other people started asking to read his memo—even people working outside his department.

After several such monthly memos, Jim's cast of characters began to grow. Each had an admittedly cheeky, but telling, name. Characters like Ed Zecutive the president; Max Profit the CFO; and Sella Case the sales director. With the growing cast of characters, the circulation grew wider as people in other functions began to see themselves in the story and learn something relevant to their work.

After five years of storytelling, Jim was appointed the company's official corporate storyteller. He continued to write one memo a month. But he spent much of his time searching the entire company for the most impactful idea he could find and then writing a story around it—a story that would captivate an audience and effect a change in the organization. Until his retirement in September 2010, his memos were eagerly read each month by between 5,000 and 10,000 people, including just about every senior executive in the company. Sometimes the CEO would even ask Jim to write a story on a certain topic because he knew people would read Jim's stories. This statistician had arguably become the single most influential person at P&G. All because one day Jim decided not to write a research report, and instead, wrote a story.

* * *

So what is the answer to the question posed in this chapter's title, "Why Tell Stories?" The simple answer illustrated by the two stories in this chapter is this—because it works! But why is that? Why is storytelling so effective? Here are 10 of the most compelling reasons I've encountered:

1. *Storytelling is simple.*[2] Anyone can do it. You don't need a degree in English, or even an MBA.

2. *Storytelling is timeless.*[3] Unlike fads in other areas of management such as total quality management, reengineering, Six Sigma, or 5S, storytelling has always worked for leadership, and it always will.

3. *Stories are demographic-proof.*[4] Everybody—regardless of age, race, or gender—likes to listen to stories.

4. *Stories are contagious.* They can spread like wildfire without any additional effort on the part of the storyteller.

5. *Stories are easier to remember.* According to psychologist Jerome Bruner, facts are 20 times more likely to be remembered if they are part of a story.[5] Organizational psychologist Peg Neuhauser found similar results in her work with corporations. She found that learning derived from a well-told story is remembered more accurately, and for far longer than the learning derived from facts or figures.[6]

6. *Stories inspire.* Slides don't. Have you ever heard someone say, "Wow! You'll never believe the PowerPoint presentation I just saw!"[7] Probably not. But you have heard people say that about stories.

7. *Stories appeal to all types of learners.* In any group, roughly 40 percent will be predominantly visual learners who learn best from videos, diagrams, or illustrations. Another 40 percent will be auditory, learning best through lectures and discussions. The remaining 20 percent are kinesthetic learners, who learn best by doing, experiencing, or feeling.[8] Storytelling has aspects that work for all three types. Visual learners appreciate the mental pictures storytelling evokes. Auditory learners focus on the words and the storyteller's voice. Kinesthetic learners remember the emotional connections and feelings from the story.[9]

8. *Stories fit better where most of the learning happens in the workplace.* According to communications expert Evelyn Clark, "Up to 70 percent of the new skills, information and competence in the workplace is acquired through informal learning" such as what happens in team settings, mentoring, and peer-to-peer communication. And the bedrock of informal learning is storytelling.[10]

9. *Stories put the listener in a mental learning mode.* Listeners who are in a critical or evaluative mode are more likely to reject what's being said. According to training coach and bestselling author Margaret Parkin, storytelling "re-creates in us that emotional state of curiosity which is ever present in children, but which as adults we tend to lose. Once in this childlike state, we tend to be more receptive and interested in the information we are given."[11] Or as author and organizational narrative expert David Hutchens points out, storytelling puts listeners in a different orientation. They put their pens and pencils down, open up their posture, and just listen.[12]

10. *Telling stories shows respect for the audience.* Stories get your message across without arrogantly telling listeners what to think or do. Regarding what to think, storytelling author Annette Simmons observed, "Stories give people freedom to come to their own conclusions. People who reject predigested conclusions might just agree with your interpretations if you get out of their face long enough for them to see what you have seen."[13] As for what to do, corporate storyteller David Armstrong suggests, "If there was ever a time when you could just order people to do something, it has long since passed. Telling a story, where you underline the moral, is a great way of explaining to people what needs to be done, without saying, 'do this.'"[14]

That answers the question, why? Next we begin our journey through stories for 21 leadership challenges, and the art of crafting compelling stories of your own.

Notes

1. Richard Maxwell and Robert Dickman, *The Elements of Persuasion: Use Storytelling to Pitch Better, Sell Faster & Win More Business* (New York: HarperCollins Publishers, 2007).

2. David Armstrong, *Managing by Storying Around: A New Method of Leadership* (New York: Doubleday Currency, 1992), p. 7.

3. Ibid., p. 7.

4. Ibid., p. 7.

5. Maxwell and Dickman.

6. Peg C. Neuhauser, original observation from *Corporate Legends & Lore: The Power of Storytelling as a Management Tool* (Austin, TX: PCN Associates, 1993). Commentary from Margaret Parkin, *Tales for Trainers: Using Stories and Metaphors to Facilitate Learning*, rev. ed. (London: Kogan Page Limited, 2010).

7. Craig Wortmann, *What's Your Story: Using Stories to Ignite Performance and Be More Successful* (New York: Kaplan Publishing, 2006), p. 44.

8. Eric Jensen, *SuperTeaching: Master Strategies for Building Student Success* (Del Mar, CA: Turning Point for Teachers Publishing, 1988).

9. Neuhauser, p. 39.

10. Evelyn Clark, original findings from *The Teaching Firm Where Productive Work and Learning Converge* (Newton, MA: The Center for Workforce Development, 1998). Clark's commentary is from The Center for Workplace Development, *Around the Corporate Campfire: How Great Leaders Use Stories to Inspire Success* (Sevierville, TN: Insight Publishing, 2004), p. 215.

11. Parkin, p. 37.

12. Mary Wacker and Lori Silverman, *Stories Trainers Tell: 55 Ready-to-Use Stories to Make Training Stick* (San Francisco: Jossey-Bass Pfeiffer, 2003), p. xxv.

13. Annette Simmons, *Whoever Tells the Best Story Wins: How to Use Your Own Stories to Communicate with Power and Impact* (New York: AMACOM, 2007), p. 28.

14. Armstrong, p. 13.

CHAPTER **2**

Set a vision for the future

"While problems can be summarized in a formula or an algorithm, it takes a story to understand a dilemma. The future will be loaded with dilemmas, so it will take a lot of stories to help make sense out of them."[1]
—BOB JOHANSEN, former CEO, The Institute for the Future

OUT FOR A WALK ONE MORNING, a woman came across a construction site where three men were working. Curious, she approached one of them and asked what he was doing. Clearly annoyed she had bothered him, he barked, "Can't you see? I'm laying bricks!"[2]

Not easily put off, she asked the next man what he was doing. He responded matter-of-factly, "I'm building a brick wall 30 feet tall, 100 feet wide, and 18 inches thick." Then, turning his attention to the first man, he said, "Hey, you just passed the end of the wall. You need to take off that last brick."

Still not satisfied, the woman asked the third man what he was doing. Despite the fact that he appeared to be doing exactly the same thing as the other two men, he looked up with excitement and said, "Oh, let me tell you! I am building the greatest cathedral the world has ever known!" She could tell he was eager to tell her more. But before he had a chance, he was distracted by loud bickering between the first two men over what to do about the one errant brick. Turning to the two of them, he said, "Hey, guys, don't worry about it. This will be an inside corner. The whole thing will get plastered over and nobody will ever see that extra brick. Just move on to the next layer."

14

The moral of the story is that if you understand the overall objectives of your organization and how your work fits into it, it not only helps you do your job better, it enables you to help others do their job better, too. In other words, it helps you be a good leader. But most important, it might actually help you enjoy what you do.

Unlike the stories in the introduction and chapter 1, this story is based on an old folktale. And it won't be the last time you come across such a fanciful tale in this book. Most of the stories you'll use in a business context will be true stories of actual events. But there is a role for myths and folklore as well. They're flexible enough to be relevant in any company and can be altered to fit your purposes without offending the truth.

This particular story is most effectively used just before new company goals or strategies are deployed. It helps the audience appreciate why it's important for them to listen, understand, and adopt the new vision and plans. It can turn what may seem to some as a boring, mandatory-attendance event into something they're eager to learn from. Like the first man in the story, at the beginning of the meeting your audience will likely feel like the job is laying bricks. By the end of the event, listeners should be building a cathedral.

It's also a good example of taking an existing story and adapting it to your own purposes. The version of the story I first heard said nothing of the second man correcting the first one for his errant brick, or their argument that ensued, or the third man correcting them both. I added those parts to deliver the conclusion that understanding how your work fits into the big corporate picture can help you lead others, not just feel good about your job.

* * *

Getting your audience to pay attention, of course, is just the first step. Now that your audience is receptive, it's time to actually describe your vision. This is where storytelling really shines! After all, a vision is a picture of the future so inspiring it drives people to action—in other words, a story. But the story must be well crafted. A story about "being number one!" isn't good enough. As organizational psychologist Peg Neuhauser noted almost two decades ago, "Beating the competition is not an inspiring enough vision to stand the test of time and trigger enthusiasm and commitment from large numbers of people."[3] It needs to be personal. Your audience needs to see itself in the future you describe. The next two examples provide a good illustration.

American Management Association • www.amanet.org

In early 2002, I was appointed to lead a group of over 100 market re-searchers at Procter & Gamble whose job was predicting the future sales of new products. Theirs was an impossible task. No matter what they predicted, the only thing they could be certain of was that they would be wrong. The only question was, would they be too high or too low, and by how far? This was exacerbated by the fact that they were typically un-dertrained and had forecasting models that were too complicated, poorly documented, and based on outmoded data.

My job was to lead this group through several changes that would hopefully improve the way they did their jobs and the tools they had at their disposal, and to help them have a more meaningful impact on the business. But these changes wouldn't be easy. They would take effort on their part to develop and implement. I needed them to understand and appreciate how much better their future could be so they would be mo-tivated to help create that future. So I wrote them a letter that included a story. I started out like this:

"I'd like to share the details of my plan and give you the opportunity to influence them. But since reviewing someone else's work detail is pretty boring stuff, I'm sending what I hope is a more interesting and vivid picture of the future I'd like to help you create. Below is one man's vision (mine) of what a day in the life of a sales forecaster could be in the near future. Some of you may feel you're already pretty close to this, and some may feel infinitely far away. Either way, I want to make this a vision we all share—either by adding your ideas to it or embracing it as is. All the major components of my work plan are represented in this vision in one way or another. So if you don't like what you see here, let me know. And if you do like what you see, let me know that, too."

I titled the story "The Vision: A Day in the Life of a Sales Forecaster." The story introduced "Sherri" as a sales forecaster two years in the future. The story line followed Sherri throughout a typical day. Only in this story, instead of meeting with frustration at every turn, she handled all of her en-counters with business partners with success and ease. It's clear in the story that the reason for each success was a change in the tools, the process, or the training Sherri had at her disposal—all, of course, the result of the plans I had just developed and hoped to get the team's help in delivering.

The story closed at the end of the day when she was walking out of a meeting. Two of the team members came up to her and thanked her for her great ideas, and commented that they liked this "new and im-proved" role the forecasters seemed to be playing in the business. She hadn't realized it before now, but she actually liked her job. It was more fun to come to work when you know that you've got something more valuable to contribute than a bunch of numbers, and that people actually seek out and appreciate your input.

The first response I got to my story was, "Wow! I want that to be my story two years from now. I'm in!" The rest of them weren't much different.

That story was sent in a simple e-mail. But you can get more creative with your delivery. In her book *Wake Me Up When the Data Is Over*,[4] Lori Silverman recounts how some very bright people at Bristol-Myers Squibb once created a future story and printed it in the format of London's *Financial Times* newspaper, their president's favorite reading material. Why? Because they couldn't get him to read their 50-page strategy document. The paper they slipped under his door had this headline: "Bristol-Myers Squibb Named Top-Ranked Global Pharmaceutical Company." He was halfway through the article before he noticed the date at the top of the page and realized it was a story about the future. When he finished reading the article, he had a complete understanding of the strategy his team wanted him to embrace, because they'd written it into the story.

Similar tactics have been used at Xerox Corporation, Braun, and Procter & Gamble, among others. It's almost always effective. After all, who doesn't want to read about themselves in a flattering newspaper article?

* * *

So you've just seen how to use a story to get your audience to sit up and pay attention to your vision, and another story to actually explain what your vision of the future is. Is there anything else you need to do? Perhaps. Sometimes a vision is so lofty or aggressive it comes across as an unachievable dream, not a realistic vision. If that's the case with your vision, congratulations on having such a worthy idea! But if people don't believe your vision will ever happen, they won't be motivated to help you deliver it. Storytelling can help with this, too, as illustrated in the following story.

In early 2010, I was appointed to lead a multidisciplinary team tasked with recommending a long-term direction for P&G's Paper Division. What type of products did we want to sell in 10, 15, or 20 years, and in what parts of the world? Despite the noble objectives, it was a hard project to get people to sign up for. By definition, nothing we came up with would get to market while we were in these jobs, and maybe not even during our working lifetimes. Meanwhile, our peers got to work on the next big product upgrade launching in the spring, and earn the usual accolades of in-market success. Besides, most people were skeptical that long-term planning had any value. I knew I had to convince my team that our mission was necessary for the company, and that it would be a rewarding experience.

At our first meeting, I told them the story of another paper company, not too different from ours. It began in 1865 when Fredik Idestam built a pulp mill on the banks of the Tammerkoski River in southwestern Finland. Soon he added a papermaking machine. As with any papermaking company at the time, much of what the company produced was used for stationery, newsprint, and books—the primary means of communication before the age of television, radio, and telephone. So in a way, it was in the communications business.

By 1900, it was already one of the biggest paper producers in Finland and was looking for growth opportunities. Electricity was a rapidly growing source of energy at the time. So in 1902 it decided to build its own electric generators and sell the current to local businesses. By the end of the 1910s, however, the company was struggling financially, so it decided to join forces with Finnish Rubber Works. Rubber (being a natural insulator for electricity) offered obvious synergies for the combined companies.

By the early 1920s, telephone service was a rapidly growing business and cables were still being laid from city to city. In 1922, the Finnish Cable Company was wisely added to this growing conglomerate. Over the next several decades, it continued to expand smartly into adjacent industries and around the world. By 2010, it had become a $40 billion company, with operations in 120 countries around the world, and a market leader in its main business line, which is still communications. You know the company by the same name it had a hundred years ago when it was producing paper in Finland—Nokia.[5]

Had it not chosen to expand into other industries at various points in its growth, Nokia would probably still be the biggest manufacturer of paper in Finland, a country about the size of the state of Minnesota. (As of this writing, the advent of smartphones like the Blackberry and the iPhone have taken much of Nokia's market share. Perhaps it will make another smart move into adjacent territory as it has in the past.)

The point, I explained to my team, was not that we should get into the cell phone business, but simply that we were already a successful paper company, with brands like Bounty, Charmin, and Puffs. To continue to grow, we needed to expand beyond our current industry definition. We could either let that happen by chance or we could *by choice* plot wise moves at each step the way Nokia did. Our management prefers the latter, and it selected us to help choose the first steps. Most businesspeople will go an entire career and never have an opportunity to impact the future of the business beyond the next fiscal year or two. We've been asked to help steer the next two decades!

"Who's interested?" I asked.

Every hand went up, and we got straight to work.

The Nokia story helped my team understand that the work was important and the goal was achievable. After all, it had been done before by a company that started out just like ours. It was the perfect preamble to the meeting. Sure, I could have responded to any skeptics by saying, "Nokia did it. Why can't we?" But that wouldn't have been nearly as compelling as the story.

SUMMARY AND EXERCISES

Stories can help with three distinct parts of setting a vision for the future:

1. Getting your audience to pay attention (building a cathedral)
2. Delivering your vision so your audience can see themselves in it:
   a. Use "a day in the life of a volume forecaster" as a springboard story. Springboard stories can serve as inspiration to write your own similar story that will be more effective for your situation.
   b. Try a creative execution to make sure your audience bothers to read your vision. One way is to format the story like a newspaper article. (According to the *Financial Times*)
3. Showing that your vision is achievable (On the banks of the Tammerkoski River)

Notes

1. Bob Johansen, *Leaders Make the Future: Ten New Leadership Skills for an Uncertain World* (San Francisco: Berrett-Koehler Publishers, 2009).
2. This is my version of an old folktale. Original author unknown.
3. Peg C. Neuhauser, *Corporate Legends & Lore: The Power of Storytelling as a Management Tool* (Austin, TX: PCN Associates, 1993), p. 123.
4. Lori Silverman, *Wake Me Up When the Data Is Over: How Organizations Use Storytelling to Drive Results* (San Francisco: Jossey-Bass, 2006), p. 149.
5. "The Nokia Story," http://www.nokia.com/about-nokia/company/story-of-nokia/nokias-first-century.

CHAPTER 3

Set goals and build commitment

> " *'Would you tell me, please, which way I ought to go from here?' said Alice.*
> *'That depends a good deal on where you want to get to,' said the Cat.*
> *'I don't much care where—' said Alice.*
> *'Then it doesn't matter which way you go,' said the Cat.* "
> —LEWIS CARROLL, *Alice's Adventures in Wonderland*

UNLIKE ALICE'S MEANDERINGS in Wonderland, in politics the goals are amazingly clear, and the level of commitment is extremely high. In fact, rarely does anyone look beyond the next election cycle, sometimes not even the next news cycle. That's because unlike business, politics is an all-or-nothing endeavor. If a company's sales only measure $228 million this year, instead of its goal of $229 million, all is not lost. Its stock price might tick down a few points. And a few executives might earn a slightly smaller bonus. But the company won't shut down and lay off all its workers. But if a politician only gets 49 percent of the vote, instead of 51 percent, the election is lost. That politician—and every single member of his or her campaign staff—is out of a job until the next election.

Just ask Ben LaRocco. After finishing a degree in political science in 2003, he went into politics as a campaign staffer for local, state, and federal candidates. He had five different jobs in his first four years out of school. A typical campaign lasts only six to nine months.

What's the work like? Campaign season is brutal. As Ben describes it, "You work long days, well into the night, and you have no social life. That's why most campaign staffers are single. There's no time for family."

20

And they constantly check their own level of commitment. "When it's 100 degrees outside in August and you've been knocking on doors for the past nine hours, you have to remind yourself that the next 10 doors could make the difference in the election. If you didn't believe that, you'd be at the bar already."

Ben learned that lesson the hard way in one of his first jobs. He was working on the primary campaign for a state congressional candidate in Ohio. The opposing candidates were well matched—politically and financially. Ben worked hard all season, right up to election night. When the polls closed at 7 P.M., his work was finally done. He watched the returns come in from campaign headquarters for the next two hours. At 9 P.M., his candidate was down by a handful of votes. He got in his car for his 90-minute drive home. Turning on the television when he arrived, he learned they were now up by less than 50 votes. When he got up the next morning, they were still up, now by 62 votes. But they weren't done counting. With such a close election, many precincts counted twice. So the candidates took turns being on top one day and behind the next. Two weeks later, one county found 23 uncounted votes. Unfortunately, it was a county that favored his opponent. In the final tally, his candidate lost by 22 votes out of over 34,000 votes cast. His margin of defeat was 49.96 percent to 50.04 percent. A tough defeat to take at the tender age of 22.

That loss taught Ben important lessons about goals and commitment. In every campaign since then, he's recalled that experience and retold the story to his colleagues. With that as motivation, he did two things differently thereafter. First, he tore out the pages of a daily calendar—five or six month's worth of them—for every day up to Election Day. He posted those pages on the wall and wrote daily and weekly goals on them: how many phone calls to make this day, how much money to raise by this week, how many people to meet, how many doors to knock on. He tracked progress against those goals every day.

Every morning when he got up, he asked himself, "What am I going to do today better than my competition? What will I do today to affect what happens on November 2?" When he went to bed at night, he asked, "Did I win or lose today? Did I do more or less than my competition?"

The lesson here is that it's easier to be committed to a goal when the assessment of success and failure is clear and unequivocal, as it is in politics on Election Day. But even in that unambiguous environment, Ben found ways to create weekly and daily goals to keep himself motivated and on track for success.

* * *

There's something in this even for those not in politics. First, in the midst of the marginal ups and downs that most companies experience, it helps to create situations where victory and defeat are clearly defined. Second, there's a benefit to having short-term milestones to measure against. But how do you do that? Obviously, you could tell your team that achieving the $229 million sales target is success and anything less is utter defeat. But that wouldn't fool anyone. One creative solution was developed at Merrill Lynch by veteran financial adviser Pledger Monk.

By 2010, Pledger had 16 years' experience in the business, and had established himself as a highly successful financial adviser—enough so that newer advisers often came to him for counsel. In April of that year, one of those people was Toby Burkett. He was doing okay but knew he could be doing better. He knew that because he had just finished a Toughman boxing competition a month earlier. Despite never having fought in his life, he came in third in a field of 25 heavyweight fighters. The reason he did so well, he explained to Pledger, was that he had a great coach, and trained every day. It reminded him that he had always responded well to coaching. Growing up and even into his college years, his athletic and academic performance improved significantly with coaching.

"I'd like to find someone to help me like that at work," he told Pledger. "Would you be willing to be my coach?"

Pledger agreed, and they arranged to meet every Monday at 4 P.M.

The first thing Pledger did was set a specific goal for the end of the year. They agreed on an audacious 50 percent increase in revenue. (Of course it didn't matter if Toby only achieved half that. A 25 percent increase was nothing to sneeze at.) Next, they created a list of the activities that lead to winning a new client and assigned a point value to each of them. Calling a prospect was worth 4 points, meeting a prospect in person was 10 points, and so on. Success was earning 45 points a day.

They started tracking points immediately. For the first few months, Toby was doing well, earning about 33 points a day on average, probably 10 points than he would have earned prior to tracking points. Both he and Pledger were satisfied with his progress, and they were seeing an improvement in his revenue production. Then in October, another adviser came to Pledger with the same request for coaching. His name was Sy Robinson. Pledger offered to have him join the Monday afternoon sessions, and the point system as well. Sy quickly agreed.

With two participants now, Pledger had the opportunity to make the point system work even harder. Now it was a competition! He declared the first person to earn a total of 2,500 points would be the winner. And that's when things got more interesting. The competition turned their business into one of Ben LaRocco's political campaigns. Now the goal wasn't just a 50 percent increase in revenue. It was to win the contest. That dynamic changed how the daily point system was viewed as well. The goal was still 45 points a day. But that didn't seem to matter anymore. Now all they cared about was earning more points than the other guy! Just like Ben, at the end of the day they asked themselves, "Did I win or lose today?" Only in their case, they knew the answer. They could compare their scores every day—and did. Some days Toby won, some days Sy won.

The competition was intense, and came down to the wire for both participants. In the end it was Toby who reached 2,500 points first, in just seven weeks. Averaging over 70 points per day was exhausting for both of them. But the benefit was clear. By the end of the year, Toby's production was up 47 percent, close enough to the audacious 50 percent goal to declare a major victory. So they continued the point system but set their 2,500-point goal for a less-grueling 12-week cycle instead of 7 weeks. And their production has continued to rise. By August 2011, Toby's monthly production was up a total of 76 percent, and is still rising. Pledger had found a way to turn the normally slower-paced business world into the high-commitment world of politics with an all-or-nothing definition of success and daily goals that are measurable.

These two stories illustrate how specific, measurable, daily goals and unambiguous success criteria can lead to better outcomes. Sharing these stories with others can give them an appreciation for the value of such goals before you assign them. They can also give people creative ideas on how to construct their own goals and success criteria.

* * *

Now let's turn our attention to commitment. Without it, nothing gets done. So how do you get people committed to your goals? One way is to get them to feel a sense of accountability and responsibility for results. Usually once that happens, people become personally committed to the goals because it's their victory if they win, and their loss if they fail. And there's nowhere better to learn about personal accountability and responsibility than the military.

In the fall of 1971, Bob McDonald joined the U.S. Military Academy in West Point, New York. Along with the traditional hazing a first-year cadet experiences, Bob learned quickly there were only four acceptable responses when addressed by a superior officer: "Yes, sir"; "No, sir"; "I don't understand, sir"; and "No excuse, sir." As Bob explains it, "Imagine I've shined my shoes, my trousers are pressed, and I go out to formation. While in line, one of my classmates rushes past and steps in a puddle, splashing mud all over my shoes and trousers. Then an upperclassman walks by and notices. 'McDonald! Why are you in formation with mud all over your shoes and trousers?'

"As a West Point cadet, I go through all four possible answers in my head. 'Yes, sir' would just restate the obvious, so that doesn't seem appropriate. And it would probably get me yelled at even more. I couldn't say 'No, sir' because it was clearly true. I'd get thrown out of the academy for lying. 'I don't understand, sir' would just make me look stupid. As a new cadet I was doing enough of that already. The only answer I had left was the fourth one, and it's the most powerful one of all—'No excuse, sir.' Even though something happened to me that was outside my control, I wasn't supposed to make any excuses. I was supposed to say, 'No excuse, sir. It won't happen again.' That's how a West Point cadet takes responsibility, which is an important part of character."

Bob was reminded of the power of that lesson 13 years later, when he and his wife, Diane, were discussing what to do about their six-year-old, Jenny. After repeatedly telling Jenny to clean up her room, they found it hadn't been done. It was a mess. Being thoughtful parents, they consulted one of the many parenting books on their shelves for advice on how to reprimand a child for an infraction like this. They discussed their options and even scripted out the conversation they would have with Jenny. With script in hand, they went and found Jenny in her room. "Jenny, we'd like to talk to you about the condition of your room." Bob started. But before he could even get to the second sentence of his prepared speech, Jenny looked up at him and with the seriousness of a West Point cadet said, "No excuse, Dad. It won't happen again."

Bob and Diane were completely dumbstruck. They stood there in awkward silence, trying to figure out what to say next. Their script was completely useless now. With seven simple words, Jenny had acknowledged the state of her room, taken responsibility for it, and promised to not let it happen again. Everything their lengthy script was supposed to help them accomplish was already done. There was nothing left to say. They kissed their little girl on the cheek and left her to play in her room.

Twenty-three years later, Bob still preaches the value of that lesson. As the CEO of Procter & Gamble, one of his primary responsibilities is to set stretching goals and objectives for the company, and get all 127,000 employees committed to delivering them. Truly committing to a goal means that if it isn't met, you take responsibility for it and promise to get it done. The "No excuse, sir" response is a clear indication of commitment and responsibility. It works as well in the business world as it does in a military academy or in parenting a six-year-old. And it works for the boss just as much as it does for the subordinate. When the boss hears "No excuse, sir"—however it's articulated—she can be certain her subordinate is taking responsibility and is still committed to the goal. For the direct report, the disarming "No excuse" response spares him a lengthy reprimand from the boss, just like it spared Jenny.

Today Bob shares these stories of his time at West Point and his daughter, Jenny, with leaders all around the company. It's his way of teaching them to accept responsibility and build commitment to goals. Share them in your organization and you'll be amazed at the level of commitment you'll generate.

* * *

Accountability and responsibility build commitment because they give people a sense of ownership of the goals and the strategies to get there— even if those goals and plans weren't their idea in the first place. But people are naturally more committed to their own ideas. As a result, another way to get them committed is to give them—all of them—a chance to influence the goals and strategies to begin with. Jeff Schomburger demonstrates exactly that in this next story.

When Jeff took over as head of P&G's biggest sales team, he knew he had his work cut out for him. The team's performance was good. But that good performance had come at a high cost to the organization. The work processes were heavy and burdensome. Customer relationships were strained. And internal competition created friction with other P&G teams. The organization was feeling stressed and out of control.

His first week on the job, Jeff took a traditional problem analysis tool and turned it on its head. Most businesspeople are familiar with a SWOT analysis—an assessment of a business's strengths, weaknesses, opportunities, and threats. It's typically completed by a single person, or a small committee at most. Jeff created a blank SWOT template and handed it out to 60 people out of the 240 on the team. All 60 filled it out. Many asked for input from their coworkers.

Once the templates were completed, he met with each of those 60 people, individually, for one hour. He probed to understand all their ideas in depth, looking for ones that could radically change the culture and performance of the team. A month later, having completed the interviews, Jeff called the entire team together and outlined the set of changes he was implementing immediately. Of course, the 60 people he interviewed could see their fingerprints all over his changes. But even more impressively, so could everyone else. The entire team embraced the changes and committed to making them a success. The culture improved overnight. A year later, the annual employee survey showed team effectiveness scores had increased significantly, and team performance along with it.

Sure, the 60 hours of Jeff's time was a huge investment. But it worked. It worked because it's far easier to get people to commit to their own ideas than to your ideas. Jeff's unconventional use of the SWOT tool made sure everyone had a personal connection to the goals.

SUMMARY AND EXERCISES

1. Goals are most effective when they meet these criteria: First, success or failure is clear and unambiguous, like a political election. Second, milestones are specific, measurable, and frequent. Consider "Did I win or lose today?" and Pledger's competition.

    a. Can you make your team's success or failure more clear by how you define the objective, or create a competition?

    b. Can you define weekly or even daily goals for your team?

2. Build commitment to your objectives:

    a. Create a culture of accountability ("No excuses, sir!").

    b. Let your team have input to and influence the goals to begin with. Humans are far more committed to *their* goals than they are to *your* goals (SWOT analysis).

CHAPTER **4**

Lead change

"Most of us are about as eager to be changed as we were to be born, and go through our changes in a similar state of shock."[1]
—JAMES A. BALDWIN

ASK ANY BUSINESSPERSON to name a superstar CEO, and Jack Welch's name is likely to be one of the first mentioned. He became the chairman and CEO of General Electric in 1981 and held that position for two decades. During his tenure, GE's sales increased fourfold, and its market capitalization increased from $13 billion to several hundred billion![2] Those are two of the reasons why, in 1999, *Fortune* magazine named him "Manager of the Century."[3]

Getting his leaders to change by facing reality was one of the hallmarks of Welch's early years as CEO. He did that by telling and retelling the story of his first successful reality check, described in his book *Jack: Straight from the Gut.*[4]

In his first year as CEO, he was on a field visit to GE's nuclear reactor business in San Jose, California. The leadership presented a rosy plan that assumed orders for three new reactors a year. Looking backward, that was a reasonable assumption, since GE had been selling three or four reactors a year since the 1970s. But the year was now 1981, just two years after the Three Mile Island nuclear disaster in Pennsylvania. What little public support there was for nuclear energy had vanished. And GE hadn't received a single new order in the two years since.

Jack listened politely for a while and then dropped a bombshell. "Guys, you're not going to get three orders a year. In my opinion, you'll never get another order for a nuclear reactor in the U.S." He told them

27

they should figure out how to make a business out of selling nuclear fuel and services to the 72 active reactors they already built.

They were shocked. They argued that if they took those orders out of the plan, it would kill morale, and they'd never be able to mobilize the business again when the orders came back. Jack didn't buy it. GE restaffed the business to focus on a service model and grew earnings from $14 million to $116 million in just two years. When Jack retired 20 years later, the company still hadn't gotten a single new order for a nuclear reactor in the United States.

The first obstacle to change is getting people to accept that change is needed. Delivering a sobering "reality check" like Jack Welch did is one way to do that. This story teaches that as a leader you need to do likewise in your organization. But it has another use as well. Telling this story prior to delivering your reality check is a good way to prime your audience to accept and appreciate being dealt the eye-opening truth you're about to deliver: "GE never did get another order for a nuclear reactor. And the reality for us is, we can't expect another year of currency fluctuations to prop up our bottom line" (or whatever your reality check is).

* * *

Accepting the need for change is not the only barrier you'll run into in trying to lead change. Even when people agree that change is necessary, human beings are still creatures of habit. Change is an unwelcome visitor. What is it about change that's so unattractive? The following story from Seattle-based author and workshop leader Evelyn Clark offers a telling insight to the cause of and cure for human resistance to change.

Evelyn learned one of her biggest lessons about managing change during a retreat she was leading for a corporate client on the West Coast. The client was about to go through an enormous change. Previously, the job of the inside sales department was to wait for the phone to ring and process orders from whomever was on the other end of the line. But as any businessperson knows, that's not sales. That's taking orders. The new plan was for them to become a real sales department—to start placing proactive, outbound sales calls to generate more customers and more revenue. The call center staff was paralyzed with fear. The retreat was designed to find ways the sales managers could help them overcome that fear. Evelyn asked the participants to get up in front of the group and tell personal stories about change. What had they learned from their own experience about managing change in their work and personal lives? She believes telling stories of personal experiences helps people find creative solutions to business challenges. One participant told a particularly insightful story about his twin six-year-old boys that proved Evelyn's theory.

As any parent knows, riding the school bus without Mom or Dad is scary enough for a first grader. But finding the way from the classroom to the bus at 3:30 by themselves is even more intimidating. There are so many buses! And they all look the same. His six-year-olds spent most of the school year getting comfortable with their exact route and pickup point every day. Then one day they were told their pickup spot was going to change. In the days leading up to the big switch, it became evident that one of the twins was very concerned, while the other seemed unaffected. Apparently, the new pickup spot was just outside one boy's classroom. He could see it from the window. But for the other boy, in a different classroom, the pickup spot was even farther away, and in a different direction.

The night before the big day, shortly after bedtime, Dad noticed one child sleeping soundly, while the other was restless. He got his nervous little boy out of bed and asked him what was wrong. "I don't know what I'm going to do, Daddy." So Dad dressed the little boy up in his school clothes already laid out for the next day, and they went on an imaginary journey. "Pretend you're in class, and the teacher says it's time to go. Walk out that door and show me which way you're going to turn." The little one did as Dad asked. "Now, let's practice walking down the hall and across the parking lot to the pickup spot." Two good attempts convinced both father and child that all was well.

"Now, who else in your class rides the same bus with you?"

"Johnny B. does."

"Okay, then you pretend I'm Johnny B. You practice asking me if it's okay if you follow me to the bus." After two or three attempts, the boy found a comfortable way to ask. Now he had a plan B. After a few more words of reassurance, Dad tucked his confident young man in bed, and he fell right to sleep.

What Dad realized—as did Evelyn's entire class from that story—was that people, even children, aren't really afraid of change. They're afraid of not being *prepared* for the change. Telling this story is helpful for an organization going through change in two ways. First, for the people in charge of the change, it's a reminder of how important it is to pro-

vide enough coaching and training so everyone can navigate the change
with confidence and success. Second, and probably less obvious, is that
this story provides comfort and motivation to those going through the
change. It tells them that their fear is really about their own preparedness,
not the change itself. The harder they work to prepare for the change,
the more their fear will abate. They'll be more likely to attend the training classes, ask probing questions, and generally take ownership for their
own preparation.

Everyone knows getting trained can help you be more successful. But
some people are comfortable with their current level of success, so they
might not be motivated to train too intently. But if they recognize that
being better prepared can also help them avoid weeks of paranoia and
sleep loss and fear, even the most apathetic of employees will be highly
motivated to prepare.

* * *

The previous two stories help address mental and emotional barriers to
change. The first helps your audience recognize and accept the rational
need for change. The second gives both leader and employee emotional
motivation to prepare for change. A third option is to change the environment so it's difficult or impossible *not* to change. Done well, this
method can be more effective than the other two combined. The following story is a simple but effective example.

Last year, file retention day was in May. The antitrust policy refresher
course was in April. And sexual harassment training was in January. Each
month, there seems to be at least one day dedicated to reminding employees of one corporate policy or another. This month, it was clean desk
policy, which requires everyone to lock up any documents you wouldn't
want competitors to see. In other words, everything!

During their monthly meeting, the leadership team discussed ways to
increase compliance with the clean desk policy, starting with a debate over
where the biggest violations were. Since most people were good about
locking up their desk drawers each night, they concluded the most violations probably came from documents left on the printers overnight. The
vice presidents and directors took turns offering up ideas. One suggested
writing a memo for the president to send out explaining why it's so important to lock everything up. Another idea was to hold a contest for the
"cleanest" department, or maybe audit the floor one night a month and
offer a prize to anyone who passed inspection 12 months in a row.

When it was Martin Hettich's turn to speak, he offered something very different. Over the phone from his office in Panama, he explained that last year his business unit was trying desperately to cut expenses. Someone decided they were spending too much money on printer paper. The solution was to charge each department based on the number of sheets its employees used. But since everybody used the same network printers in the middle of each floor, they needed a convenient way to monitor usage. Here's what they came up with. Once you click the print button on your computer, you go to the printer and type in your employee number on the printer keypad. Then it would print out your document and send a charge to your budget. When people started getting billed for their paper, usage did go down, but only slightly—probably not enough to warrant the hassle this process created.

But there was an unexpected consequence of that policy, too, which turned out to be even more valuable than the money saved. The incidence of documents left out on printers overnight dropped practically to zero. It turned out that the main reason documents were left out wasn't that people were too lazy to get them right away. It was because they just forgot about them after they clicked the print button. Now it didn't matter if they forgot for a day or two. Their document wouldn't print until they walked to the printer and typed in their employee number. Once they did that, they would just stand there and wait for it to finish printing and take it with them. They certainly didn't want to walk to the printer twice for each document.

Problem solved.

Compare that solution to the other suggested options. First, the mental one—having the president send out a memo explaining why it's so important to lock things up. Certainly some percentage of the employees would find that rationale compelling and would change their behavior. But many would remain unmoved. Option two was the emotional one—appealing to their sense of pride by offering prizes and recognition to anyone who complied. That might also win some converts, but not everyone. But Martin's solution worked on just about everyone. It's an example of what Chip Heath and Dan Heath call "clearing the path." In their bestselling book *Switch: How to Change Things When Change Is Hard*,[5] they discuss several deceptively simple ways to manage organizational change. One of them is exactly what Martin Hettich did.

Instead of using rational or emotional appeals, change the environment so it's difficult or impossible not to change. In *Switch*, the authors offer a highly recognizable example for anyone who works in manufac-turing—the secondary safety button. "Many factories use dangerous ma-chines that have a bad habit of lopping off fingers or hands that are in the wrong place at the wrong time." The solution is to design the ma-chines so they can be operated only if two buttons are pressed at the same time—the main button, and the secondary. The second button is located far enough away from the main button that you have to use both hands to press them at the same time. If your hands are pressing both buttons when the machine is operating, by design neither one can be in the dan-ger zone at the wrong moment. They offer other similar examples, such as ATM machines that make you remove your card before you get your cash, and cars that won't shift out of park unless your foot is on the brake.

The bottom line is, rather than appealing to your employees' hearts and minds, take the uncertainty out of your change leadership strategy. Make it impossible for them not to change. The next time your organi-zation is facing a major change, tell Martin's story to your leadership team. Then spend some time coming up with ideas to clear the path for your employees. If done well, you'll get great compliance to the change, and without any fingers getting lopped off.

* * *

So you've convinced your team that change is necessary, they're all well prepared for the change, and you've arranged the work environment so the path to change is unobstructed. Surely nothing can go wrong now. You've done everything, right?

Wrong. Murphy's law knows no foreign lands. Unexpected barriers to change will always pop up. How you respond to them will determine your ultimate success or failure. A good leader navigates the obstacle and minimizes its impact on the organization. But a great leader turns those barriers into agents for change, as the following story illustrates.

In early 2001, the stock market was still reeling from the dot-com bubble and burst a few months earlier. The economy was uncertain, and even many traditional companies were in turbulent times. P&G was one of them. It had been less than a year since the company's stock had lost nearly 40 percent of its value in a single week of trading. The business press was quickly losing its love affair with Internet start-ups and return-ing its interest to conventional businesses. So *BusinessWeek* decided to do a story on what went wrong with P&G.

After asking for an interview with a P&G official, *BusinessWeek* was offered Tarang Amin, the newly appointed marketing director of P&G's Bounty paper towel franchise. The brand had just finished a tough year. Tarang represented a fresh and unbiased pair of eyes to talk about Bounty's history and plans. A few uneventful weeks went by after the interview while the reporter continued researching the article.

On March 12, 2001, the article hit the newsstands, and Tarang got his first look. The title was "Can Procter & Gamble Clean Up Its Act?" The first sentence said, "For a glimpse of the daunting task facing P&G's chief executive, look no farther than the paper towel aisle." That first line hit Tarang right between the eyes. The article stated that Bounty had lost more market share in the past year than any of P&G's top brands. It went on to outline an opinion of everything the brand had done wrong in humbling detail: getting beat on product and cost innovation by its competitors, cutting its advertising spending, raising prices too much, and cutting back its in-store sales force. The article even accused P&G of rotating through brand managers too quickly.

Tarang was crestfallen. Although he was expecting a negative article, the story was much worse than he had thought. It would surely disappoint and possibly even embarrass the hundreds of employees who work to make and market the Bounty brand. More importantly, having it come out while they were in the middle of the turnaround risked undermining the plan and having people lose confidence in what they were doing. His only hope was that nobody would read the article and it would just pass over unnoticed. That hope was dashed when he arrived home at the end of the day and stepped out of his car. His next-door neighbor yelled over the hedge, "Hey, Tarang, that was a terrible article about you today, huh?"

That evening, as Tarang mulled over the article, he thought about writing a letter to the editor to complain about some of the facts that maybe weren't quite right, or statements that seemed out of context. But he thought better of it. The thought of going to work the next day and facing his teammates was overwhelming. What he really wanted to do was bury his head in the sand and pretend none of it ever happened. What he did instead was to write a memo to everyone on the team, which he titled "Bounty *BusinessWeek* Article—My Perspective." In it, Tarang admitted he was originally disappointed in the article, knowing how hard everyone on the brand had been working in the past year to put the business back on track. Yet, he had to admit, many of the points in the article were correct. For example, "We did let our price get out of target range," and some of "our key innovations didn't make it to market." In fact, several of the points laid out in the article were exactly what the brand had identified itself in defining its new strategy to return to growth.

Therefore, rather than get defensive, Tarang insisted people view this article as reinforcement that they knew exactly what their issues were and how to fix them. He reminded them of their plans to return to innovation leadership, and that they had already lowered Bounty's price to be more competitive. He concluded the memo by restating his confidence in the people and plans and his aspiration to make their great brand even greater in the year ahead.

Tarang's memo quickly circulated around the building, at first among Bounty team members but soon to other teams. His general manager sent it to the most senior executives in the company, many of whom forwarded it to people on their brands as well. Their purpose in sharing it broadly was primarily to give a response to the questions on everyone's mind, "What does management think about this article and what are we doing about Bounty's situation?" It answered both those questions brilliantly. But it did something even more important, I think. It showed business leaders how to turn a demoralizing event into a critical agent of change. Over the next few months, and even years, that *BusinessWeek* article—and Tarang's response—would get pulled back out of the file drawers. They served as a rallying cry for change. In the decade since that article was published, Bounty's market share has grown 10 points, to 46 percent, and the brand's sales have grown by two-thirds.

Today, as CEO of Schiff Nutrition International, Tarang Amin tells that story to colleagues when they're going through a tough or embarrassing situation and they want to hide under a rock. The lesson they learn is to not hide from it. Instead, publicize it. Turn it to their advantage. Use it as a tool for change and galvanize the organization around it.

SUMMARY AND EXERCISES

1. The first step to change is getting people to admit change is needed. Delivering a "reality check" like Jack Welch usually works. Tell Jack's story of the nuclear reactors; then deliver your own reality check.

2. People aren't afraid of change. They're afraid of not being prepared for it. Prepare them. And when you do, tell them the story of the "twin boys at the bus stop" so they can take comfort that their trepidation is only because they aren't prepared yet. After the training you give them, they know they will be.

3. Change the environment so it's nearly impossible not to change. Use these examples as inspiration to help you think of a way to do that with the change you're leading: Martin's printer codes, the secondary safety button, ATM machines, shift lock on a car's gearshift.

4. Barriers to change will pop up. Instead of ignoring or hiding them, turn them into change agents. An example is the *BusinessWeek* article on Bounty.

Notes

1. Larry Chang, *Wisdom for the Soul: Five Millennia of Prescriptions for Spiritual Healing* (Washington, DC: Gnosophia Publishers, 2006), p. 114.

2. "Past Leaders: Jack Welch," General Electric company website: http://www.ge.com/company/history/bios/john_welch.html.

3. "*Fortune*—GE's Jack Welch Named Manager of the Century" (April 26, 1999). Timewarner.com. Retrieved July 12, 2010.

4. Jack Welch, *Jack: Straight from the Gut* (New York: Warner Business Books, 2001), pp. 100–103.

5. Chip Heath and Dan Heath, *Switch: How to Change Things When Change Is Hard* (New York: Crown Business, 2010).

CHAPTER 5

Make recommendations stick

"There are always three speeches for every one you actually gave: the one you practiced, the one you gave, and the one you wish you gave."[1]
—DALE CARNEGIE

IN THE SUMMER OF 2000, I worked in P&G's diaper business, where we make and market the Pampers and Luvs brands. I was given a unique opportunity that summer to develop and present a five-year strategy recommendation to the president and leadership team.

After a few weeks of intense analysis and preparation, I had my big moment with leadership. They were probably expecting a traditional P&G-style presentation where I would stand up, tell them what my recommendation was, and then justify that recommendation with the details of my analysis. But that's not what I did. Instead, I told them the following.

"Every one of you in this room has been taught since you joined the company that if you deliver the sales volume, the profits will follow. And our strategy in this business unit reflects that belief. All of our plans are directed at selling more diapers. Period. So in preparation for this meeting, I decided to do some research to find out if that assumption was true.

"I looked back over our nearly 40-year history making disposable diapers in the United States and here's what I found. For the first 21 years, 1961 to 1982, there was a near perfect correlation between sales volume and profits. Every year as sales went up, profits went up. When sales went down, profits went down. It seems that assumption about higher sales

36

leading to higher profits was true, and these data are probably the reason why we'd all been taught this mantra.

"But if you look at the data since 1982, they tell a very different story. For the past 18 years, 1983 to 2000, there has been absolutely no correlation between sales volume and profits whatsoever. None. Over those 18 years, profit growth years have been just as likely to accompany sales growth as sales declines. The same is true for profit declines."

The scatter plot of this data is shocking, so I showed it and paused there while the audience took it in. I then asked the audience this question: "What do you think could have happened in 1983 that forever changed the nature of this higher-sales-equals-higher-profits industry?"

Someone answered, "Is that when Kimberly-Clark launched Huggies?" "No, but good guess," I responded. "They launched several years prior to that. Any other ideas?"

"Is that when commodity costs got out of control?" someone offered. "Another good guess," I said. "That happened in the late seventies. . . . Anyone else?"

I continued to let the audience throw out guesses until someone started getting close by asking about consumer behavior. I encouraged them to keep thinking along that direction, and steered the conversation closer with each following idea until someone found it.

"Is that maybe when the market reached full penetration?"

"Bingo!" I yelled. "That's it! Before we launched disposable diapers in the early sixties, the U.S. diaper market was composed entirely of cloth diapers that moms had to wash and reuse. Every year thereafter, more and more moms began to try disposable diapers and abandon the drudgery of cleaning dirty cloth diapers."

By 1983, the market for disposable diapers had essentially reached 100 percent of households with kids who wore diapers, and cloth diapers had almost entirely vanished from the marketplace. Up to that point, everyone making disposable diapers had rapidly growing sales numbers, and the rapidly growing profit numbers to go with them. A rising tide lifts all boats. (The cloth diaper makers, of course, were going out of business.)

But in 1983 all of that changed. Once we had successfully converted every mom in the country to using disposable diapers, the total industry sales of disposable diapers stopped growing every year, and largely flattened out. The disposable diaper business in the United States went from what P&G would call a "developing market" to a "developed market" in 1983. And apparently, we failed to notice it. We were still following the same basic "sell more" strategy we had followed during the developing-market period. An appropriate business strategy for a developed market is usually very different. And my audience knew it.

All of these conclusions—my conclusions—immediately flowed from the mouths of the audience like a well-rehearsed screenplay as soon as someone correctly identified the key observation I wanted them to spot. My conclusions had become their conclusions. Within a few minutes, my recommendations became their recommendations. Success.

I could have given them the standard-form presentation with recommendation up front. But instead, I took them on a journey so they could experience the same eye-opening discovery moment I had weeks earlier as part of my research. That "ah-ha" moment leaves a powerful mental and emotional marker in human memory. But this "discovery journey" has another benefit, too. People are naturally more committed to their ideas than they are to your ideas. This story technique turns your ideas into their ideas. Using it, your audience will be more likely to remember your ideas, be moved by them, and passionately pursue them. As a result, the discovery journey story is one of the most effective techniques I've found for making recommendations that get accepted and acted upon.

* * *

Another technique is the use of a simple metaphor. Metaphors allow you to capture the power of a complete story in just a few words. You'll learn more about metaphors and analogies in chapter 24. But the following story will show you the power of a well-chosen metaphor in action.

Alltel Corporation began in 1943 when Charles Miller and Hugh Wilbourn Jr. started installing telephone poles and cabling for telephone companies in Arkansas. By 2007, it had become one of the largest wireless telecommunications service providers in the country, operating in 34 U.S. states. On May 20 of that year, then-CEO Scott Ford announced that the company was being sold to two private equity firms: TPG Capital of Fort Worth, Texas, and Goldman Sachs Capital Partners of New York.

In his first meeting with the new owners, Scott was expected to deliver a long and detailed presentation advising them how to run the business as they took over. You can imagine the dozens of colorful charts and graphs and bullet points they might have been expecting. Instead, Scott had only two slides. The first was a picture of Niagara Falls with a tightrope walker skillfully balanced on a cable stretched across the entire width of the falls. With this as backdrop, Scott explained to the executives that running this business was a constant balance between providing the level of customer service their subscribers demand and delivering the cash flow required for a good return on investment. Better customer service meant more operators, better equipment, and the latest technology—all of which cost money that would otherwise accrue to the owners as profit. He went on to explain his experience and philosophy about how to maintain that important balance.

The second slide was even more important—not to Scott, but to his audience. Private equity firms are usually not interested in buying companies and managing them for decades. Typically, they buy companies they think will be more valuable if combined with another company, or managed differently, or simply need an infusion of cash to grow to the next level. Their objective is to rapidly grow the value of the business, sell it at the new higher value, and then repeat the process with another company. Scott knew this. So his second slide was a picture of a man getting into a yellow cab on a busy New York City street—an image all too familiar to the native New York team from Goldman Sachs. He explained the unusual convergence of events required for them to sell the company for a significantly higher price.

First, the buyer would need to be one of the big carriers, like AT&T, Verizon, or Sprint. Nobody else would value the company high enough to make any serious returns, and certainly not another private equity firm. Second, interest rates would have to be low enough for a multi-billion-dollar acquisition to make financial sense to the buyer. That, in turn, required a strong bond market. Finally, he explained, the temperament in Washington, D.C., must be just right to allow an acquisition of this size by an even larger competitor. The Justice Department monitors all mergers and acquisitions to make sure they don't result in a monopoly and unduly harm the consumer. If it sees fit, it can step in and prevent such deals, or reverse them after the fact. The point, Scott emphasized, is that waiting for that moment is a bit like trying to hail a cab in New York. You might have to wait a while. So when a yellow cab does pull over to pick you up, you'd better get in. You might not get another chance for a long time.

One year later, Scott received a phone call from one of the senior executives he had given that presentation to a year earlier. They had received an offer from Verizon to buy the company for $28.1 billion, and he wanted to know what Scott thought of the offer and if they should sell. Scott sat quietly on the other end of the phone with a knowing smile on his face. The executive finally broke the awkward silence with the answer to his own question, "This is the yellow cab, isn't it, Scott?"

For the next few minutes, the executive repeated everything Scott told him a year earlier and recognized the fortunate but unlikely convergence of events that led to the offer he had on the table. He decided he would take the offer, and thanked Scott for his counsel. Scott wished him luck, and ended the $28.1 billion phone call having only spoken a handful of words, none of which involved the sale of Alltel.

His masterful use of the yellow cab metaphor 12 months prior convinced the executive to take the offer now instead of waiting for a better one. This is the power of metaphor at its finest—to make your recommendations as compelling as possible. And it works just as well whether you're recommending what wireless carrier your small department should use next year, or how many billions of dollars to pay to buy the whole company.

* * *

A third technique to make recommendations stick is to challenge a fundamental assumption your audience has. Most recommendations start with a shared set of preconceived notions and build from there to a conclusion. But there's little you can do to make a bigger impact on your audience than to show them those assumptions are false. The following story from Joe Willke is a great example.

In 1983, Joe was still an analyst with Nielsen-BASES—a consumer research firm that specializes in predicting the success or failure of new products. Its technique starts by exposing a few hundred test participants to the concept behind the new product—just a few words to describe what it does and how it does it. Then the participants get to use the product for a week or two.

On one of Joe's first projects, the test results coming back were not what he expected. Consumers thought the concept was average at best. But once they actually used the product, they loved it! It was one of the largest differences between concept results and product results they had ever seen. Conventional wisdom for a situation like this would be to recommend a heavy sampling program. Since the concept wasn't that appealing, consumers weren't likely to try the product on their own. But if they got a free sample of this amazing stuff in the mail, they'd start buying.

In this case, however, Joe and his team had a better idea. But in order to get their client to go along with it, they'd have to get the client to admit it wasn't delivering on the promises one of its other brands had been making for years. Not an easy task. So when it came time for the big presentation, one of Joe's teammates stood up to kick off the meeting. After thanking everyone for showing up, he pulled out a piece of paper and held it up. Everyone recognized it as a nicely framed concept statement like those used in the consumer tests. He read it aloud, then said, "Just to make sure we're all on the same page, that's the concept you wanted us to test for this new brand, right?"

Everyone agreed.

That's when Joe's teammate dropped the bomb. "Actually, it's not." A hush fell over the room as everyone stared at the presenter. He continued, "That's the concept we tested for you three years ago when you launched your last brand in this category. But you could be forgiven for being confused, because it's almost exactly the same as the concept you asked us to test for this new brand."

Having everyone's full attention, Joe's colleague went on to describe the mediocre concept results and the great product results. He explained their hypothesis for why that happened. "You've been promising consumers this product for the last three years in your advertising for your current product. The only problem is, when they use your brand, they don't think it measures up to the promise. Consumers loved this concept when we tested it three years ago. The reason it tested so poorly now is that you—and several of your competitors—have been promising these benefits but coming up short in delivering it. They don't believe you anymore."

Joe and his team thought the right thing to do was to not launch a new brand at all. Instead, they wanted their client to take this amazing new technology and put it in the brand it had been selling for three years, finally delivering on the original promise. After this unexpected and unconventional presentation, the client came to the same conclusion. And that's exactly what it did.

Today, Joe is executive vice president with Nielsen, the parent company of Nielsen-BASES. He shares this story as an example of a bold and creative way to make a recommendation you know your audience doesn't want to hear. It leverages the element of surprise you'll learn about in chapter 19, and how to put your audience into the story, as you'll learn about in chapter 29. But the other reason it worked so well is that it challenged a fundamental assumption that everyone in the room had made— that this new brand had a new concept that was, well . . . *new*.

They could have simply shared the new test results in the traditional way, then shared the concept and test results from three years earlier, and drawn the comparison. But that would frame the recommendation as a natural part of the conclusion, the way it normally develops. Challenging the newness of the concept by reading the old concept at the beginning of the presentation framed the conclusion as a violation of a fundamental assumption. That's much more compelling to an audience. Consultants present results of their analysis to clients all the time, quickly followed by the conclusion they drew. Sometimes the clients agree with the conclusion and recommendation, and sometimes they don't. They don't often, however, disagree with the facts collected in the analysis. Assumptions are like those facts. Nobody expects them to be violated. But when they are violated, it's much easier—mentally and emotionally—for clients to accept an uncomfortable recommendation. After all, they've been operating under false assumptions. Surely their current course of action needs to change.

When possible, frame your big conclusion as a violation of some major assumption your audience holds. It's guaranteed to get their attention. And as Joe found out, they're much more likely to follow your recommendation.

* * *

Lastly, let's talk about a situation that happens far more often than we'd like to admit. What do you do when you're asked to give a presentation but you don't believe in the topic? It usually happens to the midlevel manager instructed to deploy the latest corporate mandate. This poor soul is stuck in between the executives issuing the mandate and the rank and file who need to carry out the new expectations. Whether you're the poor soul being asked to give it or you're the boss directing your reluctant subordinates to do so, it's a problem either way.

My answer might surprise you. Don't give it! Either get excited about it or ask the boss to get someone else to do it. If you're not enthusiastic about it, the audience won't be enthusiastic about it. The odds of them doing whatever it is you're telling them to do is nil. Your boss will appreciate your candor, and you might get off the hook entirely.

What if she says you still have to do it? Then what do you do? You figure out why you're not excited about it and fix it. Chances are it's because of one of the following three problems: You don't understand it, you don't agree with it, or you don't care about it. Let's talk about each one.

I once heard a comedian complain about a frustrating phone call he had suffered through. He had moved out of his apartment six weeks earlier and still hadn't received his deposit check. He'd left the place immaculate, so he knew he should be getting it back. He called the apartment manager's office. Sally answered the phone. He told her who he was and asked when his deposit check would be coming in the mail. She said she'd have to ask the manager. After a short pause, she returned and said very matter-of-factly, "Your deposit will be returned when those funds are released."

It wasn't her response that got the audience rolling in the aisle laughing. It was the startled look of disbelief on the comedian's face as he dramatized his reaction to it. He wasn't so much upset that she'd given him such a useless answer as he was shocked that she gave him the useless answer and then sat there waiting for him to respond . . . as if she had said anything of value to respond to! She clearly didn't understand the manager's words any better than the comedian did. But she just passed them along to him anyway. Of course, she had to go back to the manager to ask when the funds would be released, and what that depended on.

Don't be Sally. You can't explain something until you really understand it yourself. Simply repeating the words you've been given isn't good enough. Understand your topic or ask questions until you do understand.

Next you have to agree with it. If you don't, go back to your boss and share your objections. Chances are, if you have reservations about the content, so will the people you're supposed to deploy it to. Take your objections all the way up the corporate ladder until you get them resolved. That's what they get paid the big bucks for anyway—answering tough questions. Don't stop until every question is resolved. Resolved means either you finally understand the rationale or you've convinced management to change. Either way, you and your audience are better off.

Now that you understand it, and agree with it, you have to care about it. You do that by figuring out what's in it for you, your audience, or someone or something you care about. Surely it's good for one of those groups or it wouldn't be a priority for the company to deploy. You can probably figure this part out on your own just by asking yourself, "Who will benefit if we all do this?" Once you know that, you have a reason to care.

Now you're ready to present your recommendation or deploy the company policy. You understand it, agree with it, and care about it. You'll do great!

If, instead, you're the executive issuing the orders, make sure the people you ask to deploy your material have gone through all three steps. And if you find yourself having to coach or advise someone in this unfortunate position, first tell the story about Sally. Then tell the person to keep asking questions until they understand, agree, and care. They'll deliver like a superstar. For the first time in your career, you'll be an inspirational leader by repeating a professional comedian's joke.

SUMMARY AND EXERCISES

1. People are naturally more committed to their ideas than your ideas. Turn your ideas into their ideas by taking your audience on your discovery journey through story. (Think of the 1983 diaper discovery journey.)

2. Use a metaphor to capture the power of your whole story in a single word or phrase, such as the yellow cab.

3. Frame your conclusion as a violation of a major assumption your audience holds. Challenge assumptions.

4. What if you have to make a presentation or recommendation you don't believe in? Don't. Either get excited about it or ask the boss to get someone else to do it. Here's how to get excited about it:

    a. Understand it. Ask questions until you thoroughly understand the topic. Don't be a Sally. ("When will I get my deposit check?")

    b. Agree with it. State your objections and let management respond until you're satisfied. If you have issues with the material, your audience will, too.

    c. Care about it. Figure out what's in it for you or your audience.

Note

1. Lilly Walters, *Secrets of Successful Speakers: How You Can Motivate, Captivate, and Persuade* (New York: McGraw-Hill, 1993), p. 95.

CHAPTER 6

Define customer service success and failure

"A sale is not something you pursue. It's something that happens to you while you're immersed in serving your customer."
—UNKNOWN

IN THE EARLY 1980S, Sterling Price worked as a cook at Pizza Hut in Springdale, Arkansas. This was before there were any national sandwich chains in town, like Subway, Blimpies, or Quiznos. As Sterling tells the story, "A lady came in one day and asked if we had meatball sandwiches. When I told her we didn't, she got very upset—on the verge of tears. So I said that even though we didn't have it on the menu, we did have sandwich rolls, meatballs, tomato sauce, and mozzarella cheese. Since we had all the ingredients, I told her I could make it for her and just ring it up as one of the other sandwiches on the menu.

"She thanked me profusely, and then explained that her husband was very sick and had lost his appetite. She was desperate to get him to eat something, and had asked him if there was anything that sounded good. He told her he might be able to eat some of a meatball sandwich. She'd been to several restaurants already and no one could help her. We were the last stop she was going to make before going home empty-handed.

"She took the sandwich home and I didn't think much more about it until the next day when she called Pizza Hut and asked for me. She told me her husband had eaten as much of the sandwich as he could manage, and was very grateful she was able to get it for him. It was the most complete and enjoyable meal he'd had in days.

45

"Then she explained a bit more about her husband's condition. It turns out he had been diagnosed with stage four cancer a few months earlier. His loss of appetite was the least of his unpleasant symptoms, but perhaps the only one she could provide any comfort for. So it meant a lot to her that I had been so flexible with our menu.

"Then she told me that he passed away quietly during the night. That sandwich was his last meal. She was crying by then, but thanked me again and said it helped make his last day of life a little more bearable. It still touches me to this day, and is a great reminder that even seemingly small things we do for others can have a big impact on their lives."

That's the kind of story public relations managers dream of. Inside the company they help teach other employees what stellar customer service looks like. It gives them permission to think outside the box to exceed customer expectations. When shared outside the company, it makes for great advertising and builds the reputation and image of the company in the community where it happened and across the country. Unfortunately for Pizza Hut, as far as Sterling knows, none of that happened with his story. Why? Because nobody wrote it down. It was a pleasant, heartwarming story for Sterling to share with his coworkers and his shift manager. But that's as far as it went. A priceless company asset went to waste.

Compare that to the next story—equally impressive from a customer service standpoint. But leveraged far better.

When Ray Brook's flight landed at Portland International Airport on Monday morning, he headed straight for the National Car Rental counter. He had a meeting with a customer in 30 minutes and a full schedule of visits to warehouses and distribution centers for the next four days. Fortunately, Ray was a member of National's Emerald Aisle Club, which allows frequent business travelers like him to bypass the line at the counter and go directly to the lot to pick up their cars. But when he ran his card through the machine to dispense his keys, it was rejected. The message told him to see an agent back at the counter.

A frustrated but good-natured Mr. Brook went back to the counter and presented his card to the agent. After a minute of research, she said there was a problem with his profile, and asked to see his driver's license. Studying his license, she said, "Did you know your driver's license expired last week on your birthday?"

"No, I had no idea!" Ray said in genuine surprise.

Then she offered with a smile, "Happy birthday, Mr. Brook." This kind gesture certainly helped diffuse a little of the building tension but couldn't overcome what she had to say next. "I'm sorry, Mr. Brook, but we can't rent you a car because you don't have a valid driver's license." Ray was shocked and dismayed. He explained his very tight agenda for the next two days. He simply must have a car. The agent quickly called over the manager.

The manager explained the problem. "In the unlikely event you're in an accident, Mr. Brook, and are injured or injure someone else, National would be liable for renting a car to a person with an expired license. I'm sorry, but we simply cannot rent you a car."

What the manager said next, however, shocked Ray even more. "We can, however, drive you wherever it is you'd like to go."

What? Did he hear that correctly?

Ray explained that he had meetings scheduled at multiple places around Portland for two days. He then planned to fly to Sacramento, California, for another two days of meeting hopping, where he would again need a rental car. It was a very generous offer. But Ray didn't want a guest along with him for four days, any more than the manager wanted to be without an agent for that long.

After listening to Ray's agenda, the manager offered this creative solution. He noticed Ray's driver's license was from Washington State, which bordered Oregon to the north of Portland—just on the other side of the Columbia River from the airport. So despite the fact that Ray was almost 200 miles from home, the nearest Washington State Department of Motor Vehicles office was just a few miles away. He offered to drive Ray to his first appointment about 20 minutes away. Then he would come back for him at the end of the appointment and drive him to the DMV to get his license renewed. There was just enough time in between appointments to make it. Then Ray could officially rent the car for the rest of the trip.

"Brilliant!" Ray thought. And it was agreed. The manager had one of the agents drive him to his first appointment and then later to the DMV. But it was there that Ray got his third shock of that still very early day. When they arrived at the DMV, they discovered that in Washington, DMV offices are closed on Mondays.

Now what? The agent drove an increasingly frustrated Ray Brook back to the rental car office at the airport to figure out what to do next. There, Ray and the manager concocted plan B. Here's what they did. A

National agent drove Ray to his hotel to check in but didn't charge Ray anything for the day since he hadn't technically rented a car yet. With that money saved, Ray paid taxi fares to get him to the remaining calls that day. Tuesday morning, another National agent picked Ray up at his hotel and took him to his final appointment in Portland, then waited outside for him. An hour and a half later, the agent drove him to the DMV, which was now open. The agent patiently waited again for an hour as Ray slowly moved through the line and got his license renewed. They drove back to the airport just in time for Ray to catch his flight to Sacramento. Ray thanked the manager for the extraordinary customer service. But before he left, the manager personally updated Ray's profile with the new driver's license date, so he wouldn't have any trouble renting a car in Sacramento.

That was 20 years ago. Ray Brook has been a loyal National Car Rental customer ever since. Most importantly, then-president and CEO of National, Vince Wasik, used Ray's story to define customer service excellence in dozens of speeches to thousands of National employees and board members over the following years.[1] It's impossible to train employees for every possible scenario. They're infinite. But through stories like these, they can learn on a more intuitive level what great customer service looks like.

So why did National leverage Ray Brook's story, while Pizza Hut left Sterling Price's untold? Because someone wrote it down. In the case of National, that someone was Ray Brook. He was so impressed with the customer service that he wrote a detailed letter of commendation for the manager and agents at the Portland office and sent it to National's CEO directly, who recognized the value in the story and used it.

* * *

A customer's experience would have to be incredibly good (or incredibly bad) to compel most people to find the name and address of the CEO, write and print a lengthy letter, find an envelope and postage, and make a trip to the post office. Fortunately, today there are easier options. The savvy leader will find them or create them, as the following story explains.

In May 2011, Sue Soldo completed a series of chemotherapy treatments for breast cancer. Drained both physically and emotionally, she was ready for a stress-free and pampering vacation. She chose a four-night stay at the Adobe Grand Villas, a beautiful bed-and-breakfast in Sedona, Arizona. It's one of the top-rated properties in town. She picked it, however, because of the glowing online reviews with over-the-top stories about its extraordinary service. Upon arrival, Sue knew she'd made a good choice. Her room had rustic timber rafters, a hot tub, a fireplace, and a bathroom as big as the sleeping quarters of most hotel rooms. It made for a fabulous retreat. Even on the way home at her vacation's end, she was thinking what a perfect week it had been. Until she unpacked her suitcase, that is.

That's when she realized she had accidentally left a tiny but expensive mouth guard wrapped in tissue on the bathroom counter. It's the kind custom-fit to your front teeth to keep you from grinding your teeth at night. In desperation, she called Adobe. They were apologetic and empathetic but didn't offer much hope. "It could be anywhere in the Dumpster by now." Sue hung up knowing that she would never see that mouth guard again, and that a $500 trip to the dentist was in her future.

Three days later, however, a small package arrived in the mail from Sedona. Tanya, the innkeeper at Adobe, found the mouth guard! She had to wallow in the Dumpster up to her hips to find and return the missing treasure. You don't need much help to imagine how unpleasant it must be to go Dumpster diving in an industrial-sized garbage Dumpster. But suffice it to say that any business with a commercial kitchen produces some unsavory refuse.

Tanya's effort was clearly above and beyond Sue's expectations. Was it worth it? Well, according to Sue, it certainly earned her loyalty. Her next trip to Sedona, she won't think of staying anywhere else. More importantly, it so moved her that she wrote a story about it and posted it on TripAdvisor.com alongside the other raving fan posts of the Adobe Grand Villas.[2] As of this writing, almost 1,000 people planning vacations have read it.

But the benefit of Sue's story goes beyond its marketing value. Just as it shows potential guests what they have to look forward to, it shows the staff at Adobe what's expected of them. That, in turn, leads to more unparalleled service, which leads to other pleased guests leaving their own stories, starting the whole cycle over again.

Finally, this story has one more lesson to teach. When it comes to customer service, you don't even have to craft your own stories. Your customers will craft them for you—good or bad—if there's a convenient place to share them. If one exists for your industry, make sure your customers know where it is and encourage them to use it. If not, make one! Make it easy for them to share customer service stories. Then mine that database of stories often, and use them to set customer service expectations of your employees, and your customers.

* * *

It's been said that we learn more from our failures than from our successes. That's true in our personal lives. But it's often the opposite in the corporate world. The reason isn't that failures are less telling in business than in life. The reason is that we're naturally more hesitant to talk about our failures with coworkers than we are with family. So the work lessons we learn often have to be relearned over and over by everyone else, whereas our successes get documented, celebrated, and spread like ego-driven wildfire.

This story is one of a customer service failure and the lesson learned from it. Chances are, no matter what business you're in, it will apply to you, too.

"Not yet, Dad! I have to get to the next level!" That's the response I get every time I tell my 12-year-old son, Matthew, it's time to stop playing video games and go to bed. It's hard for a parent who grew up on Space Invaders and Pacman to understand. Those games were simple in comparison to today's games. Once you finished off a grid of invading space ships or gobbled up all the dots, an identical set appeared in their place. You could stop playing anytime and start again the next day and not miss any fun. But games today are highly complex, with multiple levels, each with a unique and elaborate plot played out in three-dimensional space. A game is never really over. Each time you complete one level, you're introduced to the next. You can play for months and never repeat the same experience.

The trade-off for this added complexity, however, is this. The games aren't programmed to remember every unique move you make in a given level. When you turn off the game for the night, you lose any progress since the last checkpoint and have to start that level over again the next day. Hence, the response from my son. And it's hard to blame him. He's invested maybe 20 minutes of effort already. The result is a maddening battle of will, pitting parent against child. I would think any decent game marketer would pounce on this opportunity. A huge selling point to the parents—who actually pay for these games—would be a "save" button! With a single click, save all progress to date, and remove any excuses the child has to disobey the parent. I keep waiting, but I still haven't seen it.

I was pondering this dilemma on a recent vacation while trying to rent a car. When I walked in, I saw three employees in the standard shirt and tie uniform, each sitting behind a desk working at a computer. In unison, all three looked up at me, then looked at each other, apparently determining whose turn it was to get up. Then one of them said to me, "I'll be with you in a minute, sir."

Really? I looked around the office. I was the only customer in the building. Three employees and one customer, and I had to wait on them. My wait only lasted about 2 minutes. But the lonely irony of the situation made it seem like 10. It was long enough, however, for me to wonder what would cause this misguided set of priorities. There was a competing car rental lot just down the street and they were ignoring the only customer in the room! Driving around in that rental car that day I formed my hypothesis. When I returned it the next day, there was a different set of employees on duty. Checking me in, the agent asked me all the requisite questions, and concluded with this one: "How was your customer service on this rental?"

Out of habit, I almost responded, "Fine, thanks." But I caught myself. I looked up at her and said, "Well, since you asked, actually I was a bit surprised." I told her the story of my check-in. As trained, she politely asked me if there was anything she could do to make it up to me. I thanked her and said that wasn't necessary. It was only a couple of minutes. "But I have been wondering why it happened, and I have a hypothesis." She seemed curious, so I told her of the nightly struggles with my son and his video games. "I wonder," I asked her, "if something similar is preventing your agents from responding to customers in a timely manner. If they're in the middle of completing the last transaction, or closing the books for the day, is it difficult for them to save what they're doing and take care of a customer?"

"Would you like to see for yourself?" she asked. Then she invited me around the counter to see the computer screen. "I'm in the middle of checking you in on this screen. If I stopped and rented a car to another customer right now, all your information on this screen would be lost, and I'd have to start over." I asked her if it was possible to save the information first. She said yes, and showed me how. I watched as she clicked a button to go to a different screen, then another, and then another. Three clicks to three different screens, and with each one we had to wait several seconds for the new screen to appear. On the third screen there was a save button, which she clicked. But before the save would complete, she had to enter her user name and password again. Having done that, she was now free to navigate three screens to begin the other transaction. Once that was complete, she could navigate three screens back to my transaction to complete it. In all, it would take a little over a minute of extra time.

My hypothesis was confirmed. The agent who checked me in was making a judgment call. He could stop and take care of me immediately and lose perhaps several minutes of work. He could make me wait a minute while he saved his current transaction. Or he could finish his current transaction and make me wait two minutes. The first option was understandably unacceptable for him. Of the remaining options, in his judgment, making the customer wait one extra minute and being completely done with the transaction was the best option. Either way, the customer was going to have to wait. What's one extra minute?

So why is it this way? Why is it so difficult to save a transaction and come back to it later? The answer is that computer systems are designed to be efficient for the user, which in this case is the employee. But what if in addition, they were designed with the customer in mind? What if the impact the program has on customer service was a design requirement? I know the answer to that question. It would have a "save" button at the top of every screen!

The lesson has broader implications than rental car check-in. Every modern company uses computer systems and standard work processes, and every one of them has customers. Are your systems and processes designed with the sole intent of employee efficiency, regardless of the impact on customer satisfaction? If so, you have an opportunity. Make customer service a key consideration in every system and process. You'll be amazed at the impact on customer satisfaction when customers no longer have to wait for your employees to "get to the next level."

SUMMARY AND EXERCISES

1. Great customer service stories show employees how to do their jobs with excellence, and can be great PR for the company. Don't let them go to waste like the "meatball sandwich" story at Pizza Hut. Share them at every opportunity, such as the story about the expired license.

2. Make it easy for your customers to write their own stories. Create a website; put up a "story box"; or give your customers a self-addressed, stamped envelope and blank paper for them to write their stories to you later.

3. Find stories your customers have written about you already on industry websites or customer review blogs. Mine them for stories of customer service success and failure. Use them to create more customer service success stories. Consider the story about the Dumpster-diving innkeeper.

4. People love to tell their own success stories but are less eager to share their failures. Untold, those failures are more likely to be repeated. Tell them.

5. Design your company systems and processes with customer service in mind, not just employee efficiency. Do so and you'll have much happier customers— and more of them. Tell the story about getting to the next level.

Notes

1. As reported to Portland Airport National Car Rental manager Wayne Ranslem.
2. "The Extra Mile," Trip Advisor.com. http://www.tripadvisor.com/Show UserReviews-g31352-d500771-r109386484-Adobe_Grand_Villas-Sedona_Arizona.html#CHECK_RATES_CONT.

CHAPTER **7**

Structure of a story

"Human beings master the basics of storytelling as young children and retain this capability throughout their lives."
—STEPHEN DENNING, *The Leader's Guide to Storytelling*

IF YOU ASK A 10-YEAR-OLD, "What's the structure of a good story?" the child might say something like, "Oh, that's easy! There's a beginning, a middle, and an end." True, perhaps. But not very helpful. If you ask a Hollywood script writer the same question, she might tell you there are six parts: the setup, catalyst, first turning point, climax, final confrontation, and resolution.[1] True again. And if you plan to write a screenplay or a murder mystery, that structure will serve you well. If you ask a cognitive psychologist, he will likely give you an even more complicated answer. For example: setting, main characters, conflict and resolution, initiating event, internal response, attempt, consequence, reaction, and conclusion.[2]

If you keep asking different people, you'll get different answers. The right answer is that there is no one right answer. In fact, when psychologist T. A. Harley researched the academic literature on story "grammar," as psychologists call it, he concluded, "There is no agreement on story structure: virtually every story grammatician has proposed a different grammar."[3]

What you need as a business leader is a simple structure that works. You don't need to spellbind an audience for two hours in a movie theater, and you don't need to make sure your internal response is consistent with your initiating event, whatever that means. Every adult is a natural-born storyteller. You've been studying the art of storytelling ever since your

54

parents read you bedtime stories. You already know what the structure of a good story is. All you need is to be reminded.

The simplest way to remember is to start with these words, "Once upon a time, there was . . ." When you start that way, a natural story structure is almost forced out. If you start with "Once upon a time, there was . . ." the next words can only do one thing—introduce the main character. [Once upon a time, there was a puppet named Pinocchio.]

After that, you'll naturally want to tell what happened to the main character. [Every time Pinocchio told a lie, his nose would grow. . . . And then one day, he met a cricket named Jiminy. . . .] After all the adventures are told, you'll of course have to tell how the story ends. [And they lived happily ever after.]

So, it turns out the 10-year-old might have been right after all. A story does have three parts: a beginning, a middle, and an end. But to be more useful, let's give those parts more prescriptive names and discuss what each needs to contain. Instead of beginning, middle, end, let's call those context, action, result—CAR. You may remember this mnemonic from a high school writing class. We'll take that basic structure and tailor it for a business narrative.

Context

Context is the part of storytelling business leaders most often underdevelop, or skip entirely, much to their detriment. As a result, their stories are confusing and uninteresting. So we'll spend the most time in this chapter on context.

The context provides all the necessary background for the story to make sense. If done right, it also grabs the audience's attention, convinces the audience that your story is relevant, and generates interest and excitement to listen to the rest of the story. How well your context accomplishes all this is determined by how well it addresses four questions. Where and when does the story take place? Who is the main character? What does he or she want? And who or what is getting in the way? Let's look at all four.

1. Where and when? The fundamental meaning of context is the setting—the where and when of a story. Clearly stating where and when the story takes place tells the audience if the story is fact or fiction. If it starts out like the third story in chapter 3, "In the fall of 1971, Bob McDonald joined the U.S. Military Academy in West Point, New York," it signals that this is a true story. On the other hand, if it starts out, "Once upon a time, in a land far, far away," the audience knows it's listening to a folktale of some kind. It's okay to tell a fictional story as long as your audience knows that's what it's getting. The danger of not properly starting your stories this way is that the audience might think the story is factual, only to be disappointed to find out it was fiction. Then the audience feels betrayed. As the storyteller, you've now lost all credibility.

That's exactly what happened to a consultant I once hired. We'd planned a multiday event with about a dozen managers to discuss the long-term strategy of our business. Very serious stuff. So serious, in fact, that we hired a consulting firm to help us plan the background analysis, the discussion, the tools and templates we would use, and the output of the team's work. This included a professional moderator to lead the group and guide the conversation. When he kicked off the first day of meetings, our moderator introduced himself and started into a story about an experience he had at the airport when he arrived the day before. Apparently as he was leaving the terminal to catch a cab, he noticed a police officer writing a ticket for a car that was illegally parked in front of baggage claim. Our moderator watched as a man came running out of the terminal and started berating the officer. "What are you doing? I just stopped for a few minutes to get my bags! Don't you have anything better to do!"

The officer calmly listened to the man's tirade, placed the ticket under the windshield wiper, and began writing out another ticket. This one was presumably for being a jerk to a police officer. This sent the man into an even more outraged diatribe filled with unsavory language. After the officer had written the third ticket, the man finally gave up his fight and stormed back toward the terminal. Our moderator stopped the man on his way in and asked him, "Why did you keep yelling at the police officer? All that got you was more tickets." In response, the man donned a huge smile and said, "Oh, that's okay. It's not *my* car."

It was all a big joke. That was his icebreaker. You could almost hear the *ba-dum crash* from the drummer that always followed a Henny Youngman one-liner—"Take my wife . . . please." I got the impression he took this story from a joke book and just told it as if it were his own, as if it were true. There was polite laughter in the room. But it followed an awkward pause, as people had to mentally transition from hearing what they thought was a true story to laughing at a joke.

Don't get me wrong. There's nothing wrong with putting humor in your stories. What you want to avoid is ruining your credibility by not being honest with your audience. I was left wondering what else he was going to make up or take credit for during our meetings. Remember that you're a business leader, not a comedian. You don't have license to just make stuff up. Our moderator could have told the same story with better impact if he had simply preceded it with, "I heard a funny story the other day about this guy coming out of the airport. . . ."

2. Who is the main character?
This is the *subject* of your story, the hero, or at least the person from whose perspective the story is told—the protagonist. Even the most inexperienced storytellers generally include a main character in their story. So the point here is not to remind you to include a main character, but to tell you what kind of main character to choose. The most important criterion is this: The hero of your story needs to be someone your audience can identify with. They need to be able to see themselves in the hero's situation and achieve the same result: "Hey, that could be me!" If the main character of your story is Superman, that might make for an entertaining story, but it won't make for a good leadership story. Your audience can't fly and it can't bend steel. So the fact that Superman saved the world in your story won't give them any helpful advice or confidence they can do the same thing.

In the story of the jury room tables in the introduction, the college students conducting the research were the subjects. Just about everyone Jayson Zoller has told that story to in the last 20 years was a college student at one point. The story describes the subjects as having "asked all the questions you would think a smart group of would-be consultants should ask." That further identifies our heroes with the audience. If you were a consultant, you'd probably be a smart one, right? And you'd probably have asked all the same questions they did. That could be you in that story.

With that in mind, your subject doesn't have to be a real person. It could also be a fictional person, like the woman talking to the bricklayers in chapter 2, or a typical customer of your business. But the most powerful character you could ever choose for a story is you. Stories about you have the most authenticity and are almost always identifiable with your audience.

3. What does the character want?
What is the hero trying to achieve? What is the character's passion or objective? Is he trying to save the world? Is she trying to beat the competition? Win the sale? Or just not get fired. In Jayson's story, it was trying to improve the jury deliberation

process. For me in the round room, it was trying to get the CEO to pay attention to my presentation.

For reasons that will become clear shortly, let's call this objective the *treasure* the subject seeks.

4. Who or what is getting in the way? This is the *obstacle*, the villain, or the enemy in the story. It could be a person, like your high school nemesis, or the boss who passed you over for a promotion. Or the villain could be an organization, like one of your competitors or the other department you're playing in the company softball tournament. It could be a thing, like the mountain your hero is trying to climb, or the copy machine that he finally gets his revenge on. It can also be a situation that confronts the hero, like the challenge to grow sales by 50 percent as in the Merrill Lynch story in chapter 3, or the boredom of monthly memo-writing that drove Jim Bangel to write an Earnest Engineer story in chapter 1.

The villain is a commonly excluded component in business stories. The result is a boring, useless story. It's typified by the tales of the office braggart or the self-reported results in your subordinate's performance review. You've heard them. Stories where everything that happens is great! ("After I came to this department five years ago, our sales started to skyrocket! All of our new brand launches exceeded the objective. And our profits have doubled!") Similar to Superman stories, stories without a villain won't help anyone. Their heroes didn't overcome any adversity. They didn't confront any challenge. They didn't learn anything valuable. In short, they got lucky. Telling a story about how you got lucky is no way to provide guidance and leadership, since it can't be replicated. If there's no villain in your story, you don't have a story.

In addition, your audience simply won't like your story if it doesn't have a villain. As corporate training and development expert Richard Pascoe observes, "An audience hates insincerity. And few things are more insincere than continued and unchallenged success; life is not like that."

The villain in the jury room table story was the chief judge who hired the team of college students. You were introduced to him in the first paragraph of the story, in the context. You just didn't know he was the villain until the end of the story.

So there you have the key components of the context. In addition to telling where and when, you have the subject, the treasure, and the obstacle—STO. We'll use this shortly in a single mnemonic to help you remember the story structure.

Action

This is where you tell what happened to your main character. Most importantly, it's where the hero does battle with the villain. Conflicts arise. Problems surface. The hero mounts an attempt at a solution, but fails at first. There are always temporary setbacks on the hero's journey. These ups and downs along the way provide the excitement in the story. But more importantly for a leadership story, they're also where the lessons are learned.

Unlike the Hollywood scriptwriter's story structure, the action doesn't need to be so prescriptive for a good business story. It's great if you have a catalyst, first turning point, climax, and final confrontation, but not necessary.

The action in the jury table story starts in the second paragraph: "The students interviewed dozens of judges, attorneys, former jurors. . . ." The work they did is briefly described, and then the first setback happens. After researching many possible barriers to an effective jury deliberation process, they find out "to their surprise, none of those things seemed to matter much." All the logical avenues they pursued led to dead ends.

Only after this hurdle do we find out the unlikely solution was the shape of the table. Then the team members are excited once again because they've found an effective and affordable solution. But the action isn't over yet. Our poor heroes then learn the judge ordered all round tables replaced with rectangular ones, much to their horror. So in those few paragraphs of action, the hero goes from disappointment, to excitement, to disappointment. Perhaps not a full six-step Hollywood story structure, but more than adequate for a compelling business narrative.

Result

The result is the final stage of the story where you accomplish three main things. In addition to telling how the story ends, this is where you explain the *right lesson* the audience should have learned, and link back to *why* you told the story in the first place.

Result, of course, means how the story ends. It explains the fate of the main characters. Does the hero live or die? Did the villain get what he deserved? In the jury table story, the result is the third-to-last paragraph, which explains how the semester ended for the team and how they felt after hearing the judge's decision. It ends with, "They may have finished the year with an A on their report card, but they felt completely defeated."

Right lesson. The second-to-last paragraph delivers the moral of the story. It explains why Jayson tells that story today. "He tells this story to new researchers to teach them the importance of being clear on objectives before they embark on a research project."

Opinions vary on if and when you should spell out the moral of a story. Some argue that if a story is told well, the moral will be obvious and won't need to be explicitly called out. Besides, letting the listeners consider and debate the moral on their own is part of the unique power of storytelling, and you should afford that benefit to your audience.

On the other side of the argument, some warn that after stories get repeated a number of times, the moral—the *right lesson*—could get lost if not called out specifically. And in failure stories in particular, if you don't call out the moral, it can sound like you're just complaining and didn't learn anything from the experience. I've found that in most cases it makes sense to spell out the moral. The exception to the rule is when it's important for the audience to draw the conclusion, as it was in the discovery journey you learned in chapter 5. The good news is there's not one right answer. A great story won't be ruined either way you go. Use your judgment.

Link back to why. The final four sentences in the jury table story link the moral back to the original purpose of telling the story—the *why*—to illustrate the point that storytelling is a better vehicle for teaching and leadership. It ends with, "Experience is the best teacher. A compelling story is a close second." If you want your audience to go do something as a result of hearing your story, this is where you tell them.

So there you have the basic structure of a compelling leadership story. It all hangs on the central **C**ontext, **A**ction, **R**esult (CAR) structure. It starts with the **S**ubject, **T**reasure, and **O**bstacle, and concludes with the **R**ight lesson and link back to wh**Y** it's being told. There you have the first part of a mnemonic to help you remember the structure: CAR = STORY. We'll complete the mnemonic in chapter 29. For those who prefer more of a cookbook recipe, there's a template in the appendix that summarizes each part of the story and the key components of each. Use it to craft the outline of your story before you fill in the details.

* * *

Now that we've reviewed the *context, action, result* framework, let's illustrate its importance with a story written three different ways. An inexperienced storyteller will often start with the *action*. Here's what that looks like in a story that's a brilliant example of brand marketing in the golf industry.

Version 1: Action, Context, Result

(Action) In the early 2000s, Titleist launched the NXT golf ball marketed at average and recreational golfers used to playing well above par. The NXT was designed to create less spin, have a soft feel, and deliver more consistency—exactly what 95 percent of golfers in this target audience wanted. And because it didn't deliver the short-game spin, feel, and control that Titleist's flagship model ProV1 would, accomplished golfers wouldn't consider trading down from the ball they'd been buying for years.

(Context) NXT was launched to help Titleist capture a new and growing segment of golfers. The brand already had a 75 percent market share among accomplished golfers under a 15 handicap. But that was only 5 percent of golfers in the country. It only had a 20 percent share among the other 95 percent of golfers. The NXT was a bold move because it went against this conventional wisdom: To appeal to a lower-tier golfer, launch a lower-priced and lower-quality version of the flagship Titleist ProV1. The problem with conventional wisdom, however, was that some of their elite customers buying the $5 ProV1 balls might find the new cheaper version good enough, and trade down to a $3 ball.

(Result) The NXT turned out to be a much better decision. Titleist's market share more than doubled, from 20 percent to 43 percent, among the average golfers, while still growing share among the accomplished segment.

Conclusion: Titleist delivered its growth challenge by realizing that average consumers don't necessarily have watered-down needs compared to the most demanding ones. They have different needs entirely. Understand your consumers deeply, and design a product to delight each group separately.

Not a bad story. But it suffers the most common structural error in storytelling—reversing the order of the context and action. It's easy to recognize it when you hear it, or commit the error yourself. The speaker starts telling a story with the action. Then the audience gets confused.

The speaker stops and says something like, "Sorry, let me back up. . . ." Then the speaker explains the necessary background (context). The listener's face lights up, which says, "Oh, I get it. I'm with you now." Then the teller gets back to the story, already in midaction.

Why do we make that mistake so often? Because the action is the part of the story we remember the easiest. It's the part that was exciting to live through if it happened to us, or to listen to if we heard the story from someone else. In our excitement to share the story, we jump right to it, not considering the fact that our audience didn't have the benefit of context we have. If we're lucky, the look on their face or gentle protest will remind us to stop and go back to the context. If we're not so lucky, our story is doomed to mediocrity.

Here's that same story, but in the proper order.

Version 2: Context, Action, Result

(Context) In the late 1990s, Titleist had a 75 percent market share of the golf ball market among the best golfers in the country (those with a handicap of 15 or less). But that only represented about 5 percent of golfers. It only had a 20 percent market share among the other 95 percent of golfers. To reach that other 95 percent, conventional marketing wisdom dictated that it should launch a lower-priced, lower-quality version of its flagship Titleist ProV1. The problem with that, however, was that some of its accomplished players buying the $5 ProV1 balls might find the new cheaper version good enough, and trade down to a $3 ball. What did Titleist do?

(Action) In the early 2000s, Titleist launched the NXT golf ball marketed at average and recreational golfers with handicaps well above par. The NXT was designed to create less spin, have a soft feel, and deliver more consistency—exactly what 95 percent of golfers within this target audience wanted. And because it didn't deliver the short-game spin, feel, and control that Titleist's flagship model ProV1 would, accomplished golfers wouldn't consider trading down from the ball they'd been buying for years.

(Result) The NXT turned out to be a great decision. Titleist's market share more than doubled, from 20 percent to 43 percent, among the average golfers, while still growing among the accomplished golfer segment.

Conclusion: Titleist delivered its growth challenge by realizing that average consumers don't necessarily have watered-down needs compared to the most demanding ones. They have different needs entirely. Understand your consumers deeply, and design a product to delight each group separately.

See how much better that flows?

Now, let's look at one more version. This one maintains the CAR structure but adds more storytelling elements you'll learn in other "how-to" chapters throughout the book. Note the new second and third paragraphs. Those additional paragraphs contain elements of realism, emotion, and surprise advocated in chapters 13, 18, and 19, respectively.

Version 3: (More) Context, Action, Result

(Context) In the late 1990s, Titleist had a 75 percent market share of the golf ball market among the best golfers in the country (those with a handicap of 15 or less). But that only represented about 5 percent of golfers. It only had a 20 percent market share among the other 95 percent of golfers. To reach that other 95 percent, conventional wisdom dictated that it should launch a lower-priced, lower-quality version of its flagship Titleist ProV1. The problem with that, however, is that some of its accomplished players buying the $5 ProV1 balls might find the new cheaper version good enough, and trade down to a $3 ball. What should Titleist do?

Consider this: What if I told you there was a new golf ball on the market guaranteed to fly 350 yards off the tee? The only catch is, you have to hit it dead straight or it will slice off 350 yards into the woods. Would you buy it? The answer, of course, depends on how good of a golfer you are. If you're a scratch golfer, used to playing just above par, you'd probably love it! But if you're a duffer, or even an average golfer, you wouldn't be interested in wasting your money on balls that will only get lost.

Instead, what if I offered you a golf ball guaranteed to go straight down the fairway, no matter how poorly you hit it? The catch is, it will only go a maximum of 225 yards. Would you buy that ball? Again, it depends. The duffer would fill his bag with balls like that. The pro would scoff at it.

(Action) That was the insight at Titleist that led the company to break from conventional wisdom a decade ago and launch Titleist NXT. While it didn't quite guarantee to keep you in the fairway on every shot, it was designed to create less spin, have a soft feel, and deliver more consistency—exactly what 95 percent of golfers within this target audience wanted. And

because it didn't deliver the short-game spin, feel, and control that Titleist's flagship model ProV1 would, accomplished golfers wouldn't consider trading down from the ball they'd been buying for years.

(Result) The NXT turned out to be a great decision! Titleist's market share more than doubled, from 20 percent to 43 percent, among the average golfers, while still growing among the elite.

Conclusion: Titleist delivered its growth challenge by realizing that average consumers don't necessarily have watered-down needs compared to the most demanding ones. They have different needs entirely. Understand your consumers deeply, and design a product to delight each group separately.

By fixing the structure and adding other elements of great storytelling, we've taken a story from good, to better, to best.

SUMMARY AND EXERCISES

1. A well-told business story isn't the same as a romance novel or a Hollywood movie. It has a simpler structure. But it does have one. Order does matter, and this is it: context, action, result (CAR).

    a. When you start a story with the action, you lose your audience and have to backtrack to tell the context. (Consider the three Titleist NXT stories.)

2. Context is most often skipped or underdeveloped. It provides all the necessary background, grabs your listeners' attention, convinces them your story is relevant, and generates interest and excitement to listen to the rest of the story.

3. Context must answer these four questions:

    a. Where and when did the story happen? This tells the audience it's a true story. Make sure it's yours, or give credit where it is due. ("It's okay. It's not *my* car.")

    b. Who is the main character? (**S**ubject) The hero must be relatable to your audience—not Superman.

    c. What does the character want? (**T**reasure) Your audience must find this a familiar and worthy objective—one it is pursuing or hopes to pursue someday.

    d. Who or what is getting in the way? (**O**bstacle) This is the villain. Without one, your story is useless. You just got lucky.

4. The **A**ction is where the hero does battle with the villain. It's the part most storytellers remember most vividly, because it's a recount of what they did and the setbacks they had along the way.

5. The **R**esult should explain three things:

    a. How the story ends—does the hero win or lose?

    b. The **R**ight lesson the listener should have learned. It's okay to spell it out so it doesn't get misconstrued.

    c. A link back to the reason wh**Y** you told the story in the first place. This is what you want your audience to go do.

6. CAR = STORY: Context + Action + Result = Subject + Treasure + Obstacle + Right lesson + whY

Notes

1. Michael B. Druxman, *How to Write a Story . . . Any Story: The Art of Storytelling* (Thousand Oaks, CA: The Center Press, 1997).

2. "Story Grammar," Curriculum, Technology, & Education Reform. http://wik.ed.uiuc.edu/index.php/Story_grammar.

3. T. A. Harley, *The Psychology of Language* (New York: Taylor & Francis, 1995).

CHAPTER **8**

Define the culture

"A culture is made—or destroyed—by its articulate voices."[1]
—AYN RAND

ON JANUARY 25, 2011, a revolution erupted in cities across Egypt. Millions of protesters took to the streets demanding free elections and redress from police brutality, high unemployment, political corruption, and rampant inflation.

The protests started peacefully, but quickly escalated to violent conflict with security forces loyal to Hosni Mubarak. Hundreds of deaths and thousands of injuries were reported in the ensuing days. The capital city of Cairo resembled a war zone. Many attempted to flee the city for safety. Rasoul Madadi, a Procter & Gamble expatriate (expat) from Cincinnati, was one of them, along with his wife and six-year-old son.

On Sunday January 30, Rasoul took his family to the Cairo airport. Their destination didn't matter, as long as it was out of Egypt. Two days earlier the government had announced a curfew from sundown to sunup. This slowed the movement of people and goods to a near standstill. Pilots and crew had difficulty getting to the airport, causing flight cancellations. Some foreign airlines stopped incoming flights, resulting in more outbound cancellations. The airport was overcrowded, and food and water were quickly depleting. Panic was setting in.

Rasoul, however, was calmer than most. That's because he works at a company that didn't just say its employees were its most important asset—P&G proved it that weekend.

66

Many in the airport no longer had tickets, since their flight had been canceled. They were waiting and hoping for seats on other flights to become available. The lucky ones still had a ticket. But with so many flights being canceled, even the lucky ones had only a small chance of getting out that day. Juggling three cell phones, Rasoul began calling the two company-provided travel agencies to buy more tickets. He knew that to have a decent chance of getting out, he needed to buy tickets on several flights and hope that at least one of them made it out. But that would be expensive, and access to money was limited in the wake of the revolution.

Fortunately, the day before (Saturday) he started calling for help. He called the local plant manager where he worked and asked what he was authorized to do and spend to get his family to safety. The response was, "Take care of your family first. Do what is best for you; I approve. I'm in touch with our global security contacts in Dubai and Johannesburg to advise you what to do no matter what country you land in." He got hold of a human resources manager in the United Kingdom and asked for advice. "Get on the first flight you can. We will take care of everything else." They did.

A colleague from overseas called to check on Rasoul and offer help. "I need help with travel," Rasoul said. She contacted her administrator, who was particularly adept at managing complex global travel. She spent much of her Saturday arranging alternatives for flights and accommodations in several cities that were quickly booking up.

With all of that help, Rasoul was able to secure tickets for all three family members on five separate flights out of Cairo that day. He watched and listened as other passengers desperately tried to contact their company representatives or anyone for help—many to no avail. And then they waited. The first flight was canceled only minutes before its scheduled departure time. The second one was canceled not much later. Other passengers asked him how it was that he could simply get out of line for one canceled flight and get in another. "How can you have so many tickets?"

Five hours passed. Food and water were now completely gone in the main terminal. After their first four flights were canceled, Rasoul and his family were told their fifth and last set of tickets would be honored—a Singapore Airlines flight to Dubai would soon depart with them aboard. It was only the first or second commercial flight that would actually depart from Cairo that day.

But their ordeal was not over. After landing in Dubai, Rasoul's wife was not allowed to enter the country on her Canadian passport. Apparently, a new rule allowed a Canadian to enter Dubai only as a visitor and therefore must have a paid ticket out of Dubai. Rasoul made another frantic phone call to the company travel office. They bought a new ticket on the spot for his wife and faxed it to the immigration authority. Another charge to the corporate credit card, and an hour later they entered Dubai—all of them.

After checking into a hotel arranged by the corporate team earlier, Rasoul contacted the local human resources manager and explained his situation: no cash, no access to his bank account in Egypt, and his credit card quickly reaching its limit. HR told him not to worry. "We knew you might be coming here. We'll take care of you. Just tell us what you need."

Rasoul knows what it means to be a company's most valuable asset. Today he advises people to look beyond their salary and benefits when evaluating the worth of a company. Many companies say their employees are their most valuable asset. Probably some of the less fortunate people Rasoul met at the Cairo airport worked at just such a company. His experience illustrates the difference between companies that just say it and those that prove it. That difference is what management guru Sumantra Ghoshal called "the smell of the place."[2] It's what makes employees feel valued, energized, and engaged. But it starts with feeling valued. Telling and retelling Rasoul's story at P&G helps everyone know the culture and values expected of them, and what they can expect of others.

An organization's culture is defined by the behavior of its members and reinforced by the stories they tell. The behavior and stories are more powerful than any corporate edict, policy statement, or speech from the CEO. You can't just say, "We treat people like family here," and expect it to happen. You have to actually treat people like family and hope they do the same.

But unless you work at a company with only a handful of employees who work in the same room, people can't see what's happening to everyone else all the time. That's where stories come in. Although it's clearly the behavior that has to happen first (treating people like family, for example), it's the stories about what happened that live on and create the culture and expectations for others to follow. That's why it's important for stories like Rasoul's to be heard. Often those stories circulate on their own, unprompted. But not always. If you want to create a stronger culture in your organization, find the stories that exemplify the culture you want to foster and share them broadly. In chapter 30, you'll learn many creative methods and venues to do that.

* * *

Unfortunately, stories of bad behavior can define a culture, too. You just won't like the result. Compare the following two examples from the book *Building Cross-Cultural Competence*. In it, authors Charles Hampden-Turner and Fons Trompenaars recount two starkly different tales of CEOs and how they reacted to being confronted by their own employees for violating company policy.[3]

Charles Revson, head of Revlon Corporation, insisted that everyone sign the time of his or her arrival in a logbook kept at the reception desk. A new receptionist, still in her first week on the job, noticed a man she had not seen before come into the reception area and walk off with the logbook. Chasing after him, she said, "Excuse me, sir. But that book is not to be removed. I have strict instructions." Revson allegedly turned and stared at her, then said, "When you pick up your last paycheck this evening, ask them to tell you who I am."

Contrast that with this story of Tom Watson, chairman of IBM, when he approached the gate of one of IBM's high-security buildings with a group of his senior executives. A 19-year-old security guard refused entry to Mr. Watson because he didn't have his security badge. One of the executives hissed at her, "Don't you know who that is? He's the chairman of the company!" But Watson stopped the whole party and sent someone back for his badge. "She's quite right," he said. "We make the rules. We keep 'em."

Stories like these can circulate in organizations for decades. Regardless of the official rules of conduct, such stories define the culture and the norms of behavior. If you want a culture where everyone abides by the rules, you need stories like Tom Watson's.

* * *

Does that mean there's no productive place for stories about people who aren't living up to the cultural expectations of the organization? Fortunately not. You just have to pick a story that shows that person being confronted or reprimanded for the behavior. The following story is a great example. It's been kicking around the halls of investment powerhouse Morgan Stanley long enough to become legendary. It was first recounted in the book *Blue Blood and Mutiny* by Patricia Beard.

Sometime in the 1990s, then-president John Mack was walking down the hallway at eight o'clock in the morning when he noticed a delivery boy waiting outside with a breakfast order.[4] He walked back by 30 minutes later and the same guy was there. So he asked, "Are you still waiting for the same pickup?"

"Yes," came the response.

John asked him for the phone number of his customer. He called the trader who ordered the food and asked him to come out front where he and the delivery person were waiting. When the trader arrived, John scolded him for keeping someone waiting who depends on tips for his livelihood. "Look, this guy's trying to make a living like you. You can't keep him waiting 30 minutes. Never let this happen again."

In this case, the confrontation is part of the story. But every bad culture story won't have that. In those cases, you can still use the story as long as you point out the damage the bad behavior caused—a drop in employee morale or an increase in the likelihood a valued employee will leave. What you don't want circulating are the bad stories without the negative consequences spelled out.

* * *

Another element of culture at work is the unspoken norms of behavior defined by the employees themselves, not by company management or policy. These norms trump policy every time. A classic example of that is working hours. Company guidelines might state quitting time is 5 P.M. But if everyone else works until 6 P.M. and looks at you funny when you leave at 5, you'll quickly adjust your working hours.

A more modern example—and one where storytelling is critically important—involves flexible work arrangements, or FWA. Such arrangements include things like reduced working hours or working from home. Anyone who's worked in a corporate setting knows there's a big difference between a company that has an FWA policy and one with a culture that actually allows employees to use those arrangements and feel good about it. Most companies today have an FWA policy. But at some of those organizations, the unwritten rules—the underlying culture that actually dictates employee behavior—prohibit people from taking advantage of those policies freely. Sometimes there's an overt effort on the part of management to dissuade people from using them. In other places it's less overt. Employees are afraid they'll be viewed as less committed to the company, and fear their careers will suffer because of it.

How do you make it clear that your organization's culture is one that truly embraces FWA policies? You celebrate the people who take advantage of them, publically, and share their stories. For example, in June 2011, Procter & Gamble's employee website featured a short video telling the story of three employees at its San Jose, Costa Rica, site—Silvia Porras, Annette Rodriguez, and Maria Tinoco.

Silvia joined P&G's San Jose office in March 2000 as a cost accounting specialist. She married in November 2002, and by 2005 had her first child, Antonio. As any parent knows, having a child places an entirely new set of demands on your time and energy. Silvia and her husband, Orlando, embraced those new demands, and soon were ready for another child. What they weren't prepared for was to find out they were having triplets! With such a high-risk pregnancy, Silvia went on disability leave in her fifth month of pregnancy. Then, with much anticipation, on June 6, 2007, Victoria, Catalina, and Isabel joined the rest of the family.

With four children under the age of three, Silvia had her hands full. She asked for an entire year of maternity leave, which her managers willingly granted. But a working career was still an important part of her life plan. Again, her management made arrangements to allow her the work–life balance she needed to be successful at work and at home.

After 15 months away from work, Silvia came back to work in a role in her same area of expertise, so she wouldn't have to learn a whole new job. In addition, three days a week she was allowed to work from home. That allowed her to be involved in the most intimate bonding moments with her children instead of having a full-time hired caregiver. On those days, Silvia could bathe her children in the morning, feed them at lunch, and still get her work done in between.

Annette and Maria had their own unique situations that required flexibility in work time or location. Their stories were just as poignant, and the company's FWA policies met their needs just as well. The video that shared these stories was posted on the home page of the company website, where it was surely seen by thousands of employees. To those who watched it, it was clear that the company they work for not only has an FWA policy but also a culture that supports using it. If your organization has a disconnect between the written and unwritten norms, find stories of people following the norms you want to foster and spread them far and wide.

* * *

The final lesson in this chapter on culture doesn't involve defining or changing the culture, but the importance of understanding it and conforming to it. This case involves the culture of an entire country, and one foreigner who unfortunately didn't understand it.

At 5:46 A.M. on January 17, 1995, a massive earthquake shook the city of Kobe, Japan, killing over 5,000 people, and leaving 300,000 injured or homeless.[5] Measuring 6.9 on the Richter scale, it was the worst earthquake Japan had experienced in over 70 years. One of the hardest-hit parts of the city was Rokko Island, a manmade island about two miles square that sits 500 yards off the southern coastline, in the Port of Kobe. It's connected to the mainland by only two bridges. Both were heavily damaged by the quake, and impassable. For several days, people were unable to leave the island, and food and supplies were slow to get in. P&G's Northeast Asia headquarters is located on Rokko Island, as are the homes of many of the employees who work there.

During the days after the quake, some of the only accessible food was in vending machines. When a machine was found still working, a line would quickly form in front of it until its contents were gone. At one such machine on the P&G grounds, one of the men lined up was an expat manager from the United States on a temporary assignment in Kobe. When he finally reached the front of the line, he purchased four beverages—one for each member of his family—and then left. If he had been more observant, he would have noticed that everyone else in line purchased only one beverage and then went to the back of the line to wait for an opportunity to buy a second or third.

Fairness is an important part of the Japanese culture. Everyone in line surely would have preferred to purchase several items at once. But out of respect and fairness to the others, they waited in line for each purchase. And while the expat from the United States didn't notice what the local Japanese employees did at the vending machine, they certainly noticed what he did. Even in this most extreme situation—when a man could surely be forgiven for thinking of his family first—his behavior was viewed as dishonorable. Long before the office was repaired and ready to resume operations, word had spread of his misdeed. His reputation was damaged to the point that he could no longer function as a leader. You can't lead a group of people that doesn't respect you.

He was quickly reassigned back to the United States.

CEO Bob McDonald shares that story with P&G executives to teach them the importance of understanding the local culture. He couldn't possibly explain all the things they should and shouldn't do in each country. But sharing that story teaches them the serious ramifications of not knowing the local culture. Sharing it in your organization can have the same benefit. It will probably make your audience more observant of how the locals behave as a guide. If that unfortunate expat had done so, he would have been able to finish out his assignment successfully.

SUMMARY AND EXERCISES

1. Salary isn't the only sign of how employees are valued. The culture, or "smell of the place," is an even better indicator. Management actions create the seed of that smell. But it's the stories told about them that spreads it to the entire organization.

2. Identify stories where leaders demonstrated the culture you want to foster, and share them broadly. Examples include the revolution in Egypt and Tom Watson at the gate of IBM.

3. Stories of bad behavior can support a positive culture as long as the transgressor is reprimanded in the story. (Think of the breakfast order at Morgan Stanley.)

4. Unspoken norms defined by the employees define the real rules of behavior, not corporate policy (e.g., FWA policy). Find examples of employees adopting the behavior you want to spread and celebrate them through story.

5. Never underestimate the value of understanding the local culture. It's vital to the success of any leader. If you have managers assigned to a faraway place, share with them the story of the vending machine line after the Kobe, Japan, earthquake. They're more likely to succeed.

Notes

1. Ayn Rand, *The Voice of Reason: Essays in Objectivist Thought* (New York: Plume, 1990), p. 184.

2. Sumantra Ghoshal, *The Individualized Corporation: A Fundamentally New Approach to Management* (New York: Harper Business, 1997).

3. C. Hampden-Turner and F. Trompenaars, *Building Cross-Cultural Competence* (New Haven, CT: Yale University Press, 2000), p. 45.

4. Patricia Beard, *Blue Blood and Mutiny: The Fight for the Soul of Morgan Stanley* (New York: Harper Perennial, 2008 [reprint]), p. 90.

5. The U.S. Geological Survey, "Historic Earthquakes," earthquake.usgs.gov/earthquakes/world/events/1995_01_16.php.

CHAPTER 9

Establish values

> *"'We value integrity,' means nothing. But tell a story about a former employee who hid his mistake and cost the company thousands, or a story about a salesperson who owned up to a mistake and earned so much trust her company doubled his order, and you begin to teach an employee what integrity means."*[1]
> —ANNETTE SIMMONS, *The Story Factor*

MARGARET PARKIN IS A TRAINER, coach, and bestselling author in the United Kingdom. She tells of a large supermarket chain there that claims the following story as part of its corporate heritage. A new CEO had been appointed who believed strongly in putting the customer first. One of the policies he implemented to support this value involved use of the parking lot. Until then, parking privileges were based on hierarchy. Senior managers got spots closest to the front door. Junior employees parked farther away. But the new policy required all managers to park at the farthest end of the lot to open up spaces for customers at the front. It also gave management a daily opportunity to see the condition of the parking lot and grounds firsthand.

Soon thereafter, the CEO was out for store visits and arrived at one location during a torrential downpour. Without an umbrella, he had a difficult choice to make. Does he park at the end of the lot and ruin his expensive suit? Or does he park up front in one of the many empty spaces and consider this a justified exception to the rule? You can imagine the employees nervously waiting inside for the CEO to arrive, and watching his car drive around, wondering where he would park. A few moments later, they had their answer. Through perhaps 100 yards of pouring rain,

74

they saw the dark figure of a man in a suit and tie running toward the store, completely drenched.

This particular supermarket happened to carry men's clothing—albeit only bargain brands. So he was able to buy a suit to change into before starting his tour. But the sight of the chief executive arriving at their front door, soaked from head to toe and out of breath, surely brought a round of muffled laughter. As did seeing him moments later in an ill-fitting suit much cheaper than the one he'd walked in with. The story spread like wildfire. And while much of it was good humor at the expense of the CEO, the inescapable fact behind it was that he still put the customer first, knowing full well it would cost him a new suit, as well as a healthy dent to his dignity.

In addition to its entertainment value, that story has probably done more to instill the value of putting the customer first than all the memos, speeches, training sessions, and policy documents combined. And all for nothing more than the cost of a cheap suit.

Every company has them—*corporate value statements*. Sometimes they're called company *values and principles*, or simply *what we believe*. But values are only words on a piece of paper until they're tested. That is, until someone is put in a difficult position of choosing between doing the hard right or the easy wrong. The easy wrong is usually more attractive in the short term: It's more profitable, more convenient, helps you avoid an embarrassment, or just makes you look good.

The CEO of that supermarket chain had a tough choice to make. Because he chose the hard right, he earned himself and the company a reputation of putting the customer first. It also showed that nobody is immune to the policy, not even the CEO. Putting the words "The customer always comes first" on the company's value statement posted in the break room won't do much to help keep that reputation alive. The telling and retelling of this story will.

That's why stories are uniquely called for when trying to establish values in an organization. Only a story can convey the uncomfortable predicament required to truly define a value. Annette Simmons calls such stories "values-in-action" stories. They show what happens when you put your values into action and *act* on them.

Let's look at a very typical corporate value: *Integrity*.

At most companies, each value would come with a short list of defining characteristics. Here's how Procter & Gamble defines integrity. But it's probably not too dissimilar from many other companies.

Integrity

• We always try to do the right thing.

• We are honest and straightforward with each other.

• We operate within the letter and spirit of the law.

• We uphold the values and principles of P&G in every action and decision.

Those are good values by anyone's standard. But if you find yourself facing a difficult decision, will these bullet points really help you make the right one? Instead, read the following story from one of the most admired companies in the world—Northwestern Mutual Life Insurance Company. It should give you a more clear understanding of what integrity means at Northwestern.

Northwestern was founded in Milwaukee, Wisconsin, in 1857. Two years later, Wisconsin suffered its first catastrophic train accident, killing 14 passengers, including 2 Northwestern policyholders. Together, their claims totaled $3,500. Unfortunately, the company had only $2,000 in assets. That was a tough situation for company president Samuel Daggett and Northwestern's trustees. Should they limit the settlement to each family or have the company go into debt to make up the difference? And who's going to loan money to a two-year-old company that's now technically insolvent anyway? Mr. Daggett and the trustees did what they knew they had to do. They personally borrowed enough money to make up the difference, waived the usual 90-day settlement period, and promptly paid the claims in full.[2]

This story is legend at Northwestern, and its employees still tell it today. Anytime Northwestern claims adjusters are in the difficult position of having to choose between doing the *right* thing for the policyholder and doing the *profitable* thing for the company, all they have to do is remember this story.

Stories like this give meaning to the value statement that bullet points cannot. Somewhere in your company, stories like this exist. Find them. Celebrate them. Share them.

* * *

As we've seen so far, stories are ideal for illustrating ethical or moral values. But what about company values that don't involve defining right from wrong? Read the following story from John Pepper's book *What*

Really Matters,[3] about the world's most successful retailer. What corporate values do you see?

The grocery retail chain H.E. Butt was founded in 1905 in San Antonio, Texas. Today H-E-B is one of the leading retailers in the region and operates over 315 stores throughout Texas and Northern Mexico. Fifty-seven years after H.E. Butt began, in 1962, Sam Walton opened his first store (later named Walmart) in the neighboring state of Arkansas. Within two decades, Walmart had expanded across the country and had overtaken H-E-B as the largest retailer in Texas. It would be accurate, then, to say that H-E-B's CEO (and grandson of the founder) Charles Butt and Sam Walton were fierce competitors—a fact that makes the following tale all the more impressive.

In an effort to learn from his now-larger competitor, Charles Butt once called Sam Walton and asked if he could bring his leadership team to Walmart's headquarters on a learning mission. Sam said that he wasn't sure if he could help, but he'd be happy to try. On the scheduled day, Charles Butt and his senior executives arrived and went to meet Sam at one of his local stores. As Charles walked in the front door, he could see Sam at the end of a long aisle deeply engaged in conversation with a shopper. Not wanting to waste any time, Charles walked up the aisle with his team. When Sam saw them, he said, "Charles, I'll be with you in a moment. I'm talking to this young woman." He was trying to sell her an ironing board cover.

After a few more minutes of conversation, the woman put the ironing board cover in her cart and pushed off toward the register. Sam turned to Charles and asked him with great seriousness, "Charles, do you know how many worn-out ironing board covers there are in this country? We're going to sell a million this month!"

Charles commented later that he had no doubt Walmart would sell those million ironing board covers. And in fact, it did. That's what intimate contact with the business can achieve—which is only one of many lessons Charles Butt and his team learned that day.

Now, imagine you're a current employee at Walmart. What lessons about company values could you glean from that story? Here's my list:

1. *Other retailers are our competitors, not our enemies.* We work in the same industry with a shared purpose: to serve the customer. If we can help each other achieve that goal without giving away our competitive secrets, we should.

2. *The customer is #1.* When approached by the CEO of H-E-B and his senior executives, all of whom he had invited to fly hundreds of miles to meet with him, Sam Walton chose instead to make the CEO wait while he continued a conversation with a customer.

3. *Understanding the customer's wants and needs is important.* How did Sam know there were so many worn-out ironing board covers in the country? He asked.

4. *Persistence pays off.* Valuing persistence means you don't give up until you've helped the customer find what she's looking for. Sam didn't quit until the woman was satisfied with her choice and put the ironing board cover in her cart.

5. *Passion wins.* Out of the billions of dollars of merchandise Walmart sells every year, Sam had set a goal specifically for how many ironing board covers he wanted to sell (a million this month), and he was clearly excited by the challenge. Passion is contagious. Spread it and you'll be amazed what you can accomplish.

The point is, even a simple story can convey many diverse values. Decide what values you want your organization to have. Then find and capture stories that illustrate them. Chapter 30 will have some ideas for how to find the stories you're looking for.

* * *

Stories that help define values are only part of the equation. Sometimes living up to company values requires more than just determination and effort. In some situations, it's hard to do the right thing even if you want to. In such cases, abiding by your company values requires a little creativity. Stories like the following one can give people ideas for how to stick to company values when circumstances make it difficult.

Martin Nuechtern is an Austrian who spent his final working years in the United Kingdom. After finishing his doctorate in business administration, he joined P&G as an assistant brand manager. Twenty-seven years later, he retired as the president of one of the company's global business units. He was as disciplined about his personal life as he was about his work. At one point he had a sign on his office door that read, "I work from 8 A.M. to 6 P.M., Monday through Friday. Outside those hours, I am at home with my family." The implied message was that outside those hours, you should be at home with your family, too, and not in the office working!

Part of his leadership philosophy is that "leaders should live the company values—visibly." He argues that's the best way to ensure the rest of the organization behaves the same way. "If you go out for expensive dinners and stay at fancy hotels on business trips, your people will too. If you go home at 3 P.M. every day, so will they."

Once, on a business trip to New York to meet with his advertising agency, one of the agency personnel invited Martin to the Metropolitan Opera. They knew he was a big fan. When in New York, he never missed a performance. But opera tickets can be expensive, especially good tickets. And these were very good tickets. At P&G, gifts over $25 in value are not allowed by company policy. They have to be paid for by the recipient. But not every company has such a strict policy, so it's not unusual for a set of show tickets to find their way into a client's hands.

In this case, when Martin entered the theater with the account executive, he couldn't see the ticket price. He asked several times, but the agency was deliberately evasive, determined to let Martin enjoy them as a gift. After returning home, Martin made a phone call to the opera house. He found out how much the tickets cost and inquired if they had a "Friends of the Opera" organization that accepted charitable donations. A week later, the account manager received an official-looking letter from the opera house. But it wasn't addressed to her. It was addressed to her dog, Gilda. Inside the envelope was a membership card with the dog's name on it, and a letter thanking Gilda for her generous gift to the arts. Martin had found a way to pay for the tickets anyway.

Every six months or so, Gilda gets a letter from the Metropolitan Opera announcing the upcoming shows. Her owner gets a gentle and lighthearted reminder to stay out of the doghouse by doing the right thing. And Martin gets to chuckle when he tells this story to others as a reminder that doing the right thing isn't always easy. But with a little creativity, it's always possible.

The overall lesson in this chapter is that company values are determined by the behavior of its people, and the stories that capture that behavior—not by corporate value statements buried in a file cabinet. If you don't have strong company value *stories*, then in the minds of your employees (where it matters most) you probably don't have strong company *values*.

SUMMARY AND EXERCISES

1. Values are only words on a piece of paper until they're tested. Telling the story of the test, such as the CEO caught in the rain, lets everyone see the company values in action.

    a. What are your company values and principles? List each of them on a piece of paper and make note of the events or people or situations in your company's history that best demonstrate each. These will become your company value stories.

    b. Challenge yourself to find an appropriate moment to tell at least one of these stories each week, even if it's just in rough form. You'll be surprised how often a situation comes up where good leadership requires the application of company values.

2. Bullet points cannot define company values in any actionable way to an employee. Only a story can. (Think of the train wreck in Wisconsin.)

3. While CEO of P&G, John Pepper was once asked in an interview which skill or characteristic was most important to look for when hiring new employees. Was it leadership? Analytical ability? Problem solving? Collaboration? Strategic thinking? Or something else? His answer was integrity. He explained, "All the rest, we can teach them after they get here."

    *   What's your most important company value?
    *   What stories are currently being told about that value?
    *   Are they supporting the message you want them to?

4. Having trouble thinking of value stories? Use these springboard ideas to identify some. Think of times when you, or someone else in your company:

    a. Had to make a really tough choice

    b. Made a promise, and had trouble keeping it

    c. Had to get the company policy manual out to decide the right thing to do

    d. Had to ask for help from the human resources department or the company ethics officer before making a difficult decision

    e. Were asked to do something you didn't feel good about

    f. Acted in a way that would have made the founder of your company proud

    g. Felt conflicted about two separate values

5. Stories can also help bring to life hard-to-define values like hard work, persistence, and putting the customer first. (Sam Walton's ironing board cover story is an example.)

6. Decide what values you want your organization to have. Then find and capture stories that illustrate them. Remember, if you don't have strong company value stories, you probably don't have strong company values.

7. Sometimes living up to company values requires a little creativity. Stories like Martin Nuechtern's "a dog at the Met" help people be more creative and resourceful when trying to do the right thing.

Notes

1. Annette Simmons, *The Story Factor: Inspiration, Influence, and Persuasion Through the Art of Storytelling* (San Francisco: Jossey-Bass, 2001).

2. Northwestern Mutual, "Company Overview," northwesternmutual.com/about-northwestern-mutual/our-company/company-overview.aspx#Our-History.

3. John E. Pepper, *What Really Matters: Reflections on My Career at Procter & Gamble with Guiding Principles for Success in the Marketplace and in Life* (Cincinnati: Procter & Gamble, 2005).

CHAPTER 10

Encourage collaboration and build relationships

"Coming together is a beginning, staying together is progress, and working together is success."[1]
—HENRY FORD

IT HAPPENS SO OFTEN it's almost cliché. A department in a small regional operation is reorganized, and a new big-city manager is transferred in. The previous department manager, who's held the position for years, is now the new appointee's assistant. The new manager hasn't even arrived and the team already doesn't like him—especially the assistant manager. "He's probably an arrogant, fast-talking know-it-all who doesn't have a clue how we do things out here!" This was the case for a Washington State organization that sent the department on a two-day team-building and strategic-planning retreat. Fortunately for them, the facilitator they hired was the same Evelyn Clark you met in chapter 4.

Evelyn decided to have them tell their life stories to each other, but in a playful and creative way. She provided dozens of magazines, construction paper, scissors, and glue, and asked them to create collages that represented their past, present, and future. Despite being adults, they embraced the exercise like excited schoolchildren, chatting the entire time. Once complete, they each took turns telling their stories to each other in words and pictures. Of course, everyone got to know each other much better. But the biggest impact was on the two would-be adversaries. Despite their apparent differences, they discovered they had some important things in common. When they learned they shared the same faith, tension between the two started to ease. When they learned family was their top priority, they actually started to warm up to one another. As the storytelling continued—and they learned the many values they shared—an amazing transformation took place. Over lunch they talked one-on-one and got to know each other even better. By the start of the afternoon session, they were working together as old colleagues.

The rest of the retreat was extremely productive and exceeded everyone's expectations, including the CEO's. It was also productive for Evelyn. It confirmed to her that when people have the opportunity to discover common values, they're able to build more productive, collaborative relationships. The previous example illustrates how personal storytelling can help them discover those common values. Try it in your next team-building activity and see what happens.

* * *

Finding common values is one way storytelling can help build relationships, but not the only one. The next story shows how personal storytelling can create caring, emotional bonds between employees. It also explains why those bonds help the leader be more effective, and why they result in better performance from the team.

Starting a new job is one of those infrequent occasions where you can remake yourself into a better you. Working with new people who don't have any preconceived notions about you is a gift of a blank canvass to paint the new you on. Everyone has some part of themselves they think could be better—even hardworking people with a good reputation. That's exactly what Jamie Johnson was thinking in 2008 when he joined Seek, a research firm in Cincinnati, Ohio.

Jamie is a talented consumer researcher with a strong work ethic. He's quick to laugh and has a warm smile—the kind of guy everyone likes. But by his own admission, he was somewhat robotic in the office, preferring not to mix business with his personal life. "I'm not here to make friends so much as to get my job done," he thought. As a result, the relationships he had at work were cordial, but superficial. His hallway conversations were shallow—the weather or the football game last night. On his first day at Seek, he vowed to himself to change that. He wanted to have more meaningful connections to the people he spent eight hours a day with. With the best of intentions he started his new job with a friendly attitude and a welcoming personality.

How did Jamie assess his progress? "A year in, nobody liked me." That, of course, was a humble exaggeration. But the truth is, his relationships were no deeper than at previous jobs. "Why isn't this working?" he wondered. "I'm a professional consumer researcher. I spend every day getting people to open up to me and tell me their innermost thoughts and feelings, their hopes and their dreams. And these are complete strangers I met 20 minutes earlier! What am I doing with them that I'm not doing with my coworkers?"

That turned out to be the right question to ask. Indeed, Jamie did have several techniques he used professionally to get people to open up to him. Self-deprecating humor always worked well. "Did I ask you that already? Sorry, I'm a slow learner." Sometimes he would find a common interest. "Hey, I have that same Beatles record. I stole it from my mom!" But the most effective technique was opening himself up, and letting himself be vulnerable—sharing a weakness or an insecurity.

All these things Jamie did with the people he was interviewing for research, but never with his coworkers. So he decided to give it a try. A few weeks later, Seek was celebrating its tenth year in business. After a tour around the city, visiting their previous office locations, they settled into a meeting room for the rest of the afternoon for team building. That's when Jamie got his chance. The founder of the company said, "Share something about yourself. As much or as little as you're comfortable with." Jamie took a risk and shared a very personal story.

He told them about him and his younger brother, Steven. Both had been raised by the same parents and grew up in the same house. While nobody's life is free of turmoil, Jamie had a good childhood. He had a loving family and nice friends, did well in school, and generally felt good about himself. His brother, on the other hand, suffered from an undiagnosed case of bipolar disorder. Sometimes called manic-depressive disorder, his brother's condition meant he suffered through extreme swings in mood and demeanor. One day he could be on top of the world with unbridled excitement. The next day he could be paralyzed with depression and anxiety. Untreated, the emotional roller coaster was more than his brother could handle. On April 16, 2001, at the age of 19, Steven got in his car and drove west. After crossing two state lines, he ran out of gas and pulled over to the side of the highway. He then took out a gun and shot himself in the head. Jamie describes Steven's drive that day as a final act of respect from a fantastic young man. He wanted to spare his parents the graveness of finding his body near home.

While the tragedy was certainly painful for Jamie, there was some good that came from it. He told his coworkers, "I realized I had been taking everything in life for granted. I stopped doing that." Now Jamie makes it a point to appreciate the many blessings he has. He also spends more of his time volunteering. He coaches both volleyball and football for local kids, and belongs to a group that supports families during the holidays when they can't make ends meet. Not surprisingly, he also works with suicide prevention organizations around the country to help them raise money and awareness for their cause. "It helps me remember and honor my brother in a positive way."

By the time Jamie finished telling his story, half the room was in tears. When the meeting was over, instead of a high-five on the way out, several people stopped to hug him. Some of his colleagues commented to each other later that they didn't know Jamie had so much soul and emotion. "All of a sudden," one of them commented, "Jamie had depth!" His story even earned him the respect of the most stoic men in the office. A gentle punch in the shoulder, an admiring nod, and a brotherly, "Solid, man," told him he was now in the inner circle. Within days, he realized his shallow hallway conversations had turned from the weather and sports to genuine interest in his family, his life, his dreams.

Certainly Jamie enjoys his work more now that he's better connected to his colleagues. But how has his new acceptance impacted his ability to lead? "My team performs much better now. People stop watching the clock as much when they're working with someone they care about." He knows firsthand now that it's easier to get the best out of people when you have a meaningful relationship with them. And for him, that meaningful relationship started with a single story.

As Jamie's story illustrates, one of the most effective team-building activities you can construct is also one of the simplest. Have people sit around in a circle and talk about themselves—the more personal the story, the better. And as Jamie learned with both the consumers he interviews and the colleagues he works with, the most effective will be the stories that create vulnerability by showing an insecurity, or describing a painful time in your life or a costly failure. They're exactly the kind of stories people don't want to tell to a bunch of strangers in the office— and that's the point. It's a vicious circle. We don't tell our personal stories because we work with strangers. They remain strangers because we don't tell our personal stories. You have to break the cycle. Challenge people to tell their stories, and you'll never work with strangers again.

* * *

So we've established the value of sharing personal stories at work. But those aren't the only kind of stories that foster collaboration and build relationships. Our work stories can have a similar impact on relationships, plus deliver a direct benefit to the bottom line. Tom, a partner at a major global consulting firm, knows the value of those stories firsthand, as illustrated in his story.

"I'm sorry, Tom. We're going to have to cancel your retainer—at least for a little while."

To a consultant like Tom, those are about the worst words you could ever hear from your client. It's the equivalent of an employee being told he's being laid off. Except in this case, it didn't just mean Tom was getting laid off. It also meant his entire team of 15 consultants.

"What's wrong?" Tom asked. He assumed it must be serious to warrant this kind of reaction from a Fortune 100 company. And he was right. It was serious. His client was going to miss its quarterly profit estimates, and not just by a little—enough to raise major concerns on Wall Street.

His client explained the troublesome details. In his 20-year professional career, Tom had never encountered this particular problem. But he knew in a situation like this, his client needed help. Packing up his team's things and walking away was not an option. Clearly the company needed to find people who'd been through this before. But it was an unusual problem— the kind companies don't publicize. So finding examples would be difficult.

That's when he told his client about the "monthly challenge"—a friendly competition among the consultants at Tom's company. Every month, all the partners are presented with a particularly challenging client problem, without naming the client. They're encouraged to take their teams out for a lunch or dinner, discuss the problem, and develop recommendations. Just for that hour, tens of thousands of consultants are working on exactly the same issue. But with only an hour, they don't have time for research or analysis. All they have time for is to share a few stories and brainstorm ideas. The stories they share are of when they encountered similar problems in the past, what they did about it, and how it turned out. When the meal is over, they go back to working on their own clients' projects. The winning teams and their solutions are recognized in front of the whole company.

The competition has many benefits. The client with the problem gets the collective brainpower of the entire company working on an issue. The consulting team supporting that client gets to deliver a solution and move on to the next challenge. But the competition also helps foster more collaboration and better working relationships among the consultants. The lunch or dinner events are an opportunity for team members to stop working on their separate part of their client engagement and all work together on one issue. Psychologists have long known this to be one of the quickest ways to create human bonds. And swapping stories for an hour does just as much to bring adults together as it does for children around the summer campfire. It also helps create better connections between consultants in different offices around the world. Cooperating on the same problem through the competition creates common experiences and insights they can talk about and refer to for years to come. Think of that. This consultancy has employees spread out across dozens of countries around the world. Most of them will never see each other, or ever even work with the same client. To that rich diversity of people and experiences is now added the strength of a common set of consulting challenges and solutions. It's really quite brilliant when you think of it.

Tom immediately posted his client's problem to every partner as a monthly challenge. Within 48 hours, tens of thousands of consultants began working on it. Within three weeks, they identified two other noncompeting clients that had experienced the same issue and had three creative solutions offered from across the globe. Tom presented the solutions to his client and worked with the client to implement the best one.

Tom's challenge and winning solution was added to the long and growing list of monthly challenges that makes his consulting firm stronger as a company. As for his client, it still had a tough quarter. But it wasn't nearly the Wall Street debacle it would have been without his help. And Tom never heard another word about needing to cancel his retainer.

Although new business challenges certainly pop up every once in a while, most everyday problems are ones that someone, somewhere, has experienced before. Tom's monthly challenge is a global story hunt for the best answer regardless of whether it's a new problem or an old one. Establishing a regular time and place to swap stories on just about any business challenge is sure to surface wisdom. You don't need to be in the consulting business to benefit from swapping stories with your coworkers. No matter what business you're in, it's sure to lead to new ideas, and a more collaborative, cohesive workforce.

* * *

The previous examples illustrate how you can use storytelling to create a collaborative environment. The final one here shows you how stories can convince people outside your organization that a collaborative environment exists on the inside; it's not so scary and neither are the people you'll find there. The problem isn't an uncommon one, but it's most familiar to those near the top of the company org chart.

Hierarchy in a large corporation is a very serious affair, just as it is in the military, which all modern corporate leadership structures are patterned after. The higher the rank of the officer, or level of the manager, the larger the group of soldiers or employees led. With each higher level also typically comes more authority, a bigger paycheck, and a higher degree of respect from junior officers or employees. At the most senior levels, those differences led to the observation that it's lonely at the top. That's because out of deference to the boss—and fear of saying the wrong thing—senior managers are often viewed as unapproachable and impersonal. In a military setting where senior officers have to send troops into deadly combat, that irreproachable stature is necessary. In a business environment, however, it can do more harm than good. Executives not viewed as accessible to the organization find it more difficult to lead.

So it was for Carol, a strategy director at a global Fortune 500 company and part of the company's strategy leadership team reporting directly to the global strategy officer (GSO), Ben. She was incredibly bright, hardworking, and ambitious. But to many she was an intimidating figure. Success in her role, however, required that she influence thousands of managers in the company to adopt the new business models she was developing. Deploying those new tools meant traveling around the globe to regional offices teaching the local business teams how to use them. A successful training session generally meant a successful deployment. One particular trip, however, it was the journey back, and not the training session itself, that made the biggest impact on the GSO's team and its ability to lead in the organization.

As a senior officer of the company, Ben was afforded one of the most visible trappings of high office in the corporate world—access to the company plane. Instead of flying on a commercial airline, these executives, and anyone they choose to bring with them, fly in style on a Gulfstream G-4 corporate jet. This particular trip was overseas, to the company's European headquarters. The topic was a controversial one, so they were all nervous going in. By the end of the day, however, it was obvious the training was a huge success. Feedback was phenomenal, with high praise for all the trainers.

That evening, Carol and her three peers decided to celebrate their success with a night on the town. They stayed up half the night gambling at the hotel casino and enjoying the finest French wines. Morning came early. As they settled into their comfortable seats on the jet, Ben wanted to debrief the prior day's training. He hadn't noticed the telltale signs of a hangover on the faces of his team. "Ben, we can't do that now. We're exhausted, and we won't do a quality job of it. Can we do it tomorrow in the office?" To some, that refusal would have bordered on insubordination. But his team had done a good job, and Ben graciously agreed.

Shortly after takeoff, the four night owls were sound asleep, while the boss stayed up to work. Halfway through the return flight home, the plane stopped in Nova Scotia for fuel. After the second takeoff, it was Ben who was ready for a nap, while the other four were just waking up. Here's where the hierarchy is important. The company plane is an asset at the disposal of the company officer high enough to warrant it—in this case, the global strategy officer. Anyone else on board is a guest. If the boss wants to sleep on *his* plane, protocol dictates you let him sleep in peace. But Ben's guests were now wide awake and were still feeling the lure of the casino from the night before. So they decided to continue their celebration with a game of poker—a loud game of poker.

Despite his restless sleep, Ben never complained or even said a word about it. But his four direct reports had plenty to say about it. Word spread quickly of their flight home—how they respectfully declined Ben's request for a debrief, and then probably kept him awake with their boisterous card game. The story conveyed three key messages to the organization. First, it showed the four senior leaders as regular people, with the same desires and frailties as anyone else. They were no longer stuffed-shirt corporate types. It humanized them. Second, it showed them treating their boss respectfully, but no differently than they would have treated anyone else. If four people want to play poker while one wants to sleep, they play poker. Majority rules. Third, Ben let them treat him as an equal and didn't complain or mete out any consequences for it.

In short, that one story reframed the equity of those intimidating strategy gurus into a fun, approachable group that didn't take themselves too seriously. Other managers were quicker to want to work with them and accept their guidance and counsel. They couldn't have crafted a better message if they'd tried—which is actually the point. You don't need to stage situations like the one just described. They will happen naturally. The point is that when they do, tell people about them. There were only five passengers on that plane, and Ben certainly wasn't telling this story to anyone. It got out because the other four must have. But imagine if they hadn't. Imagine if through their own sense of decorum, they'd kept their evening's excursion and airborne nap a secret. The story would never have gotten out, and their entire department might still be viewed as a haven for unapproachable corporate elite instead of a collaborative place to get some great strategy advice.

Yes, corporate hierarchy is based on a rigid military structure. But with stories like these, yours doesn't have to feel like it.

SUMMARY AND EXERCISES

1. We generally don't tell our personal stories at work because we work with strangers. They remain strangers because we don't tell our personal stories. You have to break the cycle.

2. Have people sit around in a circle and talk about themselves—the more personal the story, the better. When people discover they have common values, they form more collaborative relationships. Sharing personal stories brings out those personal values.

    a. In your next team offsite, plan time to tell such stories. Consider how well that worked with the new boss from the big city.

    b. Another way is to share a weakness, an insecurity, or a painful experience. Let yourself be vulnerable in front of others, the way Jamie Johnson did at Seek. (Jamie has depth!)

3. Sharing work stories can build collaboration, too, like it did for the global consulting company Tom works for (e.g., canceling your retainer). Hold a similar challenge at your company. Your business and clients will benefit, while you're building a more collaborative team.

4. Stories can also convince people outside your organization you have a collaborative environment on the inside. That can help with recruiting and retention. Share stories such as the one about the P&G marketing managers on the corporate jet that illustrate collaboration, and you'll get more of it.

Note

1. "Henry Ford," conservapedia.com/Henry_Ford.

CHAPTER **11**

Value diversity and inclusion

"All the data we've seen, and all of my personal experience, convinces me that a diverse organization will out-think, out-innovate, and out-perform a homogenous organization every single time. Winning will come from taking full advantage of our diversity."
—A. G. LAFLEY, former CEO of Procter & Gamble

BEVERLY KEOWN WAS BORN in 1955 on a plantation in Seaton, Arkansas, the fourth of eight children. Her father was a sharecropper. Her mother was a domestic servant in the farmer's home. Along with her siblings, Beverly spent her summers chopping cotton.

Growing up in a southern state in the 1960s, Beverly suffered indignities that would shock any thinking person today. She entered restaurants through the back door, not the front. She drank from water fountains labeled "Colored" sourced from the drain of the "Whites only" fountain next to it. She wasn't allowed at her white friends' birthday parties or sleepovers. And she didn't dare go to the only movie theater in town. But in that place and time, it was the norm. So it was all Beverly knew.

During her ninth-grade year, her all-black school closed and integrated with the white school. Four years later, in 1973, she graduated in the top 20 percent of her class and got a job as a machine operator at a shirt manufacturer. After a time, she was promoted to a secretarial job in the office. That made her one of only two African American employees in a salaried position. In the machine shop, she had been one of many. So for the first time in her life, she spent her entire day surrounded by people who were different from her. It was obvious she was the different

91

one—sometimes painfully obvious. "The other administrators laughed at me, and talked about me as if I had no feelings. They made fun of the way I talked and the way I looked. I was constantly aware of the color of my skin, and the texture of my hair. I thought to myself, 'If only I was white, I would be treated better.'" When Beverly quit three years later, her mother pleaded with her to "go beg them to give you your job back." Beverly refused.

Her next employer was not much better, and she never felt at home there. She was talked down to and treated poorly. Twenty-five years after she'd joined the company, her husband got a new job and they needed to move. Fortunately, her employer had another plant in that same town, so she was able to get a transfer. She was offered the job of payroll administrator for the 131 production operators at the site. But before she left, her boss called her into his office to give her some advice. "Where you're going, you'll have to have thick skin." Beverly didn't know what he meant. He explained, "You'll be the only black person in that whole plant. People might say things to you, or you might be targeted at times." Beverly still wasn't sure what that meant, or how it would be different from what she'd experienced for the past 25 years. But she went anyway.

She quickly found out what he meant. On her first day, her boss was outraged when he found out that as a 25-year employee, she earned five weeks of vacation a year. "I don't even get that much vacation, and I'm your boss!" Each time she would take a day off, he made snide remarks and complained. And he constantly questioned her work. "I felt like I always had to prove to him that I was good enough."

Manually processing 131 payroll checks every week, she was bound to make a mistake at some point. When it finally happened, as Beverly describes it, "You'd think the whole world was coming to an end." Her boss stormed into her office and slammed the door behind him. "What is wrong with you!" he shouted. His tirade continued as she sat in stunned silence. It was only a $100 mistake and could be fixed in a matter of minutes. So she couldn't understand his eruption. "Do you hear me talking to you? I said what is wrong with you!"

Beverly tried to get the plant manager's help, but eventually realized she was in this all by herself. After two years of similar treatment, she filed a lawsuit with the EEOC.

The reaction at the plant was unfortunate. The regional manager came down from New Jersey and told Beverly, her boss, and the rest of the department that he did not approve of what was going on. Then—in a statement obviously directed at Beverly—he reminded everyone who the boss in the department was, and said, "What he says, goes. If anyone doesn't like it, they can leave." A few days later, one of her coworkers thought it necessary to tell Beverly that several employees at the site were members of the KKK. Whether true or not, it was enough to frighten her.

Fortunately for Beverly, the company filed for bankruptcy a few months later and spared her the long legal battle. She was offered a generous severance package in return for an agreement to drop the lawsuit, which she accepted. After 27 years of dedicated service, Beverly Keown was unemployed. The year was 2002. Not 1952, or 1962. It was 2002. For 46 years, that kind of treatment was all Beverly had known.

In February 2005, Beverly got a new job as an administrator in the Fayetteville, Arkansas, offices of Procter & Gamble. Her first week on the job, she knew something was different. "I thought I'd landed on a different planet. Just looking at the faces of the people, I could tell being different wasn't going to be a barrier for me. I was no longer the only African American filling a quota. I met people from China, Japan, the Ukraine, England, and cities across the United States like Boston and Cincinnati. And I was shocked and amazed at how I was treated—no differently than anyone else!"

Beverly explained it was like "taking a starving person from an impoverished country, and moving them to the United States. It was like a breath of fresh air. Everyone had lunch together, and laughed together, and worked together. I didn't have to be ashamed of being black. Yes, they can see the color of my skin, and hear the accent in my voice. But more than that, they see *me*, my skill, my passion, my potential, and my desire to belong. Sometimes I just want to cry out of joy!"

How has the more diverse and inclusive environment made a difference to Beverly's job performance? "Now I bring the best Beverly I can bring to my work every day! It makes me want to do my job well. I love my job, and I'm proud of the team I support. And for the first time in my working career, I'm proud to be a black woman!"

If you ask Beverly how she reacted the first day in that more nurturing environment back in 2005, she'll tell you, "I tried not to act so surprised, but I'm sure it showed. . . . It probably still does." After six years with P&G, she's gotten used to being treated well. If her team members have anything to do with it, from now on that's all Beverly will ever know.

Beverly's story is a reminder of the enormous impact the work environment can have on a person's self-worth and job performance. Yes, there has been an enormous improvement in the diversity and inclusiveness of American businesses in the past 50 years. But as evidenced by Beverly's experience, that progress is not universal, nor is it complete. It would be easy for younger managers today to lack an understanding and sympathy for this challenge. Many have never seen it firsthand. That's why stories like Beverly's need to be shared.

As observed by philosopher and poet George Santayana, "Those who cannot remember the past are condemned to repeat it."[1] Get to know the history of the people you work with. You'll be shocked at how many Beverly stories you find.

* * *

Not all diversity problems are as evident and visible as Beverly's. In fact, some of the most common offenses go on without the perpetrator even knowing what they've done. Consider the following example from Bracken Darrell, president of Logitech in Silicon Valley.

Prior to Logitech, Bracken had a job reporting to a man we'll call Jack. Like Bracken, Jack was a white male, and then in his thirties. He was well educated and well traveled—a worldly guy with modern, progressive views. In other words, he was the kind of guy you would expect to treat everyone the same, regardless of gender or ethnic background. And as far as Bracken could tell—and Jack, for that matter—that's exactly the way he behaved. As evidence of this, Bracken's work group consisted of himself, an African American man we'll call Don, and a Caucasian woman we'll call Sally. Every time Jack came to the bullpen, he engaged all three of them very genuinely.

One day over lunch, Bracken was talking with Don about Jack's abilities as a leader and praising the inclusive way he worked with the whole team. Bracken was surprised when Don didn't agree. "You don't see what I see," he said. "You see him stroll onto the floor and treat us all as equals. Here's what I see. I see him come to your desk first. He cracks a few jokes, slaps you on the back, listens to your stories, smiles, and laughs. Then he goes to Sally's desk. He asks Sally, 'How's your family doing? How's your husband?' and 'What are your kids up to this week?' Then he comes to my desk, smiles, and says, 'Hello, Don.'"

Sure, he was absolutely genuine with each employee. But notice the way he related to Sally and Don very differently than Bracken. With Bracken, he carries on like they're brothers. With Sally, the only way he can relate to her is in her role as a wife and mother. "How's your *husband*? How are your *kids*?" As if that's the only thing of value she has to offer. With Don, he doesn't even have that to relate to.

Imagine you're Don or Sally. How level would you consider the playing field in Jack's department? What do you think your chances would be of getting a raise or promotion if you had to compete with Bracken for the boss's attention? Bracken shares this story today to help people understand the perhaps subtle and unintended impact their behavior has on others. Share it and you'll create more aware and inclusive managers, perhaps starting with you.

* * *

These two stories can help people understand the problem. That's a necessary first step. But stories can be part of the solution as well, as the next two stories illustrate.

Some business school professors know their students can learn a great deal from the practical experience of local business leaders. Dr. Art Shriberg at Xavier University is one of them. He regularly invites senior executives from local companies to speak to his students. And with nine Fortune 500 companies headquartered within a few miles of Xavier's Cincinnati location, he has plenty of high-profile executives to choose from.

In one of his leadership classes in the early 2000s, the CEO of one of those Fortune 500 companies was Dr. Shriberg's guest speaker. Near the end of class, one young woman raised her hand to ask a question. "What do you think about the EEOC?" The Equal Employment Opportunity Commission is the federal agency that enforces workplace discrimination laws.

"I hate it!" he bellowed. "The government's got no right telling me whom I can and can't hire! It's un-American!" The young woman's eyes grew wide, and her classmates sat in shocked silence. Even Art Shriberg nervously waited to see how the CEO would back himself out of this predicament.

But he didn't. He kept going. He continued, "About four years ago, one of my lawyers told me we were going to be in big trouble with the EEOC if we didn't start hiring more women and minorities. As much as I didn't like being told what to do, I didn't want to get in a fight with the U.S. government. So I called in my HR manager and told him to start hiring them."

He explained that within a year or two, his company was in compliance. But then during the next administration, the EEOC rules relaxed a bit. "But I didn't change a thing," he said. "By that point, we were making more money than ever! The women we'd hired in the past couple of years taught us to market to women better than we ever thought possible. And with the diversity of talent across the company, my product development teams were more creative and innovative than ever.

"I still don't like being told whom to hire," the CEO admitted. "But I can't argue with success."

Sometimes the most effective advocates for diversity and inclusion come from the most unlikely places. If the head of an affirmative action coalition or an affinity network in your company speaks out in support of the cause, that's certainly good, though not unexpected. But one story from a skeptic like the one in Dr. Shriberg's class is far more compelling. Art brought that CEO in to teach his students a lesson in leadership. What they learned was much more valuable.

Dr. Shriberg's story shows you how best to convince people that better diversity is not just the fair and right thing to do; it can actually be good for business. Tell it when you have a skeptic among you who needs convincing.

* * *

Another kind of story that can illustrate the value of inclusion is a well-crafted folktale. Folktales are wonderfully designed to show people the wisdom in valuing diversity, and encourage them to do so. By nature, these stories don't describe anyone in particular, so they can apply to everyone by extension. It's easy for people to see themselves in the mythical characters, and apply the lessons learned to their own life. Given the tension-filled nature of the topic, stories about real people are often dismissed because "that doesn't apply to me. I'm not like the guy in that story. I would never do that."

Below is a folktale you can use that just about everyone will find wisdom in. It's my adaptation of an old West African story called "the traveler."[2] The following text is from a speech I gave to a group of about 500 where I work. I share this version to illustrate how a folktale like this can be used in a real context.

Once there was a wise, elderly man who spent his days just outside his village sitting under a shady tree where he would think. One day, a traveler came up to him and said, "Old man, I have traveled far. I have seen many things and met many people. Can you tell me, if I go into this village, what kind of people will I meet there?"

The wise man replied, "Yes, I'd be happy to tell you. But first, tell me what kind of people you've met in your travels so far."

The traveler responded, "Oh, you wouldn't believe it. I have met the most *awful* people! People who are selfish and unkind to strangers. People who don't care for themselves or one another. I've met foolish young people I could learn nothing from, and old people whose lack of hope depresses everyone they meet."

As the traveler spoke, a look of sadness grew in the wise man's eyes as he nodded in a knowing way. "Yes," he said. "I believe I know exactly the kind of people you speak of. And I'm sorry to tell you, but if you go into my village, I'm afraid that's exactly the kind of people you will meet."

"I knew it!" the traveler scoffed. "It's always the same." He kicked the dirt under his feet and stormed off down the road, without ever bothering to stop in the village.

A few hours later, another traveler came upon the wise man. "Kind sir," he said, "I have traveled far. I have seen many things and met many people. Can you tell me, if I go into this village, what kind of people will I meet there?"

The wise man replied, "Yes, I'd be happy to tell you. But first, tell me what kind of people you've met in your travels so far."

The traveler responded, "Oh, you wouldn't believe it. I have met the most amazing people! People who are kind and generous to strangers; people who care for one another like family. I've met young people with a wisdom beyond their years, and I've met older people with a youthful passion for life that brings joy to everyone they meet. And I have learned much from all of them."

As the traveler spoke, the wise man smiled brightly as he nodded in a knowing way. "Yes," he said. "I believe I know exactly the kind of people you speak of. And I'm happy to tell you, if you go into my village, I'm certain that's exactly the kind of people you will meet."

"Come then," said the traveler, "and introduce me to them."

The lesson, of course, is that what we see in people is determined, in large part, by what we expect to find. So when you go back to your office tomorrow to work with your direct reports, your peers, your business partners, your boss, look for in them the traits you'd most like to see, and I believe that's exactly what you'll find.

I'm certain of this, because I believe we work at a company that hires the most amazing people. People who are kind and generous to the newest among us; people who care for one another like family. We have young people with a wisdom beyond their years, and we have experienced people with a passion for what they do that can inspire others even on their worst days. I have learned much from all of them, and I know that you have, too. After we're dismissed, there will be a happy hour where you can meet some of these amazing people that perhaps you haven't met before. I'd encourage you to stay. And if you do, come find me. Let me introduce you to some of them.

* * *

The last lesson in this chapter is for anyone charged with improving diversity and inclusion in an organization. Assembling and leading a team of people tasked with such an important but delicate task can be daunting. It's situations like these that gave rise to the idiom "You can't make omelets without breaking a few eggs." You won't make any progress until people start talking about painful and deeply personal topics. When you need people in your organization to get together and discuss a topic like diversity, you'll need some way to get them out of their shell. There's no better way to accomplish that—and get them to start thinking about the topic at hand—than to have them tell their own stories of crisis or conflict with people different from themselves. It looks similar to what Jamie Johnson did in the last chapter, except the topic of the stories would be different. Everyone will need to open up to be successful. But as the leader, you have to go first.

SUMMARY AND EXERCISES

1. When people don't feel valued or a part of the team, they can't perform their best.

2. Despite much progress in the past 50 years, ours is still not a society where all people are treated equally. Young people who recently entered the workforce may not appreciate the struggles others have endured or perhaps still endure today. Search for stories like Beverly Keown's in your organization (the sharecropper's daughter). You'll be surprised how many you find.

3. Today, some of the most common offenses occur without the perpetrator even knowing she has offended someone. Share Bracken Darrell's story ("You don't see what I see") with others so they understand the unintended impact of their behavior.

4. Diversity isn't just the right thing to do for the people in your organization. It's good for business, too. Share Dr. Shriberg's story of his guest speaker ("I hate the EEOC!") and people will understand why.

5. Folktales can be great sources to help others appreciate the wisdom of creating a more diverse workforce. Use the folktale about the travelers to help people look for the best in others.

6. Diversity and inclusion are difficult topics to get people to talk about. They're intimate and personal. The next time you run a meeting to discuss these topics, you'll need people to open up quickly. The best way to do that is with your own personal stories. Once you tell yours, they'll be more comfortable telling theirs.

Notes

1. George Santayana, *Reason in Common Sense: The Life of Reason Volume 1* (Mineola, NY: Dover, 1980).

2. Adapted from Michael Brown and Alan Khazei, City Year's *Founding Stories* (July 2004): 47–49. Used with permission.

CHAPTER 12

Set policy without rules

"Nobody, but nobody, reads policy manuals except for the person who wrote them, and then only because they get paid to do it. But there are a percentage of your employees who will read a good story."
—DAVID ARMSTRONG, author of *Once Told, They're Gold*

IMAGINE CONDUCTING this experiment. Put five monkeys in a cage with a bunch of bananas hanging from the ceiling. Underneath the bananas, place a ladder just tall enough to reach them. Then any time one of the monkeys tries to climb the ladder, spray the entire cage with cold water. Quickly, the monkeys will learn to avoid the ladder and abandon their quest for the bananas.

Then take one of the monkeys out of the cage and replace it with another monkey—monkey number six—and put down your sprayer. The new monkey, of course, has no idea about the booby-trapped ladder and water, so it soon tries to climb the ladder. When it does, the other four monkeys attack it to avoid the cold shower. The new monkey doesn't know why it was attacked. Regardless, when another original monkey is replaced, and the same thing happens, even monkey number six participates in the attack.

Continue replacing monkeys one at a time until none of the original monkeys are left. Still, all five monkeys will avoid the ladder, and attack any new monkey that tries to climb it. They all obey the same rules of behavior, even though none of them have any idea why.

This is how corporate policy is formed.

The previous story has been told in many forms and in many places.[1] The original author is unknown. But it does appear to be loosely based on an actual experiment by G. R. Stephenson in 1967 with rhesus monkeys.[2] The point, of course, is that rule books don't govern behavior in any organization. Behavior is dictated by what is rewarded or punished, even if the original reason for that rule is long forgotten and perhaps no longer present. This holds true whether the reward or punishment is witnessed in person or relayed through a story. With monkeys in a cage, of course, it must be witnessed personally. In a corporate environment of humans, it's usually a story that carries the message. Here's a case in point.

At the corner of Pike Street and Columbia Parkway in downtown Cincinnati, right across from Procter & Gamble's world headquarters, stands a 100-year-old, eight-story building. Today it serves as owner-occupied condominiums. But in the 1980s and 1990s, it was a commercial office building, known by the name of its largest tenant, R.L. Polk & Company. Every P&G new hire at the time was intimately familiar with the Polk Building because one of its floors was leased to P&G and served as the company training center. All new hires spent at least a week there during their first year learning about the company and how to do their jobs. It was also the subject of the first story I ever heard told at P&G.

Part of the training philosophy at the Polk Building was that the most effective learning takes place when the student is completely immersed in the material and isolated from distractions of the main office across the street. So the floor was equipped with a cafeteria that served a free lunch and snacks to all trainees to keep them in the building and focused on their studies. And since the only people on the floor were the trainees and trainers, they didn't even have need for a cash register.

Over one of those first free lunches, one of our trainers regaled my new-hire class with stories about the company. The first was a highly engaging one about two of our predecessors several years earlier. Two young men, just out of college, had joined P&G and spent their requisite time in the Polk Building. A few weeks later, one of them arrived at work without his wallet. Not wishing to spend an entire afternoon working on an empty stomach, and too embarrassed to ask anyone for a loan, he remembered the free lunches across the street. So he simply walked into the Polk Building, went to the cafeteria, ordered his lunch, and enjoyed his free meal. Pleased with his resourcefulness, he shared his exploit with his comrade and convinced him to join him the next day for a free lunch.

Together, they walked in and leisurely consumed their free meal without a single question or sideways glance from anyone. There were no security guards to keep them out, no signature required, no badges to swipe to authenticate their "trainee" status.

Emboldened by their success, they repeated the exercise twice more that week and several times over the rest of the month. Of course, after seeing the same faces returning for lunch so often over such a long period of time, the cafeteria staff began to wonder what was going on. Even the instructors teaching the courses were usually never in the building more than a week at a time. They had full-time jobs across the street to get back to as well. Had these two been hired as P&G's first full-time trainers? The women in the cafeteria made a few phone calls to check, and quickly realized these two were interlopers, bilking the company one lunch at a time.

Despite their pleas of ignorance, the story ended with their unceremonial exit from the company, the details of which were highly entertaining and almost certainly exaggerated by our host. The laughter at the lunch table continued among my colleagues, and ended with the coining of a new phrase that meant being fired for stealing from the company in a flagrantly stupid fashion. From then on, we referred to such an expulsion as being *Polked.*

It was never clear to us if the story was true or apocryphal. But it didn't matter. It stuck. There was no entry in the policy manual that told us we would get fired for eating in the Polk Building if we weren't in training. But after hearing that story, none of us would even consider repeating the offense. More importantly, it put us on notice that there are probably all kinds of bad behaviors that could get you fired without being explicitly told so in advance. The story taught us to use our common sense of what's right and wrong. We didn't need a rule book. If you do right, good things happen. If you do wrong, there are consequences, up to and including getting fired. The story, and the phrase coined from it, became a self-policing mechanism among my peers. If any of us ever said or did anything even remotely questionable, they would be quickly met with a probing look and the admonition, "Careful, genius. Keep that up and you'll get Polked."

As the David Armstrong quote at the beginning of the chapter indicates, rarely does anyone ever actually read a company policy manual. The purpose manuals primarily serve is a legal one. If the company is ever sued for wrongfully terminating an employee who broke the rules, the company lawyer can cite chapter and verse in front of the jury exactly the policy the now-terminated employee violated. But if your objective is to keep people from violating the rules in the first place, the policy manual will do you little good, because nobody reads it.

So how do employees learn the rules of an organization? One way is through their own behavior and experience. If they get punished for something, they quickly learn not to do it again. It must have been against the rules, written or not. If they get rewarded for something, they'll keep doing it. But nobody can possibly break all the rules themselves. So the main way people learn the rules is through the stories they hear about other people—those who broke the rules and suffered the consequences, and those who didn't and got rewarded. So in addition to your legally required policy manual, what you need are some good stories. The previous one is an example of someone breaking the rules and paying the price. But stories of positive reinforcement work just as well, as the following story about one of the oldest and most respected companies in America illustrates.

Sara Mathew joined Dun & Bradstreet in August 2001, as chief financial officer. Less than a year later, company sales projections were showing a slight decline. But nothing had substantially changed since she'd arrived. So why the drop in the sales forecast? The answer was found in several arcane accounting rules.

One of Sara's first actions as CFO was to put a new finance team in place so she could be sure the financial reporting was being done by the book. For the complex transactions in their industry, there are several accounting methods to choose from. Knowing which one is best is a complicated affair and depends on the situation. The right answer even changes over time as government regulators make new pronouncements. Apparently, the methods Sara's new team was using recognized revenues slower than other methods. Hence, the slight dip in sales. That made Sara curious. She was certain her method was correct. So she had her team look into the methods used in the past. They found the wrong method had been used in several cases. In some of them, the problems went back nearly a decade—not exactly what a new CFO wants to find in her first year.

Sara knew the company would have to restate its financials. That meant reversing all the inappropriate revenues and profits that had been reported in the past—millions of dollars out of its bottom line. And there couldn't have been a worse time for this to happen. Just months earlier,

Enron had filed for the largest bankruptcy in history as a result of fraudulent accounting practices. She went straight to the CEO.

In his office, she remembers the alarm on his face as he responded to the news. "Restatement! Like the Enron restatement?"

"Yes," she told him. "Like Enron. But in our case I don't think there was fraud—just a mistake. I won't know for sure—or how much money we're talking about—until we do a thorough investigation."

"How long will that take?" he asked.

What Sara was thinking was, "Heck, I don't know. I've never done this before." What she said, however, was, "Our next earnings release is in six weeks. I'll have it done by then." At the time, she was unaware that no restatement of this size had ever been completed in less than six months.

As the work began, Sara couldn't help but worry about the size of the problem. Hopefully, it would be small and inconsequential, and get no negative reaction from Wall Street. Her fear, of course, was that it would be big, and the share price would suffer.

In a situation like this, there are three ways a leader can respond. Option one is to ignore the problem. After all, they were using the proper accounting methods now. It's possible nobody would ever find out about the past errors. Option two is to pursue the work on the restatement, but to stop digging when the size of the problem gets too big to go unnoticed on Wall Street. For a company the size of D&B, that number is about $50 million. Option three is to keep digging until you find everything, without regard to the size of the problem. Let the chips fall where they may. Sara chose option three.

Working around the clock, the finance team completed the job in six weeks, as promised. With its next quarterly release, D&B adjusted its income going back 10 years. The grand total was a $150 million charge, with no fraud found. And despite the sizable amount, the stock price held steady. The size of the restatement and the speed with which it was announced left Wall Street certain there were no more skeletons in D&B's closet. Sara and her team received accolades and even monetary awards for completing the restatement in record time, and in a manner that left investors confident in the company and its management.

The actions of Sara and her team defined the rules of behavior in the finance department at Dun & Bradstreet. Accounting policy is defined in the rule book, written by the U.S. Financial Accounting Standards Board. But how those policies are followed at D&B was defined by the CFO, and the story that will live on even after she's gone.

Today, Sara Mathew is CEO and chairman of Dun & Bradstreet. She and others continue to tell this story to help employees understand not just the accounting policy but also the rules of behavior. Doing the right thing is rewarded at D&B. It's a policy Sara's confident she won't need to restate.

* * *

The premise of this chapter so far has been that you need stories to establish policy because nobody reads the policy manuals. But there is another reason—probably an even more important reason. Rules often lead to unintended consequences, sometimes causing more damage than the ill they were designed to prevent. Stories rarely do that. The following story illustrates the counterproductive nature of rules.

Phil Renshaw spent 17 years in banking and corporate finance before becoming a consultant and coach for finance executives with Circulus in Buckinghamshire, England. He's seen the downside of creating additional rules when the existing ones aren't working. One of his favorite examples is having senior managers personally approve all expenses, thinking it's a good way to reduce spending. It may succeed in reducing spending. But that doesn't mean it was a good idea.

In Phil's experience, here's how that typically plays out. A company has just entered the final quarter of the fiscal year and is woefully behind its earnings target. In order to save money, a temporary rule is put in place for the rest of the year. A senior executive, such as a vice president, must approve all expenses, no matter how small. The result is an absurd set of consequences. The first two are a result of the fact that such a leader might have hundreds, or even thousands, of people under his authority. Personally approving all those expenses could take several hours a day, distracting the VP from more important duties. He tries to keep up for a few days or weeks, but his work suffers because of it. Eventually the VP delegates the task to an administrator, which is the second absurdity. Expenses approval has now been delegated to an administrator less qualified to review them than the original managers who would have done so in the absence of the new rule.

The third and most malicious absurdity is that this rule robs mid-level managers of their ability to keep the organization productive and motivated. For example, let's say for the last week, three employees have worked 15-hour days on an urgent project, and complete it in record time.

At 10 o'clock in the evening on the last night, when the project is finalized and submitted, the manager wants to take the employees out to dinner in appreciation. But then she remembers the new rule. Only the vice president can approve this meal expense now. It would require a lengthy explanation to justify, and the VP might not approve it. She decides not to take the risk, and just thanks them for their hard work and sends them home. Money was saved, but at what cost? The employees are demoralized and the manager is undermined. Phil's advice is that if you can't trust your managers to make good decisions, you shouldn't have hired them. Instead, he advises companies to embed the quarterly cost or profit requirements in performance incentives like bonuses, or options, or even extra days off work. Then let individual managers decide which expenses are worth spending anyway and which are not. You'll have just as good a chance at hitting your earnings target, and without the train of absurdities.

If you ever find yourself considering instituting a new rule, consider the unintended consequences first. Ask yourself what Phil Renshaw would make of your rule. And if you happen to be one of the innocent victims of an equally toxic rule from upper management, tell them Phil's story. You might just get them to reconsider.

SUMMARY AND EXERCISES

1. Rule books don't govern behavior in any organization. Behavior is determined by what is rewarded or punished, even if the original reason is long forgotten—like monkeys in a cage.

2. Employees cannot possibly break all the rules themselves. They learn through the stories they hear about other people's behavior getting rewarded or punished. Make sure the stories in your organization reinforce the behavior you want. You should have positive stories (financial restatement at D&B), and negative ones (getting Polked).

3. Rules can lead to unintended consequences. The next time you're thinking about implementing a new rule, consider Phil Renshaw's story of expense approval. Consider telling a story instead.

4. If your boss has implemented a toxic rule, tell Phil's story. Your boss just might reconsider.

Notes

1. Dozens of similar versions of this story have appeared on the Internet for over a decade. The earliest appearance in print I've found is in John E. Renesch, *Getting to the Better Future* (San Francisco: New Business Books, 2000), where the original source is also unclaimed and unattributed.

2. G. R. Stephenson, "Cultural Acquisition of a Specific Learned Response Among Rhesus Monkeys," in D. Starek, R. Schneider, and H. J. Kuhn (eds.), *Progress in Primatology* (Stuttgart, Germany: Fischer, 1967), pp. 279–288.

CHAPTER **13**

Keep it real

"Many of the things we say to sound expert and dazzling actually distance our audience."
—JOAN LEWIS, Global Consumer & Market Knowledge Officer, Procter & Gamble

IT'S WELL ESTABLISHED in the marketing world that if you design your product or service for everyone, what you end up doing is designing for no one. You create a mass of compromises that fails to please anyone. Therefore, the theory holds, you should pick a subset of your customer base to design your offerings around. If you choose well, you'll have a group small enough that its needs are easy to identify and understand, but that represents the lion's share of your growth potential. Called *segmentation* in industry speak, that's the position P&G has taken with its own brands, and the advice it gives its retail partners about how to delight their shoppers as well.

Many retailers embraced the idea of segmentation quickly. Others found it a foreign concept, and difficult to appreciate. For them, P&G knew that the best place to start was the simplest segmentation model imaginable—a concept they called the *high potential shopper*. It's based on the classic Pareto principle. Research shows that 20 to 30 percent of shoppers in any given store are responsible for 70 to 80 percent of all the purchases. If you're going to pick a group of people to design your store around, it would be hard to go wrong starting with this group. Many retail customers quickly adopted this segmentation model for its incredible usefulness and straightforward simplicity.

108

Others weren't convinced, despite several explanations. But the P&G team in Canada kept trying with one of those holdouts. In their final attempt at one of their major retail customers, team members made the same argument they had made many times before, but this time with one simple change. Consumer research manager Monika Jambrovic removed the vague and amorphous title "high potential shopper" and replaced it with the name and photograph of one woman—Lisa. She took something abstract and made it concrete.

She gave Lisa the same demographic and attitudinal profile as the average high potential shopper they had so heavily researched. In fact, they used almost all of the same presentation materials as before, except all references to the high potential shopper were replaced with the name Lisa and accompanied by a picture of an average-looking Canadian woman.

It was a huge success! The retailer's management immediately took to the idea and began using Lisa as their primary design target. In fact, after that, anytime P&G came to them with other ideas—or, more importantly, when the retailer had ideas they wanted to consider—they would come to P&G and ask, "What would Lisa think about this?"

This was proof they had completely adopted the idea of designing to a specific target customer. And all because Monika substituted something concrete in place of something abstract.

We're often taught in the business world to "ladder our ideas up" to their highest level of generality. This makes our ideas "bigger" because they can be applied to a broader set of circumstances. This might be good advice when you're still developing your idea so you can see how far it can be stretched. But when communicating your idea to other people, that advice can turn it into abstract corporate speak that will numb the minds of your audience.

Describing your idea in specific, concrete terms is almost always more effective, for two reasons. First, it helps people understand your idea more easily. After all, what do people do when they're having trouble understanding a complex idea you've been trying to explain for several minutes? They ask you to give them an example. You do, and their eyes get wide as the light goes on in their head. The example creates the "ah-ha" moment when all the abstract theory you've been explaining actually makes sense. For the listener, struggling through all the conceptual generalities can be frustrating. Getting the oh-so-simple example at the end sometimes evokes a snide response like, "Why didn't you say that in the first place?" They could have understood much sooner if you'd given them the example up front, because the example is a concrete version of your abstract idea.

Second, concreteness helps people apply your idea to their situation. "If this is how this idea was used by so-and-so, then if I change this little thing, it will probably work just as well for me." Applying an abstract idea to an individual situation is hard if you don't know where to start. A concrete example gives people a starting place.

* * *

An even more compelling example of the power of concreteness happened at one of the top retailers in the United States, also involving customer segmentation. Unlike the Canadian example, this retailer's management has been among the foremost thinkers in the industry on segmentation. In 2006, the retailer asked Procter & Gamble to help research one of its key segments: the "achiever mom." This was a type-A personality woman who took her job running the household as seriously as running a business.

When it was time to make the big presentation to the retailer's management team, P&G researchers compiled the reams of material it had collected. But instead of presenting it in the traditional way—with PowerPoint presentations and a well-planned-out order—the P&G team leader, Mike Russell, decided to try something different. At the beginning of the meeting, he put a chair out in the middle of the room and introduced the audience to one of its achiever moms. Sitting in the chair was Julie Walker, a P&G marketing director.

Julie was, in fact, an achiever mom. She had taken the battery of segmentation questions and fit the profile precisely. She was further armed with all of the research done on the achiever mom—all that stuff they might have otherwise dumped on the audience in a firestorm of presentation slides. But they all knew her as Julie Walker, P&G marketing director. Undaunted, the P&G team prodded them with the following question: "What would you like to ask her?"

The questions came slowly at first, but then picked up. "How often do you shop at our stores? What do you buy there? Where else do you shop? What do you buy there? Why don't you buy that stuff at our store?" and so on. Each time, Julie would answer the question. Sometimes the answer came from the research, and sometimes it was just her own personal answer as a real achiever mom. But with each answer, the audience became more and more rapt with attention, and noted everything she said.

By the end of the meeting, they had a more thorough understanding of the achiever mom segment than they could have ever hoped for. Mike took a risk with this unusual presentation technique. And it worked—amazingly well. The retailer's managers got to ask the questions they were interested in, not just the ones P&G wanted them to. The retailer's management team engaged in the process of discovery. And most importantly, they met their target customer face-to-face. The achiever mom was abstract. Julie Walker was concrete.

The retailer was so intent on delighting the achiever mom and the other target segments that it reorganized its entire management structure around them. It created a senior vice president role for each of the target segments. All of the marketing and merchandising personnel who manage the product lines most important to each of those target segments were assigned to report to the appropriate senior VP. This might be the most serious organizational commitment to a customer segmentation strategy ever.

When it came time to fill the role of senior VP of the achiever mom segment, whom do you think they wanted to hire? Of course—Julie Walker. She had become the personification of the achiever mom in the mind of senior management. It had to be Julie. Now it didn't hurt that Julie was a brilliant marketer and a consummate strategic thinker. And this wasn't the first time she'd been made overtures to leave P&G to work at the retailer. But in the past, the retailer had politely accepted Julie's decision to decline the offers. This time was different. Only Julie Walker could do this job. No one else would do.

After several such requests, the CEO of the retailer went as far as to contact the CEO of Procter & Gamble, A. G. Lafley, and ask if he could "borrow" Julie temporarily to get the department started while it looked for a permanent hire. After some negotiation, P&G finally capitulated. For six months, Julie went to work as the senior vice president of the achiever mom segment.

As Mike Russell knew intuitively, being concrete can help you make your point easier to understand and more real and engage your audience more fully. And as Julie Walker found out, apparently it can also help get you a great new job.

The lesson in the first two stories is that you can always take something abstract and turn it into something concrete. The story of Lisa shows you can take words that are abstract ("high potential shopper") and make them concrete ("Lisa"). The Julie Walker story shows how you can take an entire event (like a presentation of information) and turn it into something concrete (like an interview with a real person). When in doubt, keep it real.

Fortunately, storytelling is an inherently concrete activity. You can't really tell a story about a vague generalization. You can only talk about that idea in vague, general terms. But that won't be a story. A story has to be about specific people and events. In chapter 2, the story I used to help set the vision for our paper company wasn't a general observation about vision setting, or the history of paper companies in general. It was a specific story about Nokia starting as a paper company and growing to an international communications giant. In chapter 4, the story about Tarang Amin wasn't a general discussion about how to turn bad news into a helpful agent of change in your company. It was a specific story about how he used an unflattering magazine article about his company to motivate his team to finish the changes they'd started. So deciding to tell a story that supports your ideas is the first step to making your ideas more real.

* * *

Let's look at a few examples of how to take your already real story and make it even more real with the language, metaphors, and level of candor you choose to employ.

Many young researchers I work with (and a few older ones, too) will excitedly tell their nonresearch business partners about some "ethnographic research" they have planned, or about the "attitudinal research" just completed or the "behavioral analysis" they did last month. But without defining those terms, it's likely their audience will understand very little of what they mean.

Like most humans, we want our colleagues to think we're smart. We assume tossing around some technical jargon or a few SAT exam words will do the trick. And sometimes it will. So if your goal is only to make your audience think you're smart, go right ahead with all those five-dollar words.

But if your goal is to be understood, rid yourself of such language. There are always more accessible words you could use. Instead of "ethnographic research" or "behavioral analysis," tell them you're going to "watch what people do" and "measure what they buy." Instead of "attitudinal research," tell them you asked people "what they think."

Impress your audience with the ideas in your stories, not your vocabulary.

As for events, the following table compares abstract situations to concrete ones. If your communication objective is listed on the left, the right side contains a more concrete option.

Abstract is:	Concrete is:
Having your audience read about consumer living conditions in rural Morocco.	Having them live with a poor Moroccan family for a week.
Telling your audience that many Americans live on less than $100 a week in discretionary income.	Having them make a budget and live on $100 themselves for a week.
Teaching them how to read your company's income statement in theory.	Having them produce it themselves from accounting records.
Listening to someone explain new facts.	Explaining those facts to someone else.

Let's see how these tools play out in two real stories. One is from one of the most talked-about U.S. law firms in the 1990s. The other involves one of the most challenging situations an entrepreneur faces in the early days of a business start-up—making payroll. In both cases, look for the deliberate use of concrete language versus vague abstractions.

Being a juror in a trial is a bit like being the scorekeeper at a basketball game without knowing the rules. Do free throws count the same as a 10-foot jumper? What about a last-second shot from half-court? Now imagine you're the coach of one of the teams. How do you call the plays so that your naive scorekeeper will declare your team the winner at the end?

That's how Jerry Jones describes the job of jurors and the trial lawyers who argue in front of them. Jerry spent two decades as an attorney at the Rose Law Firm in Little Rock, Arkansas, working alongside other notable partners such as Hillary Clinton and Vince Foster. He says judges don't typically give the jury instructions until after all the testimony and closing statements have been made. And even then, those instructions leave much to the jury's discretion. Then they retire to the jury room and tally up the score. That's why Jerry always found it helpful to give the jury ideas on how to keep score in his opening statement.

Like any good trial lawyer, Jerry is an experienced storyteller. He masterfully weaves in relevant metaphors and concrete examples to make his message clear and compelling. For example, Jerry recalls one particular case where he represented the plaintiff in a breach of contract case. A multimillion-dollar company had broken the terms of a franchise agreement with his client, a much smaller company, costing his client lost revenues and profits. The jury found in favor of his client, but then had to determine how much the big company had to pay in damages. In addition to the actual loss incurred, Jerry was asking for punitive damages because of the intentional and malicious nature of the breach. Here's where the scorekeeping comes in. How much a company should pay in punitive damages is left largely to the jury. Jerry needed to give the jury members a way to determine what was fair, but not too damaging to the defendant. So he told them a story they could all relate to.

"Do you remember that big snowstorm we had a couple of years ago?" Jerry asked. "Five inches, I think." The jury members all nodded. It doesn't snow much in Arkansas, so when they get a really big snow, it's hard to forget. "Well, then you'll remember there were a lot of people around here who couldn't get out of their homes to go to work or to school for about five days." More nods from the jury. "Yeah, it was tough for a few days. But we got on with life afterward, maybe even a little smarter. Because the next time the weatherman said a big snow was coming, what did you all do? You went out and stocked up on food and water and batteries, and maybe even got a generator, didn't you?

"Well, we want to do the same thing with this company. We don't want to put them out of business with punitive damages. We just want them to remember this and change their behavior in the future. Now, according to their annual report, they make about $200,000 in profit every working day. So if they had to stay home for five days like we all did with that 5-inch snowstorm a couple of years ago, that would cost them $1 million. A 10-inch storm might cost them $2 million. Your job is to decide how much it's going to snow. I'm sure you'll pick a fair number."

Jerry was hoping the jury would award one or two weeks' worth of profits. And that's exactly what he got.

The snowstorm and the days stuck at home was a brilliant metaphor to help the jury understand the value of punitive damages to teach a lesson and change behavior. Quantifying the company profits in terms of profits per day made the numbers real, understandable, and relevant to their daily lives, especially as it related to the snowstorm metaphor. All wrapped in the story, this combination of narrative tools was highly effective in Jerry's hands. With them, he taught the jury how to keep score. And his team did win the game.

* * *

Our second story dates back to the dot-com boom that made and lost fortunes for entrepreneurs of all types. Andrew Moorfield was one of them.

By 1999, Andrew had spent a decade in banking and corporate finance for companies like Citibank and Diageo. But the tidal wave of opportunities the dot-com revolution presented was too much for someone with big ideas to resist. And Andrew had big ideas. In June 2000, he left the corporate world and launched bfinance.co.uk, a London-based online lending platform for small businesses. "It was exhilarating and terrifying at the same time," he admits. As with many small companies at start-up, there were periods of time he didn't know if the company would make it. Cash flow was everything; and there were times when there wasn't enough to pay the bills.

"The first time I couldn't make payroll was the worst," Andrew explained. "Having to choose which employees got paid and which didn't was emotionally draining." Most leaders trained in big-company environments would have handled it with the veiled finesse of a corporate lawyer. First, secretly decide how much each employee deserved to get. Then talk to each employee, in private, and explain how much of his or her pay would be withheld until cash flow improved. Lastly, don't tell anyone how much the other employees were getting. But a wink and a nod from the boss leads all of them to believe they were getting more than average. The secrecy would foment doubt. Maybe they were getting less than everyone else! The result is widespread suspicion, jealousy, and complete lack of trust.

Fortunately for employees at bfinance, that's not what Andrew did. Instead, he pulled all 25 employees into a conference room and explained the predicament in brutally honest terms. He wrote a number on the whiteboard and said, "That was our bank account balance at the beginning of the month." Below that he wrote several other numbers, and explained, "Those are the revenues we expect to get this month and the expenses we have to pay to keep running the business." After adding them all up, he wrote the result underneath, saying, "That's what we'll have left at the end of the month to pay salaries," and circled the number. Just to the right of it, he wrote another number and circled it. "That's how much your monthly salaries add up to." Andrew paused and let the audience assess the stark dilemma in front of them. The number on the right was much bigger than the number on the left. In fact, there was only enough money to pay about a third of the payroll. If anyone ever told a story using more numbers than words, Andrew was doing it.

Then he did something else unlikely to happen in a big company. He asked the employees—all 25 of them—what they thought he should do about it. He assumed the fairest thing to do was to pay everyone a third of their salary. But the team surprised him with a different suggestion. They thought a better method would be to pay a third of the employees all of their salary, and the other two-thirds none. Andrew was horrified. How could he possibly choose which employees to pay and which not to pay? But they surprised him a second time when they offered to help there as well. They would decide among themselves. Their criteria were based solely on who needed the money most urgently and who could wait a month or two to catch up. Andrew left the team to discuss the matter. When they delivered their decision, Andrew got his third surprise of the day. The people on the list to get paid were not the ones he expected. He thought the younger employees with the smaller salaries would be in the most desperate position. But among themselves they'd decided that the older ones—the ones with families to feed and mortgages to pay—had the most immediate commitments. Several of the younger ones still lived at home with their parents, or in an inexpensive apartment, and had no family to support. They were the ones who volunteered to go without.

Andrew thanked them for their understanding and cooperation. He honored their decision and paid the employees accordingly.

Andrew learned a lesson from that experience he's used to this day. When faced with a difficult decision that will result in people being disappointed, do two things. First, be real, open, and honest with them about the situation. Lay all the facts out in detail. Don't shroud them in corporate secrecy or describe the situation in vague, opaque terms that might sound like this: "Unfortunately, the company's current financial condition requires that we make adjustments to employee salaries and benefits for an indeterminate period of time. Management will meet with each employee individually and determine the appropriate temporary adjustment required. Compensation will return to normal levels when key balance sheet metrics are restored." Like the legalese avoided in the previous story, this glop of corporate speak is loaded with one vague abstraction after another. Exactly what financial condition are we in? What kind of "adjustments" are you making to our salaries—a raise or a pay cut? How will the appropriate adjustment be determined? Do I get a say in it? What balance sheet metrics have to return to normal for us to get paid right again?

Corporate spokespeople sometimes prefer this kind of generalization. In the event the company does something different, it's difficult or impossible to prove they didn't follow the original plan, because the original plan lacked any real specificity. That keeps the company out of court. Unfortunately, the same lack of specificity that makes it legally defensible also makes it frustratingly devoid of real content for the audience of employees. Fortunately for the employees of bfinance, Andrew Moorfield disliked corporate weasel words as much as they did.

The second lesson Andrew learned was to ask the affected parties how they would decide if it was up to them. In Andrew's case, they suggested a solution that he wouldn't have thought of. But even if that doesn't happen, when asked to put themselves in your shoes, with all the facts at their disposal, 9 times out of 10 they'll probably come to the same decision you did. At that point, it's far easier for you to deliver the decision and them to accept it.

Andrew's start-up eventually succeeded. Ownership of the business changed twice since that first year. And Andrew has since returned to the more stable harbors of the banking world, where he is managing director at Lloyd's Bank in London. But bfinance.co.uk is still going strong. Today it is one of the largest asset management services in Europe. He shares this story when someone on his team is facing a tough decision or needs to deliver bad news to a client. Not many people have had to face a decision as tough as which employees to pay and which not to. Andrew's story lets them experience the situation almost firsthand, and learn the lesson he learned. For a banker, explaining to a client that she won't be getting the loan or line of credit she applied for is almost as difficult. Following his advice, clients are more likely to take the news well, because they appreciate the reality of the situation, and the transparency of their banker. As a result, they continue to stay a satisfied customer of Lloyd's Bank, and Andrew Moorfield never has to decide which employees not to pay.

SUMMARY AND EXERCISES

1. Concrete ideas are far more memorable than abstract ones. Take your abstract idea and explain it with a concrete story about a single example. Storytelling is an inherently concrete activity. You can't really tell a story about a vague generalization. You can only talk about it in vague, general terms. A story has to be about specific people and events.

    a. Examples: On the banks of the Tammerkoski River (chapter 2); *Business-Week* on Bounty (chapter 4); "Lisa" the high potential shopper; Julie Walker, achiever mom.

2. Avoid technical jargon your audience might not understand.

3. Make the facts, numbers, or events relevant to your audience—something they can relate to in their everyday lives, like the snowstorm in the courtroom.

4. Be brutally open and honest about difficult subjects. Avoid waffling or weasel words typical of corporate management speak today (making payroll).

CHAPTER **14**

Stylistic elements

"How do you tell stories? With passion."
—DAVID ARMSTRONG, *Managing by Storying Around*

NOTHING WILL MAKE an audience of businesspeople roll their eyes and disengage faster than overly descriptive language typical of a nineteenth-century romance novel: *"It was August in Dubai, and the sweltering mid-day heat dripped off the rooftops like hot wax down a candle. The air was oppressive and almost as thick as the despair of the local people. . . ."*

The same prose they might be eager to read at 9 P.M. while curled up in their favorite reading chair will not be welcomed at 9 A.M. in a conference room, or when reading an e-mail or a memo. "Oh, puh-lease! Just get to the point!" they'll think, or maybe even say.

That doesn't mean busy executives can't be engaged with a story. The entire premise of this book is that they can. But what engages them at work is different from what might engage them in light pleasure reading. What works in the office is plain, simple, and direct language that lets the wisdom of the story shine, not the literary skills of the storyteller. We'll spend a good deal of this chapter defining what business-appropriate writing style is. I'll also share a few key literary devices proven to turn a good story into a great story. But let's start at the beginning—literally.

Great beginnings

How should you begin your story? As the quip about nineteenth-century prose suggests, the answer is not with a string of colorful adjectives and

118

adverbial phrases. Instead, there are three options to get the attention of a business audience early in a story. The first is the element of surprise. You'll learn about that in chapter 19 so I won't repeat those lessons here.

The second method is to create a mystery. Mysteries are highly engaging story lines. Listeners stay engaged because they want to solve them. For example, in the chapter 5 story about the diaper business, the mystery was posed early about the strange relationship between sales and profits, and why it suddenly changed in 1983. The mystery wasn't solved until much later in the story. In chapter 2 you read a folktale about a woman who came across a construction site and wondered what they were building. As the reader, you surely wondered what they were building as well. But like the woman, you didn't get to find out until almost all the way through the story. Mysteries make a great beginning to great stories. Open with a question important to the story line, and leave it open as long as possible.

The third method is the most powerful one of all, and also the simplest. You've seen many examples of it in this book already. The best way to get the attention of a business audience is to quickly introduce a main character they can relate to, and put the character in a challenging situation or predicament. It's really nothing more than the context you learned in chapter 7. Introduce the relevant hero (Subject), Treasure, and Obstacle, but do so quickly with little or nothing else prior.

For example, the opening story in chapter 1 started with the statement that in my first presentation to the CEO, I learned a valuable lesson about how *not* to do it properly. Almost every businessperson either already does make presentations to the CEO or hopes to someday. So the main character in this story is highly relatable. The challenging situation is that I obviously made a mistake the audience can learn from without having to make the same embarrassing mistake themselves.

In chapter 10 you read the story of the consultant, Tom. In the very first sentence, you learned that his client wanted to cancel his retainer— in other words, to fire him. There's probably no more common fear in the working world than the fear of getting fired. Everyone can relate to that. In each case, the stories started with a main character relatable to just about any businessperson, and a predicament they might typically face and hope to navigate successfully. When opened this way, listeners are eager to hear the rest of the story in hopes they'll learn how to succeed in the situation next time they face it. So they listen—intently.

In each story you craft, use at least one of these attention-grabbing tools.

Writing style

Ironically, even the ideas of gifted speakers can miraculously transform into a complex swamp of words when they commit their idea to writing. There's something about the formality of writing that makes us want to fluff up our communication. We're under the misconception that long, elaborate sentences full of big words are more professional. They're not. The result is something like the following paragraph, originally written to describe the accomplishments of two managers accepting an award for exemplary performance. (I'm not making this up.)

"Ashley and Dana's business model portfolio reinvention that drove a fewer-bigger-better-balanced-integrated strategy with boutiqued, optimally supported new launches balanced with increased commercial initiative and base business activity led to maximizing category incremental sales and return on investment. This reinvented portfolio strategy addressed opportunities such as 10+ new initiatives per year with suboptimal support, few restages, no year two sustaining media, and no base business support. As a result, 2007 initiative bundle sales were up 29 percent, profits were up 109 percent, all with fewer initiatives."

You've seen this kind of writing before, and maybe even written something like it a time or two. It makes complete sense to the author when writing it. But the reader has to read it several times to understand. That's not effective communication. And can you imagine ever saying those words to another person face-to-face? Of course not. Your listener wouldn't let you get away with it. You might be accused of being crazy, or a corporate automaton at best. That realization leads directly to the single most effective piece of advice to fix this sort of fluff: *Write the way you speak.*

Sure, that's a bit of a simplification. But as a solitary guideline to better writing, it can't be beat. Better to be too simple and informal than too complex and formal. To illustrate that advice, below is a translation of the fluff into readable English.

"Historically, we've launched 10 to 20 new products a year. Most had too little marketing support, and even less support in year two. Everyone thought new items kept the category growing. So we launched a lot of them—more than we could afford to support. And we neglected our base business entirely. But Ashley and Dana convinced management to try a new business model. They suggested bigger initiatives, but fewer of them; more marketing support for each, even in year two; and restages of the base business to keep the parent brand growing as well. And it worked—

amazingly well! Sales in 2007 were up almost 30 percent and profits doubled, all with fewer initiatives. Congratulations, Ashley and Dana!"

Now do you have a better idea of what Ashley and Dana did to deserve their award? Why did the second version make more sense than the original? First, because I rewrote it in the proper story structure of *context, action, result.* Note the first version starts out with the action—what Ashley and Dana did. "Ashley and Dana's business model portfolio reinvention . . ." Then it gets to the context—what was going on before Ashley and Dana did anything. "This reinvented portfolio strategy addressed opportunities such as . . ." Lastly, it shares the results.

My version starts by putting the context in its proper place—at the beginning. "Historically, we've launched 10 to 20 new products a year. . . ." Then I get to Ashley and Dana's action. "But Ashley and Dana convinced management to try a new business model. . . ." Then it ends with the results.

The second thing I did was to write it as if it were a conversation I was having with someone in person. It's what I would say to someone to explain very briefly what Ashley and Dana did to deserve the award. To understand that, let's have a look at the difference between the way most people write and the way they speak. Specifically, I mean how people speak when they're speaking at their best. That is, in a relaxed, thoughtful conversation. Not a rushed, rambling monologue, or nervous patter riddled by "uhs" and "ers." Good spoken language uses these tactics:

1. *Shorter sentences.* The first "Ashley and Dana" paragraph averages 27 words per sentence. The corrected version averages less than 13. Most experts recommend between 15 and 18 words per sentence for effective business writing. If your sentences are longer than that, break them up into smaller ones. As a benchmark, this book averages 15.3 words per sentence. This paragraph has only 10.3 per sentence.

2. *Smaller words.* For some reason we are less tempted to throw in impressive-sounding words when speaking than we are when writing. So for writing, you'll have to exercise more discipline to keep those high school SAT words from sneaking in. Words that draw attention to themselves—or to you as the storyteller—are a barrier to good storytelling. They distract the reader's attention from the story. Use mostly words with one or two syllables. Words of three or more syllables should be no more than 15 percent of all words. The bad paragraph above has 21 "big words" out of 83, or 25 percent. The improved paragraph has only 9 percent big words. As political poll-

ster Frank Luntz says, "Avoid words that might force someone to reach for the dictionary—because most Americans won't."[1]

3. *Active voice.* In conversation, you would never say, "The contract has been won by Newton Corp." You'd say, "Newton Corp. won the contract." But most people have no issue using that first sentence in writing. The first sentence is in passive voice. The second is active. In active voice, the subject is doing the action. "Newton" is the subject of the second sentence, and "won" is the action. In passive voice, the subject receives the action. "The contract" is the subject of the passive sentence, and the action of "being won" is happening to it.

   Passive voice makes your writing sound pretentious and unnatural. For example, in the following sentence there are three passive phrases. "It did not go unnoticed by the board that the recommendation lacked top management support, and therefore, their approval was withheld." Compare that to the same sentence converted to active voice. "The board noticed top management didn't support the recommendation, so they rejected it." The active voice sentence is more direct and natural and communicated the same message with 38 percent fewer words. Ninety percent or more of your sentences should be in active voice. This book is 95 percent active voice.

4. *Getting to the verb quickly.* Go back and read the first sentence in the bad "Ashley and Dana" paragraph. You have to read a jaw-dropping 32 words into that sentence before you get to the verb! One reason it's so cumbersome is that you have to keep the 31 words prior to that in short-term memory waiting to find out what's happening to them. Compare it to the first sentence in the improved paragraph. The verb is the second word. In fact, the first three sentences have the verb as the second or third word. If your verbs are trapped in the middle or end of your sentences, move them forward. Your audience will appreciate it.

These guidelines aren't new. They're similar to those you'll find in classic writing guides like *Strunk & White's Elements of Style* or Reader's Digest's *Write Better, Speak Better.* So why repeat them here? Because not enough business leaders read those books—or perhaps haven't for two decades. Either way, they need to be repeated. For those wanting a short, modern guide to writing style at work, I recommend *The Language of Success* by Tom Sant.

Is there an easy way to know how readable your writing is without counting your words by hand? Yes! Some word-processing programs can compute your average sentence length and use of passive voice. More helpful, some compute standard readability scores on your documents. For example, Microsoft Word can calculate your Flesch-Kincaid Grade Level automatically. (In Spelling and Grammar check options, select "Check grammar with spelling" and "Show readability statistics." After you run the Spelling and Grammar check, a window will pop up with the readability report. Warning: As of this writing, some versions of Microsoft Word have a defect in their Flesch-Kincaid Grade Level calculation. Scores above 12 are not reported properly and simply read 12.0. If that's the case with yours, check the "Flesch Readability Ease" score instead. It ranges from 0 [impossibly difficult to read] to 100 [very easy to read]. You'll want to score a 60 or higher.) The program counts to see how long your sentences are and how big the words are. Long, complex sentences with bigger words result in a higher "grade level." But unlike a school exam, a high score here isn't better. The score doesn't reflect the intelligence of the ideas, just the complexity of the writing style. So a high score doesn't mean you're smart. It means you're a bad writer.

For comparison, articles in the *Wall Street Journal* and the *New York Times* typically score between grade level 8 and 10 on this scale. That's about right for impactful, decisive business communication. Even popular fiction writers like John Grisham and Tom Clancy write around a 7 or 8 on this scale, which is one reason their books are such good reads. The book you're reading right now scores grade level 8.

Unfortunately, many businesspeople write at a 12 to 15 on this scale, which is much too complex. You want your audience to read your writing easily and enjoyably. It shouldn't be a chore. Save their brainpower to think about the meaning and impact of your idea. Don't make them waste it trying to interpret your syntax and grammar. As an example, the bad paragraph about Ashley and Dana scores a grade level of 21. The improved version scores at a grade level of 8. In general, writing that scores above 15 is unreadable in the first pass. Anything over 20 will be judged either offensively pompous, or a rambling, run-on mess. Both are likely to be abandoned before completion.

For those of you who don't have access to a program that calculates these readability scores, there's a simple method developed by an organization famous for creating great leaders—the U.S. Army. In the pamphlet *Effective Writing for Army Leaders*, it defines a writing "clarity index" as follows. Calculate the average number of words per sentence. The target should be around 15. Then calculate the percentage of words that are three or more syllables. The target should be 15 percent. Add those two numbers together for the clarity index. Ideal is around 30. Below 20, and the army considers the writing too abrupt. Over 40 it considers difficult to understand.

A final piece of advice that's *not* typical of spoken language is to *be concise*. Said most succinctly by Strunk & White, whenever possible "omit needless words."[2] That means never use a sentence when a simple phrase will do. Never use a phrase when a single word will do.

My favorite illustration of that involved one of my college roommates, Ed Tanguay. He burst into laughter the first time he listened to a local radio station in our small college town. Hearing only the weather report, I asked him what he found so funny.

Ed replied, "Did you hear the way that guy announced the temperature? He said, 'The current temperature reading at the station here in downtown Conway is 65 degrees.' The guys at the big stations back in Denver report the weather, too. But they would have just said, 'It's 65 degrees,' and then got back to playing music." In other words, the big-city radio host would have replaced 12 words with 1 word: *It's*. Think about it. Why would you need to say, "The current temperature reading . . . ?" Would the listening audience be confused and think you're talking about the temperature yesterday? And why, "at the station here in downtown Conway"? The station had a broadcast radius of about five miles. There couldn't be much fluctuation from one side of town to the other. None of that was necessary. It's 65 degrees. That's it.

French writer and poet Antoine de Saint-Exupéry once observed, "A designer knows he has achieved perfection not when there is nothing left to add, but when there is nothing left to take away."[3] Think about your writing the same way. Strip parts of it away one at a time. When you can't take out anything else without making it unrecognizable, you're done. This traditional Indian folktale, as recounted by Garr Reynolds in *PresentationZen*,[4] is a good illustration.

When Vijay opened his store, he put up a sign that said: "We Sell Fresh Fish Here." His father stopped by and said that the word *we* suggested an emphasis on the seller rather than the customer, and was really not needed. So the sign was changed to "Fresh Fish Sold Here."

His brother came by and suggested that the word *here* could be done away with. It was superfluous. Vijay agreed and changed the sign to "Fresh Fish Sold."

Next, his sister came along and said the sign should just say "Fresh Fish." Clearly, it's being sold; what else could you be doing?

Later, his neighbor stopped by to congratulate him. Then he mentioned that all passersby could easily tell that the fish was really fresh. Mentioning the word *fresh* actually made it sound defensive as though there were room for doubt about the freshness. Now the sign just read "*Fish*."

As Vijay was walking back to his shop after a break he noticed that one could identify the fish from its smell from very far, at a distance from which one could barely read the sign. He knew there was no need for the word *fish*.

As with most things in life, "all things in moderation" is probably good advice. One could argue whether or not Vijay should have gone all the way to having no sign at all. As Einstein is often quoted as saying, "Make everything as simple as possible, but no simpler." Following both the admonitions from de Saint-Exupéry and Einstein, Vijay might have stopped with "Fresh Fish." Anything more is not simple enough. Anything less changes the core of the message. Ruthlessly take things away from your message. But know when to stop.

* * *

The other benefit of being concise is that it makes it easier to explain your idea in a short amount of time. It's an often-observed fact that the more senior the manager, the shorter the attention span. It's not that senior executives are less intelligent than the rest of us. They're just busier. A Fortune 50 company recently hired a new CEO. In his first week, he offered many of the vice presidents an opportunity to meet with him one-on-one to share the most important things they were working on in their departments. They started putting together presentations to highlight all their fabulous projects and ideas. They were assuming they'd have at least the standard one-hour meeting to get through it all, but were hoping they'd get more time if the CEO was particularly interested in the content. After all, how can you possibly show off a whole department's worth of work in any less time than that?

Most were shocked when the CEO's administrator called to schedule the meetings and offered them a maximum of 15 minutes each!

Storytelling shouldn't take a long time. Most of the stories in this book can be told verbally in two to four minutes. Some take less than one minute. As a rule of thumb, a comfortable speaking pace is about 150 to 180 words per minute. So a 500-word story will take about three minutes to tell.

Literary devices

Dialogue is the single most engaging literary device you can put in a story. It has benefits for the story, and the storyteller. First, it signals the audience that this is a story, not a lecture. It's the most natural way humans tell stories, even from a young age. Listen to a kindergartener at the end of the day talk about what happened at school, and you're likely to hear, "Johnny said . . . and then Jane said . . . and then the teacher said . . ."

Second, it turns a dry account of the facts into a story about the impact the facts had on real people. People say what they think and feel. When you quote people in stories, you'll be sharing what they think and feel. As a result, dialogue delivers the emotional content in your stories.

Third, dialogue grabs the listener's attention. There's something that happens in that brief pause after you say, "And then my boss said . . ." that focuses the listener's attention with anticipation of what's coming next.

Lastly, it makes it easy to craft the story. If you rely on what was said by the people involved, you'll need to create less of your own historical account.

Let's look at a new story as an example. This story follows the one in chapter 12 about Sara Mathew, then-CFO of Dun & Bradstreet.

Getting D&B's books restated in six weeks left Sara feeling the high of success still early in her tenure as CFO. But that high was short-lived. Once a year, everyone at D&B completes an employee satisfaction survey. Sara had just gotten the results for her department. They were among the worst in the company. Her organization was sending her a clear message about how she had gotten the restatement done. The long hours and unyielding focus had taken its toll. Quickly, she was back in the CEO's office, and he was not happy. His opening line was, "You're not leading well, Sara."

Of course Sara was disappointed in the survey results. But in the light of what happened with the restatement, it seemed inevitable to her. She assumed the end result justified the means it took to get there. Her response reflected this belief. "You need to make a choice," she said. "Which do you want—great results, or happy people?"

The CEO's simple, but profound response was, "Great leaders do both."

Those words hit Sara like a freight train. It forced her to reflect on her own methods and the impact she can have on others in her urgency to deliver. Like most people, she was aware of her own foibles. She was a strong strategic thinker, and a natural problem solver. But she was also a terrible listener. She was direct—to the point of being blunt. She was tough, demanding, and played to win. If you were on the other side of the table from her, it could be intimidating. But she had assumed that was just part of who she was and a requisite part of how she got things done.

Her boss convinced her otherwise. She decided to have several round-table discussions with her employees to gather direct feedback on the shortcomings of her leadership style. It was a painful, humbling process. But she didn't just gather the feedback. She actually accepted it and acted on it. Two years later, her employee satisfaction scores were among the best anywhere.

Sara shares this story today to teach the value of being a learning leader. Even bosses need to continually learn, whether they are the CFO, CEO, or chairman of the board—all roles Sara has held. If she hadn't learned the hard lesson she did as CFO, she would have never been given the chance to have the second two.

How would that story have sounded without dialogue? Imagine the first paragraph closed by saying that "the CEO called her into his office to express his displeasure with her employee survey scores." That's not nearly as engaging as hearing him say, "You're not leading well, Sara." You can put yourself into her shoes when you hear her boss telling her she isn't doing her job well. Without the dialogue, it's more removed and impersonal.

Similar with her response: "Which do you want—great results or happy people?" That's a very bold question to ask the CEO. It's clear from the dialogue Sara disagreed and was standing her ground. That's more effective than writing, "Sara believed happy people and great results weren't possible at the same time, so she stood her ground."

Finally, the CEO's response was poetic in its simplicity: "Great leaders do both." Compare that to, "The CEO disagreed, and insisted Sara could do both if she tried." Is there any doubt the dialogue made this story more engaging?

* * *

Another helpful device when you have a story about real people is to use their real names. Unless you have a reason to protect someone's anonymity, using a name makes your story more real, believable, and interesting. Plus, sometimes the people you'll be telling a story about will be in the audience. People like hearing their names in stories. It's flattering.

The last literary device worth mentioning is repetition, which can greatly enhance the effectiveness of a story. Consider the story of the three men building a cathedral in chapter 2. Each time the woman turns to one of the men to ask what he's doing, the story repeats almost the same language: ". . . she asked one of them what he was doing . . . asked the next man what he was doing . . . asked the third what he was doing." It would have been simpler to just say, "She asked all three men what they were doing and their responses were: the first man said this . . . the second said . . . the third said . . ." But the repetition helps build the cadence of the story and anticipation for the surprise ending. You'll see the same device used in the story of the three researchers in chapter 20.

As any parent knows, repetition is comforting to children in bedtime stories and nursery rhymes. Adults appreciate it for similar reasons. Don't be afraid to use it.

* * *

The final thoughts in this chapter involve the attitude of the storyteller. I've seen too many business managers, executives, and even trainers and keynote speakers lessen the effectiveness of their stories by apologizing for them, or asking permission to tell them in the first place. You've probably heard someone say, "I hope you'll forgive me if I tell a personal story. . . ." I've even seen a paid professional speaker ask several times in his speech, "Can I tell you a story?" and then proceed only after a few obligatory nods from the audience.

That kind of language signals to the listener that you don't value the story as much as what you would have been saying otherwise. If that were true, you should skip the story and get on to the bullet points on slide number 72. Your story is a valuable gift to your audience. They're lucky you took the time to craft it and share it so they can learn something important in a way they'll remember and perhaps even enjoy. Leaders don't ask permission to lead. They just do it. Never apologize for or ask permission to tell a story. Deliver your story with the confidence that your listeners will thank you for it later.

In fact, while you're not apologizing for or asking permission to tell a story, go one step further and don't even tell your audience you're about to tell them a story. Some people (including me) bristle when a speaker announces he's going to tell a story, and then tells it in third-person perspective, constantly referring to "the story." It sounds something like this: "I'd like to tell you a story about when I was a college student . . . and so the story goes like this . . . and then the story gets interesting because . . . and the story ended when I . . ."

Stop making such a fuss about "the story" and just tell it!

Doubtless you've noticed that almost every chapter in this book starts with a story. The chapters don't start with an explanation about the story that follows, or a hint about where it came from. They don't even start with a statement that what follows is a story. As the reader, you just suddenly find yourself in a story. And that's the way it should be. When you find yourself in a situation that requires a story, just start telling it.

SUMMARY AND EXERCISES

1. *Great beginnings.* Start your stories with one of the following three devices:
   a. A surprise (see chapter 19).
   b. A mystery (see 1983 discovery journey in chapter 5; building a cathedral in chapter 2; three researchers in chapter 20).
   c. A challenge—introduce a relatable character facing a difficult challenge (e.g., how not to present to the CEO in chapter 1; canceling your retainer in chapter 10).

2. *Writing style.* Write the way you speak:
   a. Use short sentences (15 to 17 words per sentence).
   b. Use small words (15 percent or fewer words over two syllables).
   c. Use active voice (15 percent or fewer passive voice sentences).
   d. Get to the verb quickly (place the verb at the beginning of sentences).
   e. Omit needless words (e.g., Fresh Fish). Most stories should be 250 to 750 words, or two to four minutes when told orally.
   f. Find the automatic spell-check setting in your e-mail and word-processing programs. Turn them on and leave them on.
   g. Find the grammar checker in your word-processing software. Use it on every document before you publish it.
   h. Set the grammar checker to automatically run the readability scores (i.e., Flesch-Kincaid Grade Level). In Microsoft Word, click on the pull-down menu Tools, then click on the Spelling and Grammar tab, then the Options button. Check the boxes in front of both the "Check grammar with spelling" line and the "Show readability statistics" line.
   i. Target a reading grade level of 8 to 10. If your document is higher than that, rewrite it and check it again.

3. *Literary devices:*
   a. Include dialogue.
   b. Use real names of characters.
   c. Repeat words or phrases (e.g., building a cathedral story in chapter 2; three researchers in chapter 20).
   d. Don't announce or apologize in advance of a story. Just tell it.

Notes

1. Dr. Frank Luntz, *Words That Work: It's Not What You Say, It's What People Hear* (New York: Hyperion Publishing, 2007).
2. William Strunk, Jr., and E. B. White, *The Elements of Style*, Third Edition (New York: MacMillan Publishing, 1979), p. 23.
3. Antoine de Saint-Exupéry, *Wind, Sand, and Stars* (Boston: Houghton Mifflin Harcourt, 1992), p. 44.
4. Garr Reynolds, *PresentationZen* (Indianapolis: New Riders, 2008), p. 111.

CHAPTER **15**

Inspire and motivate

"Smart, clinical, sterile leadership doesn't inspire anybody, no matter how right they are."
—JEFF STRONG, Executive Vice President, Sun Products

MEXICO CITY IS A world away from the East African country of Tanzania, where John Stephen Akhwari lived. But that's exactly where he found himself in October 1968, representing his country in the Summer Olympic Games as a marathon runner. Unfortunately, Akhwari suffered a fall during the race. And it wasn't a gentle tumble on a grassy knoll. He fell hard on rough concrete, badly cutting his right leg and dislocating his knee. Medical personnel arrived quickly and bandaged his wounds. But the dislocated knee required more treatment than they could provide in the city streets. He needed to go to the hospital. But against their advice, Akhwari instead stood up and started down the road behind the rest of the runners.

Given the severity of his injuries, he couldn't run his normal pace. With a combination of jogging, hobbling, and walking, he pushed ahead. At 2:20:26 into the race, Mamo Walde of Ethiopia crossed the finish line in first place. Most of the remaining competitors finished within a few minutes. Akhwari was nowhere close.

An hour later, the Olympic stadium had only a few thousand people left in it. The marathon was the last event of the day, and the sun had already set. Mexico City was brutal on the marathon runners. At over 7,400 feet in altitude, the air has 23 percent less oxygen than at sea level.[1] As a result, 17 of the 74 runners failed to finish the race that day. Akhwari, bloodied and injured, was determined to not be one of them.[2]

131

Followed by a police escort, and clearly in great pain, Akhwari finally arrived and limped his way onto the track, his loosening bandages dangling from his leg. As the diminished crowd cheered in awe and disbelief, John Stephen Akhwari made his way around the track and crossed the finish line at 3:25:27, in last place. The few remaining reporters rushed onto the field to ask him why he continued running in his condition. He responded simply, "My country didn't send me 5,000 miles to start this race. They sent me 5,000 miles to finish it."

Akhwari's dedication became an inspiration to millions, and earned him the title "King without a crown." To this day, his story is legendary among Olympic athletes and nonathletes alike.

"Yes, it's an inspiring story," you might protest. "But I'm not running a marathon. I'm running a business. How can that story help me?"

I'm not a marathon runner, either. But I use it all the time. Here's one example. At many companies, managers are expected to rotate to new assignments every few years. It helps them develop skills needed for higher levels of responsibility, and brings fresh thinking to the business. Managers might find out what their next assignment will be two or three months in advance. Inevitably, when that happens, they begin to emotionally and mentally detach from their current responsibilities and start thinking about what's next. The boss faces the challenge of keeping them focused on their current job until it's time to leave.

Having faced that challenge many times as a boss, I often tell the story of John Stephen Akhwari to the junior manager eagerly awaiting the next assignment. The point, I explain afterward, is that once your next assignment is announced, others know you're emotionally compromised. They know you're running injured. But they also know the difference between a starter and a finisher. If you slack off these last three months, most people will forgive you out of sympathy. But if you want to make an impression that will last a long time, finish strong. People will notice.

The other benefit is that once told, that story also makes it easy to check up on your injured player and gently remind him to stay focused. Simply ask this question: "Hey, John, how's your knee?"

* * *

The Akhwari story is helpful for keeping people motivated and focused on their normal job. But what if you've asked them to do a job that isn't normal? A job without the typical and recognizable rewards—that atypical role off the standard career path, or a "special assignment"? The uncertainty and lack of a common experience make it difficult to get people to take those jobs, and harder to get them to stay. If that's your situation, you need the following story.

Delaine Hampton was always a few years ahead of her time. Or, more correctly stated, ahead of everyone else's time. Throughout most of the 1980s, P&G based the decision to launch a new brand on the results of long and costly test markets. By 1990, the company had chartered a small team to globally expand *simulated* test marketing. This method used only a few hundred people and product samples and cost a fraction of the time and money of real in-market tests. Delaine was chosen to lead that team.

A decade later, the practice was commonplace, and Delaine had moved on. Now she was investigating the use of virtual testing capabilities to make simulated test markets even more powerful. It couldn't always replace the traditional method. But when it was used, it could assess not just the new product launch, but the competitive reaction as well.

Delaine convinced her management to afford her a small team to turn the vision into a reality. She pulled out some of the same people who had helped her expand simulated test markets 10 years earlier, and added some new blood, too. They started in earnest and began the creative process all over again. But Delaine knew it would be hard to keep her team motivated. Development takes a long time, and the required secrecy means the work is lonely. By contrast, other teams were using their skills to launch new products. It was rewarding to see tangible results in the market. Celebrations were frequent. Rewards were real.

So every six months, Delaine took her team aside and celebrated milestones on their way to completion. At those celebrations, she often shared stories and used analogies. The one the group liked hearing the most was this one.

When the central and western United States was being settled in the 1800s, there were two kinds of people brave enough to leave the comfort of the eastern seaboard: pioneers and settlers. Pioneers were the first ones out to the new territory. The terrain was uncertain; danger lurked around every tree. Their job was to find the next inhabitable space, with workable land for farming, access to water, and timber for making shelter. They were skilled at crossing unbridged rivers and trailblazing through thick forests. Their most important assets were courage and the ability to fend off a hungry wolf.

After they established a new post, it was time for the settlers to come in. Instead of horseback, settlers arrived in covered wagons—luxury transportation at the time. Their job was surveying the land, expanding on the crude buildings put up by the pioneers, and establishing trade with merchants back East. Their skills were more refined than the pioneers'. They were craftsmen, blacksmiths, farmers, and bankers.

Once the settlers arrive, life for a pioneer changes. Their skills are in less demand. They feel crowded in the streets. Their days are slow and lack challenge. Eventually, it's time for them to move on. They're happier under the stars, charting out the location of the next frontier town, and creating a legacy for other men and women to follow.

"You," Delaine would tell her team in her most earnest voice, "are pioneers. Nobody has been where we're going. So it's our job to go there and leave a trail."

It's almost impossible to hear that story and not feel the pride of a pioneer, no matter how many times you hear it. At some point in their careers, most businesspeople find themselves in the position to lead a team with a similar mission as Delaine's—create something new or try something that's never been tried before. When you do, keep this story handy. You'll need it.

* * *

The two previous stories are helpful for keeping a team inspired and motivated to do its job. In normal times, that can be hard enough. Hence the need for stories like these. But what about when bad things happen? When your organization suffers major setbacks or losses, how do you keep team members motivated? These stories don't seem appropriate. The following one will.

In January 1993, the U.S. Ninth Circuit Court of Appeals considered the case of *Cal-Almond, Inc. v. the Department of Agriculture* (the government agency overseeing the Almond Board of California).[3] As the Almond Board's CEO, Rodger Wasson followed the hearings with particular interest. At issue was the constitutionality of one of the primary functions of his organization.

The Almond Board represents almond growers and handlers. Since one farmer's almonds are basically the same as any others', it makes sense for farmers to pool their resources for things like research, crop forecasting, generic advertising, and public relations. At issue in this case was the advertising and PR.

The Almond Board works like most other commodity boards. The members all contribute to a central fund, which pays for the advertising and PR that benefits all of them. It's the same kind of arrangement that created the familiar "Got milk?" campaign from milk producers and "Beef—it's what's for dinner" from beef producers. But what if one particular almond grower, or milk producer, say, didn't want to pay into the fund, and just opted out? That really wouldn't be fair to the other members. The one holdout would, of course, benefit from the marketing just like everyone else, but without paying its fair share. As a result, in all such commodity boards, membership and paying dues is not optional. It's mandatory. And that was the rub for some of the almond growers in California. Their attorneys argued that by making membership and dues mandatory and using those funds to pay for marketing (a form of speech), it violated their First Amendment right to free affiliation and free speech, and was therefore unconstitutional.

When the court reached its decision in December 1993, it was not a good day for Rodger Wasson. The court held in favor of the holdouts. The Almond Board was ordered to cease all marketing activity and refund all the dues paid to it by the almond handlers since 1980. Rodger was forced to eliminate marketing and PR jobs on his staff. This was not only disappointing for the Almond Board but for most of the almond growers and handlers as well. High almond prices in the early 1990s had encouraged growers to increase almond tree acreage. So, there was now more supply of almonds than demand. To keep the growers from financial disaster, they needed to increase demand—a seemingly impossible task with your advertising and PR efforts outlawed.

But that wasn't the end of the bad news for Rodger. A newly elected board of directors thought it would be best if he and his staff moved from Sacramento, the state capital and home of their biggest member, to a more independent location in Modesto, about 90 miles east of San Francisco. None of his staff members would leave Sacramento. So he lost all but two employees.

What now for Rodger? Almost all of his employees were gone. And one of the primary functions of his organization was just deemed unconstitutional. For most of us, that would be a good time to polish up our resume. But not for Rodger. That only strengthened his resolve. He moved the office to Modesto and promptly started hiring new staff. He even hired new marketing and PR professionals! Of course, they weren't allowed to do any actual marketing, yet. Rodger found other work for them to do for the time being. Much of the board's focus shifted to research on the health benefits of almonds. But he was still confident that the court's decision would get overturned on appeal. Or at least that's what he told himself, and everyone else. To Rodger, there wasn't any other way to work. Move forward boldly, or get out of the way and let someone else. Rodger was all in. As was his Modesto-based staff—many of whom had accepted a position knowing their type of work was currently banned by federal court order.

The case was appealed in May 1995; part of the earlier decision was reversed, but other parts were upheld.[4] The appeal eventually made it to the United States Supreme Court. On June 25, 1997, Rodger's bet paid off. In a 5-to-4 vote, the Court ruled in favor of the Almond Board, and its efforts to promote the sale of almonds were once again allowed.[5] Staffed and ready to go, he switched his team into high gear, implementing the plans they'd only theorized for the past many months. The Almond Board approved a fivefold increase in funding to bring the plan to fruition. The results speak for themselves. During the seven years from 1995 to 2002 (when Rodger left the Almond Board), the annual sale of California almonds tripled from 367 million pounds to 1.1 billion.[6]

He and the Almond Board staff attained a level of success in only a few years that takes most organizations decades to achieve, if ever. The almond growers and handlers prospered. And millions of Americans added healthy servings of almonds to their diets.

It's not uncommon for businesses to run into legal difficulties. Competitors can challenge the accuracy of your advertising and get it taken off the air. A regulatory agency can impose fines on you. The Safety Commission can even force a temporary closure of a manufacturing site. These can be frustrating and burdensome to the people affected. Keeping them focused and motivated (and employed with you!) during such times is the job of a leader. Stories like this that tell people how others successfully navigated similar waters—maybe even tougher waters—can help. I'm no lawyer. But it seems to me on a scale of legal seriousness where a parking ticket sits at one end of the spectrum, having your work declared in violation of the U.S. Constitution would be as far to the other end as possible. If Rodger Wasson and his team had the strength to stay committed, despite the overwhelming barriers against them, there's no reason why your team can't survive your next legal challenge (or any challenge) with just as much success.

* * *

The Almond Board story helps motivate the team after something bad happens. But is there a way to motivate a team to avoid the bad thing to begin with? Is there a story that can inspire your team to face each opportunity as if it were the last, and not accept failures as temporary inevitabilities? Fortunately, there is. In fact, I'm sure there are many. Here is my favorite.

The 2004–2005 season was destined to be a rebuilding year for the Fayetteville High School boys basketball program in Arkansas. Most of the guys on the starting lineup were juniors. In fact, the entire squad had only one returning senior. This wasn't a team anyone expected great things from. As anticipated, the first half of the season, the Fayetteville Bulldogs won some and lost some. But in the second half they won almost every game, earning a birth in the state playoffs. It was an exciting time for a bunch of kids who weren't supposed to be there in the first place.

Winning in the first round made their presence feel justified instead of a fluke. When the Bulldogs won their second and third games by double-digit margins, it became clear they had a legitimate shot at the state title. When they won the semifinal game and landed in the state finals, it was like a scene out of the movie *Hoosiers*. This team of young, unproven juniors would play the defending champions—a team full of college prospects. It was a real David versus Goliath matchup.

The game was tight, going into double overtime. With about 15 seconds left, Fayetteville had the ball and called a time-out. The coach called the play. The Bulldogs inbounded the ball to their star player, the point guard who had played a great game and rarely made mistakes. His job was to let the clock run down a few seconds before starting the play to take the last shot. In the excitement, however, he made a mistake. He let his defender stay too close to him for more than 5 seconds without passing. West Memphis took possession with less than 10 seconds left. Its star player drove to the basket, was fouled, and sank two free throws to win the game.

Having been so close to victory after such an improbable string of wins, it was a crushing defeat for the players and their supporters. One of those supporters was Jeff Strong. His daughter was a good friend of one of the players, so he followed every game with anticipation. Jeff asked the player, "So, what'd you think about the game?"

The young man's response was surprisingly nonchalant. "No big deal. We're all juniors. We'll all be back next year and win it for sure."

It was exactly the kind of thing caring parents would say to console their child after a bitter loss. No doubt, every player on the team was repeating the same mantra within hours of the game. Jeff agreed with the boy and offered his own words of encouragement for next year. But inside, he couldn't help but think that this team had been given a great gift. And perhaps, unfortunately, the Bulldogs had missed their opportunity. The chance to play for state championships, even for great teams, is a rare thing, indeed.

The next year, the whole starting lineup was back, this time as seniors. This year, they were the team to beat, the heavy favorite to win the state title. The season started just like everyone expected. They went undefeated the entire season and earned the number-one seed in the state championship. As is typical, the highest-seeded teams are paired with the lowest-seeded teams early in the bracket to give the best teams the best chance to win and ultimately reach the finals. Unfortunately, in the first round—against a team they were highly favored to beat—the Bulldogs lost. Those players never got that second chance in the state finals they'd hoped for.

Does this disappointing end suggest the well-meaning parental advice that consoled the boys a year earlier was in poor judgment? Of course not. Nothing would be gained by brooding over a lost opportunity once the opportunity truly is past. But what if someone had that attitude *before* the opportunity was past? How would it affect people's behavior if they thought, "There will always be another opportunity"? The answer, of course, is that they wouldn't try as hard. If there's always another opportunity, then there's nothing to lose by letting this opportunity slip. That's the thought that stuck in Jeff's head after that bitter defeat in the state finals, because he's seen that attitude in business many times—people failing to seize an opportunity because they think, "There's always a next time." What this experience taught Jeff was that there isn't always a next time.

Today, as executive vice president of Sun Products in Salt Lake City, Jeff tells that story when he comes across someone who isn't engaged as much as he or she needs to be. Every lost sale is a lost sale. You might win the business back next year, but you can't ever get back the lost sale from this year. Jeff's story helps people appreciate the opportunity they have today as a gift and motivates them to perform like it's the last game of the state finals, with no "next year" to fall back on.

SUMMARY AND EXERCISES

1. There are a countless number of things to distract people from their work. Keeping them motivated and focused on their objectives requires inspirational leadership. The next time one of your employees faces a major distraction, share the story of John Stephen Akhwari (finishing the race). People can tell the difference between a starter and a finisher. Finish strong.

2. Getting people to appreciate that special assignment off the proven path is an even tougher task. Delaine's story of pioneers and settlers could be just what you need.

3. Keeping employees motivated in good times is hard enough. In tough times it's even harder. Having your business declared unconstitutional is about as tough as it gets. If Rodger Wasson and the Almond Board made it through, so can your company. Share Rodger's story. Then get to work. (U.S. v. California Almonds)

4. Stories can even help your team avoid hard times in the first place. Jeff Strong's story of the Fayetteville Bulldogs inspired his organizations to stay engaged and face each opportunity as if it were their last. It can do the same for yours. (There isn't always a next time.)

Notes

1. "Altitude Air Pressure Calculator," www.altitude.org/air_pressure.php.
2. "Who Is John Stephen Akhwari Who Ran in the Mexico City Olympics?" Answers.com, wiki.answers.com/Q/Who_is_John_Stephen_Akhwari_who_ran_in_the_ Mexico_City_Olympics#ixzz1EKLsDbfJ.
3. U.S. 9th Circuit Court of Appeals abstract, law.justia.com/cases/federal/ appellate-courts/F3/14/429/613125/.
4. U.S. 9th Circuit Court of Appeals, *Cal-Almond v. U.S. Department of Agriculture* (October 10, 1995), caselaw.lp.findlaw.com/scripts/getcase.pl? navby=search&case=/data2/circs/9th/9417160.html&friend=oye.
5. U.S. Supreme Court, *Glickman v. Wileman Brothers and Elliott Inc.* (October 1996), supreme.justia.com/us/521/457/.
6. Dale Darling, "Strategic Thinking for Global Operations: The Case of Blue Diamond Growers" (February 16, 2006), Almond Board of California, www.scribd.com/doc/1671008/USDA-Darling.

CHAPTER 16

Build courage

"You may have to fight a battle more than once to win it."
—MARGARET THATCHER, former Prime Minister of England

WHEN HE WAS SEVEN YEARS OLD, his family was forced out of their home and off their farm. Like other boys his age, he was expected to work to help support the family.

When he was nine, his mother died.

At the age of 22, the company he worked for went bankrupt and he lost his job.

At 23, he ran for state legislature in a field of 13 candidates. He came in eighth.

At 24, he borrowed money to start a business with a friend. By the end of the year, the business failed. The local sheriff seized his possessions to pay off his debt. His partner soon died, penniless, and he assumed his partner's share of debt as well. He spent the next several years of his life paying it off.

At 25, he ran for state legislature again. This time he won.

At 26, he was engaged to be married. But his fiancée died before the wedding.

The next year he plunged into a depression and suffered a nervous breakdown.

At 29, he sought to become the speaker of the state legislature. He was defeated.

At 34, he campaigned for a U.S. congressional seat, representing his district. He lost.

140

At 35, he ran for Congress again. This time he won. He went to Washington and did a good job.

At 39, when his term ended, he was out of a job again. There was a one-term-limit rule in his party.

At 40, he tried to get a job as commissioner of the General Land Office. He was rejected.

At 45, he campaigned for the U.S. Senate, representing his state. He lost by six electoral votes.

At 47, he was one of the contenders for the vice-presidential nomination at his party's national convention. He lost.

At 49, he ran for the same U.S. Senate seat a second time. And for the second time, he lost.

Two years later, at the age of 51, after a lifetime of failure, disappointment, and loss (and still relatively unknown outside of his home state of Illinois), Abraham Lincoln was elected the sixteenth president of the United States.

Despite being elected to a second term, he served only four years in office before meeting his final defeat at the hands of an assassin, in April 1865. But during those short four years, President Lincoln successfully led the country through its greatest internal crisis (the American Civil War); preserved the Union; ended slavery; and rededicated the nation to the ideals of equality, liberty, and democracy.

So the next time you think about quitting because you've already tried and failed, ask yourself this: How different would this country be if Abraham Lincoln had stopped trying after his first defeat . . . or his fifth . . . or his tenth?

It takes a great deal of courage to keep trying after a defeat. This story of Lincoln has surely helped millions gain courage to face their own struggles and setbacks in the many decades it's been circulating. The original author is unknown, but it has been written in various forms in countless newspaper articles, magazines, and books. I use it when a team has suffered repeated setbacks and needs a boost of courage to try yet again. Similar to the story of the bricklayer building a cathedral in chapter 2, it's a piece of the public domain of stories that I've rewritten to serve my own particular purpose. In chapter 19, I discuss the changes I made to make it a better story.

* * *

Certainly persistence in the face of defeat is a required character trait in politics. You have to lose a few races on the road to Washington. But is it useful in business? Absolutely! A prime example of that is the story of Pringles snack chips.

P&G first test marketed Pringles in September 1968 in Evansville, Indiana, and began shipping it to grocery stores across the United States in 1971. It was an instant success. By 1975, it had become a household name, had a 15 percent market share, and more than 10 million cases a year were being sold. A year later, however, sales dropped 20 percent— enough to send any brand manager into panic mode. The following year, sales dropped another 10 percent. That's probably when speculation began that the brand would be put up for sale. P&G wasn't used to such steep sales declines. Certainly not two years in a row.

Another year went by, and another 10 percent of sales vanished. Can you imagine how hard it must have been to recruit employees to accept an assignment on Pringles with sales plummeting and rumors of a sale looming? By 1979, the brand was in free fall. Sales dropped over 30 percent, and were now down to 4 million cases a year—a 60 percent decline in four years! That's when a line was drawn in the sand. P&G executives declared they would either fix the brand, or sell it, in five years.

Over the next 18 months, management put several major changes in place. It commissioned new research to develop a ground-up understanding of the consumer. Product improvements gave Pringles a better taste and more variety. New advertising touted the unique benefits of the saddle-shaped chips. A price reduction made Pringles more competitive with traditional potato chips. And a major cost savings project helped the brand afford the price reductions and product improvements.

Sales continued to decline, but at a much slower rate. In 1980, sales were down about half a million cases, to 3.4 million. And in 1981, they bottomed out at 3 million. The next year, sales started to grow—slowly at first, and then faster. By 1984, Pringles sales were 5 million cases. In 1986, they were up to 7 million. By 1989, sales were back to their 1975 peak of 10 million cases. And by the end of the 1990s, sales of Pringles were over 50 million cases.

In December of 1984, just after the turnaround started, the head of P&G Sales, Mike Milligan, gave a speech to a group of employees, shareholders, and members of the press. In it, he shared five key lessons the company learned from the experience. In hindsight, the first three shouldn't be too surprising: (1) know what your consumer wants, (2) develop a product and marketing messages to meet those expectations, and (3) organize a strong team to deliver results. The fourth lesson was a little more interesting: Set realistic goals. They adopted a five-year plan, not a one-year plan. They realized the magnitude of the changes they needed to make were too ambitious to accomplish in a matter of months. Despite that, they succeeded two years ahead of schedule.

The final lesson Mike explained, however, is the most telling of all, and the key point I want to make. He summarized it in two simple words: "Don't stop." Don't give up too soon. Imagine how easy it would have been for management to give up on the Pringles brand. And how many times had they probably considered it in the late 1970s? Instead, they persevered. They pushed on through six years of nerve-wracking sales declines and fixed the business. Compare this to today's quarterly-profit-obsessed CEOs who flinch at the earliest signs of trouble and kowtow to Wall Street with promises of a quick exit.

As a result of that perseverance, Pringles became a star in the P&G stable of iconic brands, with a rich history of perseverance and courage.

Thomas Edison summarized the wisdom of the perseverance shown in both the Abe Lincoln and Pringles stories in a single sentence when he observed, "Many of life's failures are people who didn't realize how close they were to success when they gave up."[1] My advice: Don't be one of them.

* * *

Of course, perseverance in the wake of repeated failure is not the only situation in business that requires courage. More typically, we're struggling with the fear of failing in the future. We're afraid to tackle that seemingly impossible task, so we don't ever start. If someone in your organization is in that situation, share the following story.

Once upon a time, in a land far away, there lived a very bright and trustworthy young woman.[2] Having learned all she could in her own village, she set out to explore the neighboring lands. After some time, she came upon a great city surrounded by a huge castle wall. "Surely I can learn something new from the people here," she thought to herself. But after entering the city, she found its people too frightened and depressed to share any wisdom. "Why is everyone here so sad?" she asked.

One trembling citizen answered, "Today is the day the giant comes."

"Giant?" she scoffed in disbelief. "There's no such thing as giants!"

"Oh, but there is," came the response. "He stands over 10 feet tall! So tall, he can't rightly be called a man at all."

Skeptical, but intrigued, the young woman pleaded, "Tell me more of this giant."

So the frightened citizen nervously explained to her, "Every year, on the same day, and at the same hour, he comes down from the mountain where he lives. He stands at the edge of the clearing and yells, 'Send out your bravest man for me to fight, or I will knock down these walls and kill everyone inside!' Each year, one poor valiant soul steps out to face the giant, and there he stands, mesmerized by the giant's enormity and the impossible task ahead. And every year, the giant slays the poor warrior where he stands before he even has a chance to draw his sword. The warrior doesn't even move. It's as if he is hypnotized."

Eyes wide with fascination, the woman begs, "Can I see this giant?"

"The only way to see the giant," the citizen explained, "is to face him in battle."

Still in disbelief but eager to learn, the woman responded, "Then that is what I will do!"

Shortly thereafter, at the appointed hour, the giant's distant but powerful voice was heard over the castle walls, "Send out your bravest man for me to fight, or I will knock down these walls and kill everyone inside!" Unshaken, the young woman stepped out through the castle gate to face her opponent.

She looked out across the clearing to the edge of the forest at the foothills of the mountain. Sure enough, there stood an enormous giant! For a moment, she just stood and stared at him from a distance. There was a gentle rise in the ground separating the two, so she could only see him from the waist up. It was difficult to tell exactly how big he was, but he was clearly taller than any man she had ever seen or heard of. She was struck with the same awe and terror all of her predecessors surely felt at that moment. The giant was real. And facing him today, she would surely die. She considered running back inside the castle walls. But she had given her word to the good people inside to face their giant. So with all the bravery she could muster, she began to walk tentatively toward the giant. And the giant began to walk toward her.

After a few paces up the gentle incline, she gained full line of sight to the giant, and could see his whole form. With this better angle she could tell he was not nearly the 10 feet in height she first believed, perhaps only 7 feet tall. He was still massive, but at least now in human proportions. She was still no match for him, but at least she would meet her defeat at the hands of something recognizable.

With that element of the unknown removed, she was able to walk at a normal pace. And after a few more steps, the giant appeared to be smaller still. Was this some strange optical illusion? The giant appeared to be not much bigger than she was now. She might actually have a fighting chance! With this new hope, her pace quickened. And with every step she could tell it was no illusion. The giant was actually shrinking before her very eyes, and the faster she ran, the faster the giant shrank.

Her terror had turned to hope, and now that hope had turned to confidence. Certain of her victory, she was now in an all-out sprint toward the giant. As she reached the middle of the clearing she stopped and stood toe to toe with the giant, who was now only 12 inches tall and still shrinking quickly. She reached down and picked him up in the palm of her hand. She only had time to ask him one question before he shrank down to the size of a grain of sand and blew away in the next gust of wind.

"Who *are* you?" she asked earnestly.

The giant responded in a tiny and dwindling voice, "I am known by many names. To the Chinese, I am *kǒngjù*. To the Greeks, I am *phobos*. But to your people, brave one, I am known simply as *fear*."

She had come to this village to learn something. And indeed she had. If you face your fears and confront them with confidence, they will shrink before your very eyes.

Whether facing a giant in battle or simply using the company's new accounts receivable system, the fear of failure can be debilitating. It can paralyze us and prevent us from even trying. But once you start making honest strides on the task, the size of the challenge begins to shrink. Once we've made progress, no matter how little, we earn some small amount of confidence, and the remaining work is diminished. It becomes less daunting with each step.

Even in today's world, there are still giants. They just take a different form. No matter what the challenge that has people in your organization frightened or intimidated, use this story to help them break the grip of fear and take those first steps.

* * *

A final situation that requires courage in the workplace has nothing to do with a fear of failures past or future. It's based on an even more human frailty present in all of us since childhood—the ever-present concern about what other people think of us. To a 10-year-old, it might be what the other kids will think of her new tennis shoes. Are they cool or not cool? To a teenage boy, it might be what the girls think of his moves on the dance floor. To the adult, it might be what his peers think of his work, or what her boss thinks of her leadership potential. At any age, an unhealthy concern about what others think about you can stifle your creativity, sap your energy, and keep you from doing what's really important. That's a lesson Richard Feynman learned while standing at his wife's hospital bed.

Feynman was a Nobel Prize–winning physicist known in scientific circles almost as much for his sarcastic wit and bongo playing as for his brilliant science. Publically, he was a bold character remembered for his defining role in the investigation of the 1986 Space Shuttle *Challenger* disaster. Characteristic of Feynman, he refused to go along with the prescribed inquiry arranged for him and the other 11 congressionally appointed investigators. His unapproved conversations with NASA engineers led to the correct conclusion that the cause of the shuttle disaster was a tiny rubber O-ring on the fuel line. During the congressional panel—unannounced—Feynman flamboyantly illustrated his theory by pulling a similar O-ring out of his glass of ice water and throwing it on the dais, shattering it in front of hundreds of journalists and television cameras. Apparently, the temperature on the morning of takeoff was well below that of any previous shuttle launch. Too cold, in fact, for the rubber O-ring to maintain its flexibility, causing it to shatter under pressure.

Was Feynman just born a brave soul? Probably. But there was at least one defining moment that shaped his life and his science by building on an already courageous character. In the early 1940s, Feynman was working at Los Alamos National Labs on the Manhattan Project, the top-secret government effort to build the atomic bomb. Feynman's young wife, Arlene, was undergoing treatment for tuberculosis in nearby Albuquerque, New Mexico. Feynman would hitchhike to the hospital on weekends to visit her.[3]

Arlene knew Richard was frustrated at his own inability to comfort her or heal her terminal illness. So one weekend when he arrived, she presented him with an 18-inch charcoal grill she'd ordered through the mail. She desperately wanted a home-cooked meal instead of the hospital fare. So she asked him to cook her a steak.

Always the pragmatist, Feynman protested, "How the hell can we use it in the room, here, with all the smoke and everything?"

Arlene suggested he just take it out on the lawn in front of the hospital. But the hospital was located right on Route 66, one of the busiest highways in the country at the time. Richard again protested that with all the automobile and pedestrian traffic, he couldn't just fire up a grill and start cooking steaks. People would think he was crazy!

"What do you care what other people think?" Arlene asked.

Those words struck a profound chord with Richard. Not only did he cook Arlene the steak she asked for, he did so every weekend thereafter.

Feynman must have realized the wisdom in her words. Why *should* he care what other people think? He cared about Arlene! Her comfort and happiness was more important.

Being overly concerned about what other people think can distract you from your primary objectives and paralyze you with indecision. His wife's words helped Richard Feynman realize that. Telling his story can help you and the ones you tell let go of the confining anxiety over what other people think.

SUMMARY AND EXERCISES

1. Perseverance in the face of repeated failure is one of the hallmarks of great-ness. Unfortunately, it's also rare and unnatural to most living creatures. The story of President Lincoln has been providing courage for over 100 years with-out getting old. Use it. (A lifetime of failure)

2. The Pringles story shows how perseverance applies to business challenges. It makes a great pairing with the Lincoln story for a business audience, even if you don't work on the Pringles business. Your company probably has its own similar story. Find it.

3. "Many of life's failures are people who didn't realize how close they were to success when they gave up." Don't be one of them.

4. Fear of failing the first time is an even more common obstacle to action. Small steps shrink the size of the challenge. Use the story of the shrinking giant to bolster courage to take those first steps.

5. Being worried about what other people think of you can stifle your courage and creativity. When you see someone holding back from trying something daring for fear of embarrassment or ridicule, share Richard Feynman's story. Then ask the person, "What do you care what other people think?"

Notes

1. Deborah Hedstrom-Page, *From Telegraph to Light Bulb with Thomas Edison (My American Journey)* (Nashville, TN: B&H Books, 2007), p. 22.

2. Original author unknown. I first heard this story from Margaret Parkin, *Tales for Trainers* (London: Kogan Page, 1998), pp. 136–137, but have adapted it for my own purposes.

3. Richard Feynman, *What Do You Care What Other People Think?* (New York: W. W. Norton & Company, 1988), p. 46.

CHAPTER **17**

Help others find passion for their work

> *"If a man is called to be a street sweeper, he should sweep streets even as Michelangelo painted, or Beethoven composed music, or Shakespeare wrote poetry. He should sweep streets so well that all the hosts of heaven and earth will pause to say, here lived a great street sweeper who did his job well."*
> —MARTIN LUTHER KING JR.

EVER HEARD THE ADVICE "You really need to love your job"? It's usually offered unsolicited by an overconfident boss who thinks the rank and file will find it inspiring, or somehow turn their drudgery into a rewarding experience. Does it work? Of course not. You can't order people to love their job. That just gives them inspiration to quit and go somewhere with more exciting work! Far better to help them *find* the passion for their work.

In spring 2009 I needed to find that passion myself. I had just been asked to take a new position as director of consumer research for P&G's paper business. That meant I was going to be in charge of consumer research for, among other things, *toilet paper*. That didn't sound very glamorous, or even interesting. I immediately formed a host of prejudicial notions about what it would be like to work in the toilet paper business. I couldn't think of a less important product in terms of impacting people's lives. Plus, for a marketing researcher like me, there couldn't be many unexplored ways you could talk about how soft and absorbent a piece of paper was, right? Fortunately, my first stop with the news was to see my good

148

friend and fellow P&Ger Jeff Brooks. After suffering through the obligatory potty humor, he ended up telling me the following story that helped me appreciate my new role in a way neither of us expected at the time.

At the end of a weeklong business trip to Budapest, Hungary, Jeff had a short train ride to the airport for his return home. He sat next to a fellow American, now living in Budapest, so they struck up a conversation. When she found out it was his first trip to Hungary, she asked him what he thought of it. In a very cordial manner, he replied that he liked it very much, and that there was much to do in Budapest. After finishing the socially graceful answer, however, he began to tell her a little more about what he really thought.

"The people were very nice," he said, "but they all seemed a bit melancholy. Depressed even. And the weather was beautiful, so that wasn't the problem. Most of them just seemed irritable and unhappy." He went on to describe in detail the behavior he saw that led him to his dreary conclusion. As he did, the woman nodded and smiled knowingly, as if to agree with his assessment. When he finished his story, the woman turned quietly and looked out the window in a contemplative manner. After a long pause, and without even looking back at him, she sighed, and said matter-of-factly, "I think it's the toilet paper."

Okay, it's funnier when you hear the story told in person. But the woman was dead serious. Here's the point. Toilet paper may seem like a pedestrian, unimportant part of people's daily lives. But imagine what your day might be like if all you ever had to use for toilet paper was the thin, rough, cheap tissue you might imagine to be typical in Budapest 15 years ago. If that's all you ever used, you might be constantly chafed and slightly irritated in your nether region. Perhaps not so much that you thought about it constantly, but enough that it might just make every day a little less pleasant. And that might make you a little more short-tempered with a visiting businessman from the States, as well as anyone else who crossed your path.

The implication to me for my new job was this. We may not be curing cancer. But what we do matters to people probably more than we realize, perhaps even more than they realize. One of my prejudicial notions had just evaporated. The toilet paper business still wasn't going to be glamorous. But at least it felt more meaningful now.

What I came looking for when I entered Jeff's office was a sympathetic ear to commiserate with. What I left with was an eagerness and passion for my work that I hadn't even started yet. Since then, I've told this story to dozens of other newcomers to the paper business. Most of them, it turns out, came with the same preconceived notions I did. Conclusion: If stories can help someone get excited about working on toilet paper, imagine what a good story can do for the business you're in.

* * *

So what if the business you're in is even less glamorous than toilet paper? (Yeah, I can't imagine what that would be, either. But let's just say there is, and you're in it.) And let's say you can't think of a story to help the people you work with find any passion for the products you make, or the service you provide. Then what do you do? You tell the following story of someone who already learned that lesson.

In 2009, Daniel Dorr attended a marketing conference in Bloomington, Indiana. As a marketing leader, he usually learned something at these conferences he could apply to his work. And if not, he would at least boost his passion for his profession. At this particular conference, however, he wasn't getting either. At what he thought was the low point of the event, he was listening to David Beré, CEO of Dollar General. Those are the retail stores that sell just about everything for one dollar, or a low multiple of it. Daniel didn't work in the retail business, so he thought he wasn't going to learn much from this guy. And he couldn't think of anything he was less passionate about than marketing products designed to be sold for a dollar. But he listened respectfully as Mr. Beré told the audience about a recent visit he made to one of his stores.

Of course, it's not unusual for CEOs of a retailer to spend time in their stores. When they do, they often walk the aisles, check out the merchandise and the condition of the shelves, look for out-of-stocks, and talk to employees about what's selling and what's not. If you've ever been in a store and seen a congregation of executive-types wearing suits and corporate badges clogging up an aisle, you've seen this in action. The employees prepare for such visits weeks in advance and have their talking points ready for the big brass.

But Beré's story was different. He described how he entered the store and walked up to the first shopper he saw. He offered to carry her shopping basket for her if she would let him accompany her around the store and ask questions. She agreed, and as they walked he asked her what she thought of the condition of the store, the prices, the selection of merchandise, and so forth. After she was done and about to leave, she stopped and turned around. "I'd like to show you something," she stated. "Interested?"

"Of course," he replied.

"Well, then come get in my car and take a drive with me."

This was an unusual request, and one many CEOs would turn down. But he was intrigued, so he joined her. She drove him several miles down the road and eventually pulled into the parking lot of another one of his company's retail outlets, with a similar banner over the front door. They got out of the car and walked inside together. That's where the similarities ended. The first store was clean and tidy. This one was messy and dirty. The first store was well lit. This one was dark and unwelcoming. The first store was well stocked and had plenty of cashiers. This one had bare spots on the shelves, and long lines at the few registers that were open. The difference between the two stores was both obvious and stark.

"This store is only a few blocks from my house," she told him. "But I drive an extra 10 minutes to get to the other one because I don't like shopping at this one. I'm a single mom and don't make a lot of money. I need to shop at your stores because I can't afford to shop just anywhere. But that extra 10 minutes is time I don't have. It's time away from my kids, who get far too little of my time as it is."

Beré apologized to her for the condition of the store and promised to fix it.

At the conference, he probably went on to talk about retail marketing or some other element of strategy, but Daniel doesn't remember any of those details. What he remembers is the compassion and interest that CEO showed for his customer. Daniel realized Dollar General wasn't in the business of selling cheap merchandise. It was in the business of serving underserved people—people who need products in those price ranges, and who can't afford to shop elsewhere. It wasn't about what Dollar General was selling. It was about whom it was selling it to.

Daniel understands now that having passion for your work doesn't have to be determined by what you do or the products you sell. It could be determined by whom you're doing it for. So if you or people in your organization are having a hard time developing a passion for the work, try developing a passion for the customer you're working for. Create your own stories about them and you'll ignite passion in anyone who hears them.

Oh, and that store a few blocks from that shopper's house that was such a mess . . . I'll bet you a dollar that David Beré fixed it.

* * *

The previous stories are examples of helping people find something about their work they can be passionate about. Another way to help people be more passionate about their job is to remove the things they are decidedly dispassionate about. The following story illustrates one way to do that.

As a small-business owner and mother of four, it's not unusual for some of Melissa Moody's employees to also know her as their mom. That can sometimes lead to very unusual meetings. Here's a case in point. One afternoon during a typical staff meeting, Melissa was discussing something that mostly involved one particular employee, so her comments were directed primarily his way. Out of the corner of her eye, Melissa noticed Brooke Moody, her 30-year-old daughter, slowly sinking lower in her chair. Like any good parent whose child is misbehaving, Melissa ignored it so she wouldn't encourage her any further.

Eventually Brooke disappeared entirely behind the desk that separated them. Melissa continued with the meeting, not saying a word to Brooke or even looking in her direction. "If I just ignore her, eventually she'll sit up and start paying attention," she thought.

A few seconds later, an unexpected movement entered her peripheral vision. It definitely was not Brooke straightening up in her chair. So this time she looked. Through a small space between the edge of the desk and the door, she could just make out the form of her daughter—crawling on all fours—slowly inching out of the room and down the hallway!

Brooke was insanely bored. The dramatic exit was her unique form of protest. And since her mom was the boss, she knew she could get away with it without getting fired, or probably even reprimanded. And she was right. In fact, the whole family gets a huge laugh every time the story is retold.

Here's the point. How many employees have desperately wanted to slink out of one of *your* staff meetings but didn't because it would be unprofessional? Probably more than you'd care to admit. The reason is likely no different from Brooke Moody's. They're bored. The discussion during much of the meeting doesn't involve or affect them. They're in the room for two hours just to hear the 30 minutes that actually matters to them.

Why does this happen? Because staff meetings are typically arranged to be convenient for the boss, not the staff. It's the easiest way for the boss to hear what's going on from everyone and provide direction to the group. What the boss doesn't realize is that the time she's saving by doing it this way (her time) is more than offset by the collective wasted time of her staff. More importantly, the cost to morale is immeasurable.

That's the lesson Melissa Moody learned that day. Since then, her staff meetings have been much different. Now they're very short and only cover a summary of the business that's important to everyone. She then follows with detailed one-on-one meetings with her staff members to cover the information important to them in particular. Yes, it takes a little more of her time to do it that way. But her staff is happier, more engaged, and has more time to work on the things they are passionate about.

Brooke Moody hasn't crawled out of a meeting since.

It's hard to hear this story and not rethink the way you run your staff meetings. In fact, if you're the boss where you work, ask yourself this in your next meeting: "If my daughter worked here, would she be crawling out the door right now?" If the answer is yes—and it probably is—take a piece of advice from Melissa and change the way you run things. And if you're not the one in charge, and it's you who feels like crawling out during the meeting, take this story and read it to your boss!

SUMMARY AND EXERCISES

1. You can't order people to love their job. But you can help them find that passion with some well-chosen stories, such as the train ride in Budapest. What is it that makes you come to work every day? Tell your story to others. Ask for theirs. Find the best ones and share them with everyone else.

2. Can't find a good passion story for your product or service? Then find passion for the customer you're serving. Like the Dollar General CEO, meet your customer face-to-face. Understand his or her life. Share the story.

3. Use the story of Brooke Moody crawling out of the staff meeting to teach your leaders to remove the things that drain the passion from an organization. What you'll be left with is more likely to engender passion and commitment.

CHAPTER **18**

Appeal to emotion

"It is useless to attempt to reason a man out of what he was never reasoned into."[1]
—JONATHAN SWIFT

IF YOU'VE MANAGED other people in your career, you're bound to have run into this situation at least once or twice. One of your direct reports comes to you and asks for a promotion. This person is a hard worker and good at his job. But the next level of management requires a number of skills he doesn't have. More importantly, it comes with expectations he's not likely to be willing or able to meet: more working hours, out-of-town travel, and flexibility to be relocated to other company offices in faraway cities.

You explain all about those skills and expectations necessary for success, and the person is still interested. So you ask why he wants to get promoted and you get these kinds of responses: "If I don't get to that level, I won't feel successful." "Most of my friends are already at that level." "Everyone keeps telling me that's what I should do."

Sound familiar?

This is the profile of employees who could be very productive and happy at their current level but have let other people's opinions convince them to be dissatisfied with where they are. And, unfortunately, if they get what they're asking for, they'll end up frustrated, unsuccessful, and unhappy.

Instead of all the by-the-book career coaching I've tried in the past, today I simply tell them the story of Karen Armitage, a Disney Imagineer,

154

from an inspiring little book called *The Imagineering Way*. Karen tells the story like this.[2]

I saw a call in the newspaper for volunteers for the Special Olympics at the Los Angeles Coliseum, so off I went. They put me to work, and I found my main job was to monitor this one young lady in the 100-yard-dash. Like many of the folks who competed that day, "Penny" was a Down's syndrome kid—about twelve years of actual age and somewhat delightfully younger in reality. And that is exactly what I was to learn from her—all about reality.

There were five girls in the race. They were nervous. They each had an adult, like myself, individually assigned to them, to get them in the starting blocks and to calm them while waiting for the starting pistol. There were probably 3,000 to 4,000 people—family and fans—in the stands.

The guy shooting the starter's pistol was Southern California's answer to breathtaking beauty. Model material, this guy had a smile and a voice that would soothe a frightened tiger. The girls were mesmerized. Concentration was difficult, even for those of us who only qualified for Ordinary, not Special.

There were several false starts. Nerves were high. Finally, "Beautiful Bob" had all five runners relaxed and we had a clean start with a bang on "go." The girls took off running. But after about twenty-five yards my little one stopped in the middle of the track and got down in the starting position again!

Meanwhile, the crowd is cheering and roaring. I run onto the track and start yelling, "Run . . . Go!" She's stagnant, planted firmly, crouched in the start position. The other runners had all crossed the finish line. Now the crowd sees my girl and starts yelling, "Go . . . go . . . go!" Beautiful Bob sees this and throws me a questioning look. I run out to my girl and say, "Sweetheart, run." She looks at me with her biggest smile and says, "After the gun goes bang!"

I speed back to Beautiful Bob and yell, "Shoot the gun! Shoot the gun!" As I hurry back to my eager young athlete, I see Bob run to the in-field up alongside her. We all three yell, "Ready, set, go!" Bob shoots the starter pistol and she was off again—and after another twenty-five yards she's down again. So now, finally, we get it.

Bob and I get abreast of her again. The crowd is chanting, "Go . . . go . . . go . . ." We holler, "Ready, set, go!" With another bang of the starter pistol, off she goes, and after about twenty-five yards, she's down again. By now, everyone in the stadium has got her game. Bob motions me to take the pistol on the infield. He runs to the finish line, gets another huge ribbon strung across—and he kneels on the track dead center, arms open wide—his huge smile just for her. I raise the pistol.

The crowd now yells in unison, "Ready . . . set . . . go!" I shoot on "go" and she's off, hurtling herself as fast as she has ever gone—through the ribbon to a screaming crowd. Bob caught her on the other side and throws her skyward. I will forever remember her grin—open and wide with exultation, her face to the heavens above, yelling, "I WON!"

There was not a dry eye anywhere in that coliseum. For she spoke absolute truth, and there was not one person out of those 4,000 fans who would have argued the point.

Talk about power. She single-handedly changed everyone's perception—to her own—without malice, force, or any hint of "victimhood." What everyone else would have previously perceived as failure was now perceived as success, simply because my beautiful young athlete could see it no other way.

After finishing the story, I turn the conversation back to the person in my office seeking the promotion he really isn't ready for. I close the conversation with a single sentence. "Never," I insist, "let someone else define your personal success." He decided he wanted that promotion for emotional reasons, not rational, logical ones. He needed an emotional "out." Karen's story gives it to him.

* * *

Emotion is so important to a story, some storytelling experts consider it a defining element, without which you don't even have a story. In their book *The Elements of Persuasion*, Richard Maxwell and Robert Dickman define a story as "a fact, wrapped in an emotion that compels us to take an action."[3] That's it. Fact + Emotion + Action = Story. Novelist E. M. Forster defines a story even more narrowly as only the fact plus an emotion. A pithy example of his illustrates the point: "To say, 'The king died, and then the queen died' is not a story. To say, 'The king died, and then the queen died *of grief*'—now *that* is a story."[4] Like metaphors you'll learn about in chapter 24, those last two words, "of grief," carry the emotion and concoct in the listener's head an entirely plausible story to explain the fact given. The point is, if you don't generate an emotional reaction in your audience, you haven't told a story. It might be a good memo, or perhaps a case study. But it's not a story.

Some leaders think the modern workplace should be an emotion-free zone, restricted to rational thought and logical decisions. That might be true if your job is limited to managing machines and processes. But leading people requires something more. Humans make emotional decisions. Good leaders recognize that and aren't afraid to lead with both sides of their brain.

Emotion was the primary ingredient in the previous story. More typically, it's only part of the equation. Either way, it's important that you pick the right emotional content that will both resonate with your audience and further your objective. A sad story about cute puppies might tug at the heartstrings of most people. But unless you're trying to find a home for unwanted puppies, that emotion will be wasted on your audience and won't further your purpose in telling the story. The next story is an example of one that's perfectly suited for the audience it was designed for. It taps into what that audience wants most at the point in life when it hears it. And it contributes directly to the objective of the story.

Fifteen years ago, a 16-year-old girl and her mother showed up at Excel Models & Talent in Little Rock, Arkansas. Mom was interested in signing up her daughter, Elissa, for a four-day camp in modeling and personal development. Elissa was tall, clumsy, and lacking in what her mom thought of as traditional feminine qualities. Mom wasn't really interested in making her into a model. But she thought the four days might help her develop more ladylike qualities. Elissa agreed.

Elissa ended up liking the class so much that she signed up for the advanced class a few weeks later. During that session, she was selected to be among only four girls to go to New York to attend an international showcase for models. She did so well, she received over 30 callbacks from modeling agencies the next week, including an immediate contract offer from an agency in Japan. Although Elissa had a wonderful experience in New York, she still wasn't interested in modeling as a career. "But," she said, "I've never been to Japan before. And I don't know when I'll ever have another opportunity to go." So she went. It changed her life forever.

While in Japan, she developed a keen interest in international studies. When she came back and graduated from high school, she selected a college with an exceptional international studies department. That launched her into the career she really wanted. That's also where she met the man of her dreams. They fell in love and got married. Today she can't imagine life without him.

She continued to model off and on to pay her college bills. On one fashion assignment in London, her parents decided to come with her. There they met one of the clothing designers, and the foster child he was parenting. Mom, dad, and Elissa fell in love with that child, and eventually adopted her into their family. Mom and dad got another daughter. Elissa got the baby sister she always wanted.

A typical meeting with a prospective student at Excel involves owner Melissa Moody sitting down with a 14-year-old girl and her mother. They're obviously somewhat interested, or they wouldn't be there. But training and photos cost money. So Melissa has to help them understand why it's worth the investment. Elissa's story is one she typically tells in this setting for two reasons. First, she wants them to understand that her school really does change people's lives and opens up opportunities for them they might otherwise never have. They get the chance to travel abroad, learn new languages, and experience a business and culture few people have access to.

But the other reason she tells this story is that it connects with both prospective student and mom emotionally. Think about it. What do most 14-year-old girls want more than anything else? To meet Prince Charming and have him sweep her off her feet! What do most moms of teenaged girls want more than anything else? Two things. First, for their daughters to grow up, perhaps go to college, and get a nice job so they can be self-sufficient. (Marrying a caring husband is a nice plus, though.) Second, they long for the baby daughter they once had who's now turning into a woman. In this story, both mom and daughter get what their hearts desire most. When Melissa tells this story, it almost always ends in tears of joy from at least two people in the room—and sometimes three.

* * *

In Melissa's case, most of her prospective students already care a great deal about becoming a famous model or actor. Her story gives them several more emotional connections to her school. But what if your audience doesn't naturally care about your product or idea? Answer: Figure out what it does care about and connect your idea with it. In their ground-breaking book *Made to Stick*,[5] Chip Heath and Dan Heath describe a classic example of doing exactly that.

In the 1980s, none of the antilittering campaigns were working in Texas. Even the highly successful national TV campaign showing a Native American shedding a tear over a littered highway didn't work there. Why? Research by Dan Syrek's Institute for Applied Research found that the people in Texas who did most of the littering were 18- to 35-year-old, pickup-driving males who liked country music, didn't like authority, and certainly didn't care about weepy Native Americans. This was their target market. They called this demographic "Bubba."

What did Bubba care about? Bubba cared about Texas. Everything is "bigger and better" in Texas. And like all of us, Bubba cared about himself. The solution, then, was to appeal to Bubba's love of his home state, and his natural self-pride. Thus, the campaign "Don't mess with Texas" was born. It included celebrity endorsements by people Bubba would care about and respect (Dallas Cowboys football players, Houston Astros baseball players, even country and western singer Willie Nelson). The message in all the ads was the same. When you litter here, you're "messin' with Texas." And when you mess with Texas, you're messing with anyone who cares about Texas. "Hey, that's me!" This association turned the worst litter offender into the biggest antilitter advocate. Not only was Bubba not littering, but if he saw someone else littering, he'd call him out on it!

Litter dropped 72 percent over the next five years.

The lesson again is this: If your audience doesn't naturally care about your idea, find out what it does care about and associate your message with that. Later in the chapter, we'll discuss ways to find out what your audience cares about. For now, let's talk about which emotion is most effective for business narratives.

* * *

There are, of course, many emotions you could use in your stories: love, guilt, fear, pride, greed, and so on. But a powerful emotion that's largely underutilized in the workplace, and that stories are ideally suited to deliver, is empathy—vicariously experiencing someone else's thoughts, feelings, or attitudes. Empathy is so potent because almost every business decision affects other people and how they think and feel. Leadership stories are usually designed to affect those decisions. So the better you enable the decision maker to empathize with the people affected by the decision, the better you'll be able to influence their decision. If you want the CEO to lower prices because some of your customers are struggling to afford your product, your best bet is to demonstrate how much you're losing in sales because your prices are too high. Short of that, your best weapon is to generate empathy on the part of the CEO for the plight of your customer. If you want the plant manager to offer a concession to the labor union, generate empathy for the average laborer.

Let's explore empathy a bit and contrast it with a related emotion it's often confused with—sympathy. Both sympathy and empathy are acts of feeling. But with sympathy, you feel *for* the person. With empathy, you feel *with* the person. For example, you can sympathize by feeling sorry for people who are hurting, even if you don't know why they hurt. Any stranger can sympathize with a patient in a hospital. To empathize, however, takes more work. You have to understand why someone feels the way she feels or thinks the way she thinks. To empathize with that stranger in the hospital, you'd need to visit him and find out he's suffering from clinical depression resulting from the death of his only child in a tragic auto accident he feels responsible for causing. Now you can empathize, because you can imagine yourself in that same situation. You can imagine the kind of guilt and shame and regret that would cause.

The following story illustrates empathy through the eyes of a business executive and her five-year-old son in one of the most dangerous cities in the world. As with all stories in this book, it also teaches a valuable lesson.

In the early 1990s, Kim Dedeker lived in Caracas, Venezuela, with her husband and five-year-old son, Bryan. Kim's job as an executive on foreign assignment with a U.S. company made them quite wealthy by local standards. Per capita income in Venezuela is about $13,000 a year, with 30 percent of the population living on less than $2 a day.[6] In addition to being a poor country, it's also a dangerous one. Caracas has one of the highest homicide rates of any large city in the world.[7] Accepting the assignment there was a difficult decision, but a deliberate one. Kim believes it's only by taking such risks that some of life's greatest rewards are possible. One of the most touching examples of that happened in Caracas on her way to the toy store.

Bryan had been saving his money for months to be able to buy one of the wildly popular Teenage Mutant Ninja Turtle figures to add to his collection. He'd finally accumulated the required 800 bolivars—about 20 U.S. dollars. Kim strapped Bryan into the backseat of their car and started the drive to the toy store for the much-anticipated purchase. Unlike a drive to a toy store in the United States, however, there is no way to drive across Caracas without coming face-to-face with the reality of local life. Poverty is all around you. But it was danger that was on Kim's mind as they ventured outside their compound of largely U.S. expatriate homes and apartments. Kidnappings and carjackings are not unusual. As a result, it's common practice to not even come to a stop at an intersection if you can avoid it. And you certainly don't roll down your windows.

En route to the toy store, Kim came to an intersection and had to stop for a red light with oncoming traffic. She noticed a woman on the corner who appeared to be homeless or at least severely impoverished. In her arms she held a baby about 18 months of age. Standing beside her was a young boy, about the same age as Bryan. The two mothers made eye contact—one destitute and one well off. Both surely considered what life might be like for the other for that brief instant.

While still waiting for the light to turn green, the boy outside began walking toward the car. As any protective mother would, Kim's immediate concern turned to her own safety and that of her son. Is this how the many unfortunate incidents start—with the distraction of a child? But the mothers had not been the only ones who'd made eye contact. The boy saw Bryan in the backseat as well, and it was his window he was approaching. Before Kim could react, Bryan rolled down his window. The two boys were face-to-face with each other, separated by only a few inches of space, but separated even further by language and the harsh contrast of their economic realities. Without exchanging a single word, Bryan reached into his pocket, pulled out his 800 bolivars, and handed it to the young boy through the car window. The traffic light turned green, and Kim cautiously continued through the intersection.

The next few minutes passed quietly with both driver and passenger processing what had just happened. Kim finally broke the silence by asking, "What are you feeling right now?"

Thoughtfully, he responded, "I'm feeling really good, Mom, because I think that little boy needed that money a lot more than I needed another Teenage Mutant Ninja Turtle."

As you can imagine, Kim was marveling at the selflessness her five-year-old had just shown. She debated in her head what to do when they arrived at the toy store. Should she reward her son's generosity by buying him the toy anyway? Or should she afford him the full experience of giving by feeling the loss required to be truly benevolent? When they arrived, Bryan found the exact figure he was after—a rare one imported from the United States, unlikely to be there on a future trip. That made Kim's decision even harder. Bryan looked at the price tag on the figure and said to his mom, "It's 810 bolivars."

"You're right," Kim responded. "You almost had enough."

"But I don't have any now," he said, just fully realizing the impact of his decision in the car a few minutes earlier.

Having made her decision, Kim offered, "I could buy it for you, if you want."

After a thoughtful pause, Bryan said, "No. I don't think I want it today."

"Are you sure? I don't mind getting it for you."

"Yeah, I know," Bryan answered. "But I can probably get that turtle anytime I want. I can save my money, or you can afford to buy it for me. It just doesn't feel important now."

Sharing the day's story with her husband that night, Kim realized Bryan never would have had that experience or learned that life lesson if they had stayed in the United States. But because they took a risk and exposed themselves and their child to a part of the world he might not ever see otherwise, he developed a sense of selflessness beyond his years.

As a young man now in his twenties, Bryan has told that story hundreds of times to teach a personal lesson about what's important in life and what's not. Kim has done the same. But as chair of the Americas at Kantar—the second largest market research company in the world—Kim also tells that story at work when people need the strength and motivation to put themselves in an unfamiliar and perhaps scary environment or challenge. Maybe it's a new assignment they didn't ask for, or new job location they're afraid of, or promotion to a new level they're not confident about. It's easy to see all the negatives that might lie ahead in the new situation. But the positives are usually harder to see ahead of time, so people tend to dwell only on the negatives. Kim's story helps people look forward to their new challenge or environment as an opportunity to find those unforeseeable positives. Like it was with Bryan in his new environment of Caracas, Venezuela, when he found something in himself he didn't know was there—something wonderful. In their next scary environment or intimidating challenge, what will they find within themselves they didn't know was there?

The power in the previous story comes from the empathy felt by young Bryan for his street-side acquaintance and felt by Kim for the boy's mother. If they had been asked to think of a homeless woman and her five-year-old son, they both could have felt sympathy for the hypothetical family. But by coming face-to-face with them on the street corner, they were able to empathize with them. They saw the clothes they were wearing, the look on their faces, the body language in the mother's posture, and the gait of the boy's walk. They looked into the eyes of these fellow human beings and knew their plight. Empathy requires a personal knowledge of the subject of your empathy. Kim and Bryan's encounter—brief though it was—gave them that personal knowledge.

So how do you help your audience feel empathy? You have to introduce them to the people you hope they will develop empathy with. Either you can arrange to do that literally, like Kim and Bryan meeting the boy and his mother on the Caracas streets, or you can do it through your story by giving a glimpse into their lives.

You've seen this in several stories in this book so far, including two in the previous chapter. The story of Brooke Moody slinking out of the staff meeting generates empathy not just for Brooke but for employees in any company trapped in meetings they shouldn't be in. The story allows the listener to connect with the mindless frustration the hapless attendees suffer through. After hearing that story, you (and anyone you tell it to) will think twice about who's invited to the next staff meeting. The story of the Dollar General store visit where the CEO met a frustrated customer worked solely because you could empathize with the plight of the mom struggling to care for her family on a limited budget. What Dollar General employee wouldn't feel more passion for the job after hearing that story?

In all of these cases, the story allows you to know the characters more deeply than the stranger in the hospital with an unknown malady. As you can see, it doesn't take much. A three-minute story can contain enough context and plot to move the audience from sympathy to empathy. With whatever decision you're trying to influence, identify the people the decision influences most. Tell their story to your decision maker.

* * *

So where can you go to find emotional content for business stories at your company? One of the best untapped sources is your customers. In fact, you probably have loads of emotional content buried in consumer studies that never sees the light of day. Most consumer surveys have at least one or two open-ended questions—ones that don't have multiple-choice answers. Instead, the respondent is asked to write (or type) the answer in his or her own words, referred to as verbatim responses in the research business. The seeds of highly emotional stories can be found in those verbatim responses. Qualitative research—like focus group discussions with four to eight people in a conference room—is generally summarized in some way, too. It's also filled with high-potential content. Stories are in there waiting to be discovered. Find them.

For example, let's say your great idea is to introduce a new-line extension on your brand priced much lower than the rest of the brand. The reason, you argue, is that with the worsening economy, consumers are choosing to trade down to lower-priced brands and private label. If you had an offering in that price range, they might buy it and at least stay loyal to your brand. If you don't sell something at that price, they'll buy someone else's more affordable brand. As you've just learned, if you want to generate passion and commitment to your idea, it needs to have an emotional element. So what is it?

Ask your research department for recent studies that asked any questions about how consumers are coping with the worsening economy, or about the price of your brand, or about other low-priced brands. Ask for the verbatim responses and any focus group summaries, too. Read them—all of them. You're likely to find something like the following verbatims from a 2008 study Procter & Gamble placed asking about the impact of the economy on people's lives. Consider these comments from consumers around the world:

UNITED STATES: "We have one adult child unable to find work living with us. And it's become a family project to try and keep our granddaughter in the local community college. The sad thing is that my husband is having to put off retirement by at least four years."

ITALY: "I'm particularly suffering for my children: I feel bad because I always need to say no to their requests of new and nice clothing or toys like the ones of their schoolmates."

PHILIPPINES: "Mothers are mixing rice water with baby milk to compensate for the high price of dairy."

UNITED STATES: "We've had to remember how to live like we did nearly 26 years ago when we first got married. I've gone back to saving bacon grease to cook."

CANADA: "I lost my house because of high interest rates and a high payment; and I haven't been able to find a steady job, just temporary."

UNITED STATES: "I'm scared to death. I'm currently in a Chapter 13 to save my condo, but I don't even think that will work for me. The payment to the trustee every month is too high along with the mortgage payment."

The new brand you plan to launch will help these consumers save a little money so they won't have to dilute their baby's milk with rice water or deprive their children of play toys; or perhaps it will help them make their mortgage payment so they don't lose their home. Telling their stories will create the empathy you need.

Emotional content is all around you, if you know where to look.

SUMMARY AND EXERCISES

1. Emotion plays a huge role in decision making. Sometimes reason and logic won't help you influence people nearly as much as an emotional appeal. Nothing delivers emotional appeal better than a story. Use stories like the Special Olympics narrative to engage the right side of your audience's brain.

2. Not just any emotion will do. The emotion and the context must be relevant to your audience and to your objective in telling the story in the first place. Elissa's story at Excel Models & Talent is a great example of both relevant emotion and context. ("I've never been to Japan.")

3. What's in it for your audience? If your audience adopts and supports your idea, what does it get out of it? How will this advance your listeners' goals, their careers, their interests?

4. If your audience doesn't naturally care about your idea, figure out what it does care about and associate your idea with it. One example is the story about the slogan "Don't mess with Texas."

    a. If you don't know what your audience cares about, find out. Your research department can help.

5. A powerful and underutilized emotion in business is empathy. If you want to influence someone's decision, find out whom that decision will affect and generate empathy through a story.

    a. Kim Dedeker's story of the Teenage Mutant Ninja Turtle illustrates the difference between empathy and sympathy. Empathy requires more work. You need a personal knowledge of the subject of your empathy. To get your audience to empathize with someone, introduce your listeners to that person's story. (Consider the staff meeting and the Dollar General stories.)

    b. A great source for empathy is verbatim consumer research and qualitative research summaries. Ask for them. Find the most emotional responses and craft a story around them.

Notes

1. Maturin Murray Ballou, *Treasury of Thought: Forming an Encyclopædia of Quotations from Ancient and Modern Authors* (Nabu Press, 2010; print on demand), p. 433.

2. The Imagineers, *The Imagineering Way: Ideas to Ignite Your Creativity* (New York: Disney Editions, 2003), pp. 151–153. Used with permission.

3. Richard Maxwell and Robert Dickman, *The Elements of Persuasion: Use Storytelling to Pitch Better, Sell Faster & Win More Business* (New York: HarperCollins, 2007), pp. 122–131.

4. Jack Maguire, *The Power of Personal Storytelling: Spinning Tales to Connect with Others* (New York: Tarcher/Putnam, 1998), p. 105.

5. Chip Heath and Dan Heath, *Made to Stick: Why Some Ideas Survive and Others Die* (New York: Random House, 2007).

6. "The World Factbook: Venezuela," Cia.gov.www.cia.gov/library/publica tions/the-world-factbook/geos/ve.html. Retrieved January 18, 2011.

7. El Pais, "96 homicidiosporcada 100.000 habitantes." Retrieved November 3, 2009.

CHAPTER **19**

The element of surprise

"A true leader always keeps an element of surprise up his sleeve, which others cannot grasp but which keeps his public excited and breathless."
—CHARLES DE GAULLE, former French president and military general

IT WAS THE FIRST DAY of fall semester at Conway High School—Jim Owen's world history class. Mr. Owen had a reputation for being one of the toughest teachers at CHS, but also one of the best. Class started the way most others do on the first day: The teacher introduced himself, explained what the class was about, how many tests there would be, how the grading would work, and so on. About 20 minutes into class, four teenaged boys burst into the room, all wearing ski masks and brandishing weapons. "Nobody move!" they shouted. They went directly to the front, where they proceeded to knock Mr. Owen to the ground, relieve him of his wallet, steal the grade book off his desk, and leave as quickly as they came in. It was all over in less than 15 seconds, leaving the students paralyzed in shock.

When the dust settled, Mr. Owen rose to his feet. "I'm fine. Is everyone okay?" We assured him we were. He then explained that what we had just witnessed was not real. Those teenagers were his students last year and had agreed to take part in a mock criminal activity. And they had done their job well.

"Your first assignment," he continued, "is to take out a sheet of paper and write down everything that just happened in as much detail as possible." Still somewhat in shock, the class complied. Ten minutes later, he asked the students to hand in their papers. He then read each one aloud

167

to the class. That's when the third shock of that fourth-period class hit. The stories were astonishing in their differences in the account of the facts. One story claimed there were four boys; another claimed there were three. Some said there were three boys and one girl. One said the weapons were all real guns; another said they looked like plastic water pistols painted black. Somebody thought one boy had a knife. Some insisted Mr. Owen had been hit during the mugging. Most said he wasn't touched at all. Mr. Owen continued to read while we sat and listened.

When he finished, he put down the last paper and said, "History is recorded from the perspective of the people who write it. As we've just learned, that can be very different, depending on the author. The victors in war will surely tell a different story from that of the vanquished. The groups in political power will surely write a different perspective from those not in power. Please keep that in mind as we begin our journey through world history. Now . . . open your books, and turn to chapter 1."

That was 26 years ago. But I remember it like it was yesterday.

Studying history taught many important lessons that year. But the most valuable and lasting one may have been learned on that first day, because of Mr. Owen's bold and surprising teaching technique. (Unfortunately, Mr. Owen had to discontinue this annual dramatization after the tragic shootings at Columbine High School in 1999 made such a specter all too real.)

You can tell this event was amazing and impactful for the students it actually happened to. But it also makes a great story when you hear it told. That's because the surprises elicit similar physical and emotional responses in the listener or reader as they did in the students it happened to. As everyone knows, the element of surprise plays an important role in the drama and excitement of a story. What you may not be aware of, however, is the vital role it plays in the effectiveness of a story that's told with a purpose. In this story, there are three key surprises: first, when the four masked boys burst into the room; second, when you learn it was staged; and third, when you find out how differently the students recorded the event. The first two surprises, near the beginning of the story, serve one purpose. The third surprise, near the end, serves an entirely different one. Let's discuss both purposes, starting with the surprises at the beginning.

The purpose of putting a surprise at the beginning of a story is to get your audience to pay attention. It shakes people out of their focus on whatever it was they were doing, and gets them to listen to you more attentively. A good example was the first sentence of the consultant's story in chapter 10, when you found out his client was firing him. That's enough to make most business leaders take note. Or in the first sentences of Bev Keown's story in chapter 11, when you learn she was born on a plantation, daughter to a sharecropper. That's certainly not the way you're introduced to a typical character in a business narrative. These aren't the kind of surprises you see in a horror movie. They won't elicit a scream or audible guffaw. But they can widen your eyes; quicken your pulse ever so slightly; and, importantly, trigger the release of a small amount of adrenaline in your body. Just enough to get you to pay a bit closer attention.

Of course, if your story does involve a shocking topic worthy of a prime-time news headline, certainly lead with it. That's exactly what I did with two stories in chapter 8. One opened with a scene of violence and pandemonium on the streets of Egypt during the 2011 revolution; the other with the devastating earthquake in Japan in 1995.

* * *

So, is it necessary to have over-the-top story lines like the Jim Owen story to create impactful surprise? Fortunately not. In fact, one of the most attention-grabbing, memory-trapping surprises you can give your audience might also be the simplest. And it can be delivered with as little as a single word. Consider the following examples from Gary Cofer.

Gary is executive vice president at dunnhumby USA, an analytics consultancy specializing in retail sales data. In 2010, he was concluding a meeting with one of his clients. As they were walking out, the CEO asked him what Gary describes as an "affirmation-seeking" question. You know the type—the kind of question people ask in hopes you'll say yes and reaffirm whatever flattering notion they have about themselves. In this case, the question was this: "I understand we're best-in-class among your clients at using your data. Isn't that right, Gary?" It's a pretty safe question for the customer to ask the hired help. The customer is always right, after all.

Gary's answer stopped the CEO in his tracks—literally.

"No." Gary told him directly. "You're not."

The CEO stopped walking, turned and looked at Gary with wide-open eyes. "Oh," was all he could manage at first, and then followed with, "What do you mean?"

Gary's response was equally surprising. "Actually, I don't even think you're getting your money's worth out of us."

The CEO couldn't believe what he was hearing! "Really? That sounds like something I should be complaining to you about, not the other way around."

Gary explained that in addition to basic sales and loyalty data, dunnhumby offers dozens of advanced analytical services to help its clients make better decisions about how to price and promote their products. Many of them are included in the fee they were paying already. But for some reason, they just hadn't been fully taking advantage of them.

Twenty-six years of sales and general management experience have taught Gary there are two ways that clients typically find out they're not getting enough value from one of their agencies. First, they figure it out for themselves, and complain about it. Second, a competing agency approaches them and points it out. Either way, it usually ends up with the agency losing the account. Gary prefers a third option. Tell them about it yourself, and then fix it. And in this case, that's exactly what he did.

In a similar situation with another client, Gary was even more direct. He told the client, "You should fire us." Can you imagine a more arresting statement from an agent? Me, neither. But for Gary, it prompted the same kind of conversation that led to the client better leveraging the capabilities his company had to offer.

In both cases, business for the client and dunnhumby increased significantly. And in both cases, it was due in large part to Gary Cofer's jaw-dropping candor and the brilliant use of surprise it elicits.

* * *

Surprise isn't the only device you can use early in a story to get your audience's attention. But it is an effective one. You'll learn others in chapter 29. What you're looking for is something unexpected or unusual to lead with—like the CEO being told no. Just about any story worth telling will have something unexpected in it—usually more than one. Find one of them, and put it near the beginning of your story.

A surprise near the end of a story serves another purpose entirely. Since your story is over, you don't need your listener to pay attention any longer. The purpose of a surprise at the end is to sear the entire story in your audience's long-term memory. Memories don't form instantly in the brain like a photograph. They form over a period of time shortly after the event happens—a process psychologists call *memory consolidation*.

I learned that the hard way at the age of 16. I was playing a game of pickup football in an empty field near the house I grew up in. Unlike organized sports, we didn't have helmets or pads, and the players' ages were determined by who showed up that day. In the opening kickoff, I caught the ball and was running it back at full speed. A boy of 19—much bigger than I—met me head-on. My head hit the ground unusually hard, causing what my doctor later confirmed was a concussion. I didn't lose consciousness. But when I got up, I knew something was wrong. I walked over to the huddle that was forming to listen in on the next play. The other players looked at me like I was crazy and yelled, "Smith, get back on your side!" I'd joined the wrong team's huddle! I knew every boy on the field by name but couldn't remember what team I was on. Choosing up teams in a backyard football game happens immediately before the game starts. With my concussion happening on the first play of the game, those team rosters hadn't permanently formed in my memory yet. My concussion interrupted the consolidation process.

The scientific proof of this was first shown by Dr. James McGaugh, a neurobiologist at the University of California at Irvine.[1] While training rats to navigate a complex maze, he discovered they could remember the patterns quicker if given a mild stimulant. That might not be too surprising. A cup of coffee makes most of us pay attention better. Only in his experiment, he gave the rats the stimulant *after* they finished running the maze, not before. After the stimulant wore off, the rats were tested on their memory of the maze pattern. The rats with the postadministered stimulant remembered the maze patterns better than the rats without. This was the first proof of the memory consolidation theory that memories form shortly after the event happens, not during.

The second discovery resulting from Dr. McGaugh's work was the impact of the stimulant on forming stronger memories. As he would discover later, adrenaline had the same effect on memory consolidation that his administered stimulant did. And unlike his stimulant, adrenaline is a chemical the body produces naturally. Specifically, it's released when we experience strong emotions or surprises. It helps the body prepare for either fight or flight in case the surprise is dangerous.

The conclusion: A surprise at the end of your story helps your audience remember it better because adrenaline will be present in the brain during the important memory consolidation period. In the Jim Owen story, finding out all the historical accounts were different accomplishes this. In Jayson Zoller's story in the introduction, finding out the judge ordered all the round tables removed is the surprise ending. And in chapter 16, you had to wait until the end of the story to find out the giant's name was "Fear." All of these surprises at the end make the stories much more memorable than if you learned those facts earlier on.

* * *

You may be thinking that some stories just naturally lend themselves to having a surprise ending. That's certainly true. But you can take a story that doesn't seem to have a surprise ending in it and turn it into one that does. I've done that in several stories in this book already. Let's look at three examples.

In chapter 16 you read a story about Abraham Lincoln. You just didn't know it was a story about Lincoln until the end, which gave it a powerful surprise ending. Every version of that story I've seen, however, identifies the main character as President Lincoln in the first sentence. Some start, "Abraham Lincoln faced many challenges in his life," and proceed to list all the events by the year they happened. Some of them even have his name in the title: "Abraham Lincoln Didn't Quit."

For the version I wrote, I didn't use a title. I didn't open with a statement about Mr. Lincoln. And I converted the years into what his age would have been at each event, further masking the subject. A history buff might have figured it out early in the story. But most of you were probably surprised at the end. I also added the last three paragraphs myself after only a few minutes of research. Would the story have been effective the way it's traditionally told? Certainly. But the surprise ending sears it into memory much more effectively.

I do the same thing with the story of "James and the teakettle" in chapter 26. (But you'll have to wait to see who that is when you get there.) The story originally came from a publication in 1905 that bore the name of the subject in the title of the book. Clearly there was no surprise about who the main character was. In my version, I simply didn't mention his last name. Then I added a paragraph at the end divulging his true identity and explained the historical significance of his contributions. Presto! Surprise ending. In that case, and with the Lincoln story, I created a surprise where none existed by keeping a critical fact in the story a secret until the very end.

Sometimes a surprise naturally exists in a story, but you can make the story more effective by changing where it occurs. For example, in chapter 2 you read the story I told my team about Nokia starting as a papermaking company in Finland. But I chose not to tell them it was Nokia until the very end. Perhaps a more natural way to start the story would be, "Did you know Nokia started out as a papermaking company like us? It all started in 1865 on the banks of the Tammerkoski River in southwest Finland. . . ." In that case, it's still surprising that Nokia started by making paper. And we've just learned that surprises at the beginning of a story do serve a purpose. But if you can choose between placing the surprise at the beginning or the end, always choose the end. It's much more important in making the story memorable and maintaining listeners' interest throughout the story while they wait to find out the detail you're hiding from them.

* * *

Of course, a surprise doesn't have to be at the beginning or end of a story to add to its impact and memorability. A surprise anywhere in the story is better than no surprise at all. The last story in this chapter is one where the surprise is roughly in the middle. More importantly, it's a case where a surprise is not only of tangential importance, it's the entire subject of the story.

It's 6 A.M. in Queretaro, Mexico, about 130 miles north of Mexico City. Most of the residents are just waking to the sound of an alarm clock. But one woman is already dressed and has visitors in her kitchen. However, this isn't the typical time or type of guests she normally entertains. These are senior executives from the Kellogg Company visiting from their Battle Creek, Michigan, headquarters in the United States. As the world's largest cereal maker, they have a vested interest in understanding how consumers go about their breakfast routines. In-home research like this is one of the primary ways they gain that understanding in countries around the world. But this visit had several of the executives scratching their heads.

One of those executives was John Bryant, CEO of the company. He watched as the mom went about preparing the meal for her household of five. It was what John calls a "heavy" breakfast: eggs, ham, cheese, toast, juice, and some fruit. As he watched the family enjoy the meal, he noticed two boxes of Kellogg's cereal on top of the refrigerator. After they finished breakfast, he asked the mom, through an interpreter, if she ever ate cereal.

She responded, "Yes, every day."

John first looked at his interpreter—not sure he'd gotten the right translation—and then back to the mom. His look of confusion must have crossed the language barrier quite easily, because she responded unprompted, "Para la cena."

John looked back at his interpreter, sill confused, and then heard the unexpected translation: "For dinner."

The words hung in the air for a few seconds as the executives' eyes jumped from the interpreter, to the mom, and then to each other. For a breakfast cereal maker, finding out your consumer is using your product for dinner is a bit like a winter coat manufacturer finding out people are wearing its products in the summer. It just wasn't what they were expecting. On further research, Kellogg's learned that this mom wasn't unusual. Thirty percent of cereal in Mexico is consumed for the evening meal. Imagine how different the company might think about the ingredients in the cereal, or the way it communicates in its advertising, knowing a third of its consumers eat cereal at night.

Today, John tells that story to keep managers from thinking too dogmatically about how consumers use their product. "It's too easy," he explains, "to think of cereal only being consumed for breakfast, between six and eight o'clock in the morning, at home, with milk, from a bowl, with a spoon, and so on." It could be in the afternoon, straight from the box, and dry! His lesson: "Don't force your assumptions on our consumers. Our products are more versatile than we give them credit for. And so are our consumers."

In this case, the entire story is built around that ah-ha moment when the Kellogg's executives first realized their product was being consumed for dinner instead of breakfast. The surprise is not only the central event in the story; it was the inspiration for creating the story in the first place. Surprises in business usually represent significant learning moments, like when a longstanding paradigm is challenged, or a sacred cow is exposed for its flaws. Situations like that beg for a story to capture the moment. If one is created, like John Bryant's, the learning moment is passed on from person to person so the wisdom can spread throughout the organization, driven by the compelling nature of a surprising story. Imagine instead if it was only captured in the form of a fact or bullet point in a research report. It would still be as true. But only a fraction of the number of people would know about it.

SUMMARY AND EXERCISES

1. Grab your audience's attention with a surprise at the beginning. What's unusual or unexpected about your story? Open with it. Examples: Tom getting fired in "canceling your retainer" (chapter 10), Bev Keown being born on a plantation (chapter 11), moonlighting at Blackbook (chapter 26).

2. Does your story involve a newsworthy event? Lead with it. (Think of the revolution in Egypt, chapter 8; earthquake in Japan, chapter 8.)

3. Use unexpected candor. Gary Cofer's disarming "No" and jaw-dropping "You should fire us" comments stopped his clients in their tracks. Hearing about it in a story does the same thing to an audience.

4. Memories aren't formed instantly like a photograph. *Memory consolidation* happens over a period of time after the event.

    a. An injury, like a concussion, can interrupt that process and create memory loss.

    b. Conversely, heightened attention from an adrenaline rush enhances memory formation.

    c. Surprises trigger the release of adrenaline. Therefore, a surprise at the end of the story helps the audience remember it better. (Examples include finding out the judge ordered the round tables removed in the introduction and finding out the giant's name is "Fear" in chapter 16.)

5. No natural surprise at the end of your story? Create one. Hold back a key piece of information in your story until the very end, like the name of the person or company the story is about. Examples include finding out it was Abraham Lincoln after a lifetime of failure in chapter 16, finding out who James is in "James and the teakettle" in chapter 26, and finding out the papermaking company from 1865 was Nokia on the banks of the Tammerkoski River in chapter 2.

6. The next time you have an eye-opening ah-ha moment, write a story about it. These surprise lessons are the most impactful moments in business. (Breakfast in Mexico)

Note

1. Richard Maxwell and Robert Dickman, *The Elements of Persuasion: Use Storytelling to Pitch Better, Sell Faster & Win More Business* (New York: HarperCollins Publishers, 2007), pp 122–131.

CHAPTER **20**

Teach important lessons

"Learning is not compulsory. But neither is survival."
—J. EDWARDS

BARRY STARTED WORK as a financial analyst at P&G the same day I did in 1993. He was more proud than most to have gotten the job offer, having grown up just a few miles from P&G's world headquarters in Cincinnati, Ohio. Following in his father's footsteps, Barry was a diligent student, went to college, studied business, and graduated at the top of his class. In addition to being well prepared academically for a career in business, he also had a very strong mental image of what success looked like. That image was formed from visits to his dad's office as a child in the 1970s, and from television and movies in the 1980s. Images like the corner office, mahogany desk, and a secretary at your beck and call were the markers of success in his mind.

A typical first assignment as an analyst was working on a brand team, doing financial analysis of product upgrades or new brand launches. You sat in the bullpen of cubes where the rest of the team was, and aspired to be in your boss's chair someday, over in the corner office.

That was my job. Barry, however, lucked into a very different first assignment. He worked in what most companies would call the accounts receivable department. With millions of dollars of sales every day, it took a lot of people to make sure we got paid correctly for all those truckloads of product shipping to retailers around the country. The department was staffed with dozens of hourly paid employees who spent most of their time on the phone with the people who pay the bills as our customers.

176

Managing those throngs of receivables experts were a few newly hired managers, like Barry. Each one led a team of five or six people, who had their own version of a bullpen sitting right outside—you guessed it—Barry's big office with a mahogany desk!

Instead of having to work his way up the ladder for 15 years like his dad, Barry's first assignment had the trappings of success he'd been dreaming of since childhood. He'd hit the jackpot. He walked into his office that first day with his feet barely touching the ground. He sat back in his chair, kicked his feet up on the desk, leaned back, and smiled a satisfied smile as he surveyed his good fortune.

Sometime during that first hour, Sally came in to introduce herself. She was one of his direct reports. Although Barry didn't have a secretary per se, all of the people who reported to him were the same level as secretaries. And while Sally had her own accounts receivable responsibilities, if there were any copies needed or meetings to be scheduled in the group, it was her job to do it. So she was the closest thing he had to a secretary.

After they finished a brief get-to-know-you chat, Sally turned to leave. That's when Barry uttered the words he'd wanted to say to someone since he was 12 years old. Words that completed the trifecta of his personal success vision: "Hey, Sally, while you're out there, get me a cup of coffee, would you?"

Sally paused briefly, grimacing. She then continued on her way, throwing a "Sure, I'd be glad to" over her shoulder in a strained attempt at cheerfulness. Barry went back to his executive's chair oblivious to the insult he'd just leveled on Sally.

Word traveled fast. Before the week was out, the legend of his misstep morphed him into a sexist, patronizing ogre who'd slapped her on the rear end, smiled and winked, and said, "How about fetching me a cup of coffee, sweet cheeks?"

He never fully recovered. Although that comment certainly wasn't responsible for his short tenure with the company, when he did leave less than two years later, it was still haunting him.

Compare Barry's behavior his first day on the job to Mike Parrott's.

The same year Barry was making a name for himself in accounts receivable, Mike was appointed the leader of P&G's club channel sales team. With customers like Costco and Price Club on the West Coast, and BJ's on the East Coast, a Midwest location in Cincinnati didn't seem like a bad idea for the boss. In a couple of hours he could visit his team on either coast. But within a year, somebody decided it would be better if Mike picked one of the two coasts to work from as home base. Mike chose the West Coast office outside Seattle, Washington.

In October 1994, Mike arrived at the office complex where P&G rented space for the one manager and four hourly employees working there. Most of the sales associates worked out of their homes. The part of the floor P&G rented only had five permanent cubicles and a small kitchen that served as a break room. So it wasn't clear where Mike would work while they looked for more office space across town. But the cubes were big enough that two people could have shared one of them if necessary. So most people assumed that one of the administrators would have to share with another one to make room for the new boss.

You can imagine the surprise on that first day when Mike brought in a folding card table and set up his new "office" in the kitchen! And not just for a day or two until the others doubled up and emptied a cube for him. He insisted on staying in the kitchen until they moved to a bigger office complex, six months later.

That selfless gesture on Mike's part won him the respect and admiration of his team that normally takes months to earn. It showed him as genuinely humble and focused on what he, as the boss, could do for his team, and not the other way around.

People new to their jobs or new to the company often look to their leader for advice on how to be successful. Clear direction and coaching on their job responsibilities is certainly part of that. But you can't tell people how to handle every situation that might come up. Stories like the previous ones give people a picture of what success and failure look like so they can decide for themselves what future they want to create. It's one of two story forms I'll cover in this chapter that are most effective at teaching important lessons. I call this kind "two-roads" stories, after the Robert Frost poem *The Path Not Taken*, which begins, "Two roads diverged in a yellow wood." This kind of story illustrates two different paths the audience could take. It clearly leads them toward one path, but still allows listeners to draw that conclusion themselves, which is far more powerful than being told what to do.

I'll cover the second form later in the chapter. For now I want to demonstrate three different varieties of two-roads stories. The one above uses two different stories about actual people in the situation you want to teach about. This is the one to use if all of the following things are true—when you have real examples (1) that involve heroes (subjects) your audience can relate to, (2) with villains (obstacles) they are likely to face, (3) where one hero was successful and one failed, and (4) the logical conclusion would lead your audience down the path you want to recommend. In other words, when you have the perfect good and bad stories for the situation. But that's difficult to come by, which is why the other two varieties are useful to have in your storytelling tool kit.

* * *

The second variety works even if you can only meet the third and fourth criteria. It's a true story about real people who succeeded and failed. And it will lead you to the right conclusion. But it doesn't involve the actual situation your audience is likely to encounter. And the hero might not be immediately relatable. The only reason this can work is if you use the entire story as a metaphor for the real situation. The following example is one I've used many times.

As part of their annual review process, managers at many companies are given a performance rating indicating how well they did their job that year. At P&G, for example, the top 15 to 20 percent receive a 1 rating, with the remaining 80 to 85 percent sharing the 2 and 3 ratings. I've often been asked by junior managers, "What do I need to have on my work plan next year to get a 1 rating?" It's an impossible question to answer, mostly because it depends on how well the other managers do. Since it's a forced curve, if everybody has a great year, it will be much more difficult to get a 1 rating than in a typical year. After many years of managing and rating employees, I can usually provide some coaching to make sure their work plans for the next year will at least get them in the top half of the bell curve. But I've noticed that most of the people who get the 1 rating did so because they accomplished something they didn't plan on. A problem came up or an opportunity presented itself and they jumped on it, turning it into a victory. After years of trying to explain that to people in a satisfactory manner, I finally came across a story about a scientist who captured the essence of the idea. At almost 200 years old, the story may be at least partially apocryphal. But since I'm not teaching a science class, I still find it useful. Here's what I tell those aspirational and inquisitive young managers today.

Hans Christian Oersted was a Danish physicist at the University of Copenhagen in the early 1800s. On the night of April 21, 1820, Oersted was giving a lecture to his students on electricity. He had a simple wire circuit connected to a battery and a voltameter to show the level of current. As legend has it, sometime during the demonstration, Oersted noticed a magnetic compass on the table and picked it up to move it out of the way. As he did, he noticed the compass needle jump wildly as it passed near the electric circuit. Oersted moved it back near the wire and it jumped again. After the demonstration, Oersted asked one of his assistants if he had ever seen that happen. His assistant responded very matter-of-factly, "Sure. It happens all the time."

Intrigued, Oersted continued to experiment with it over the next several months and conclusively demonstrated a direct relationship between electricity and magnetism. Electric currents generate magnetic currents, and magnetic currents generate electric currents. This phenomenon is now known as electromagnetism and is the underlying mechanism that explains the light we see, the television and radio waves that entertain us, the cell phone signals that keep us in touch, the microwaves that cook our food, and the X-rays that help diagnose our ailments. Much of modern physics—including Einstein's Theory of Relativity as well as Quantum Mechanics—has its roots in electromagnetism.

The lesson is that Hans Christian Oersted didn't become the discoverer of electromagnetism because he was looking for it. It wasn't on his "work plan." He also wasn't the first person to notice the fact that magnetic compasses freak out when they pass near an electric current. He discovered electromagnetism because he was the first to recognize the significance of the jittery compass. And he pursued it.

So if you want a 1 rating, first have a strong work plan and accomplish everything on it. But then, pay attention to what's going on around you. Watch for something interesting to happen in your business. Be curious. Ask yourself if there's something significant going on. If so, jump on it.

In this story, Oersted represents one path, and all the other physicists who had seen jittery compass needles represent the other path. If you can think of a relevant metaphor, this can be an effective option. In chapter 24, you'll learn a technique for generating good metaphors.

* * *

What if you can't think of a story that meets any of the four criteria? Do you have to give up and revert to nonstorytelling techniques? Fortunately not. Here's where you get to be really creative. Just make one up! Really. The third kind of two-roads stories uses fictional characters to create the different paths for the listener to consider. In the next example, there are actually three paths, not two. I created it to help young research managers understand the difference between good and great.

Once there was a market research manager who had three bright young researchers working for her but was able to promote only one of them.[1] To determine which it would be, she gave each of them this challenge. "The one who best helps the next brand manager who comes through our door will win the promotion."

Soon an eager brand manager came to the research department with this request, "I have several new ideas for my brand, and need you to place a concept test to pick the best one." The research manager explained the competition and asked that the brand manager meet with each of her researchers separately. At the end of the week, the research manager called all three researchers in to present their recommended plan. The first researcher had designed the perfect concept test—a survey where different groups of consumers each evaluate one of the test concepts. It included a separate test leg for each of the brand manager's new ideas, plus one for the current concept to compare against. The test called for just the right number of respondents in each leg to be statistically reliable. The age, education, income, and ethnicity of the respondents was perfectly representative of the country's population. And he had included every conceivable question in the survey to help pick the winning concept.

"Well done," said the research manager.

When the second researcher stepped up to make her presentation, she proposed an entirely different test. "But the brand manager asked for a concept test. Why have you designed something different?" asked the boss.

She responded, "Well, when I looked at the new concepts, I realized they were all very similar. In fact, I don't believe them to be testably different. They all describe the same product benefit as the brand currently offers, with only minor differences in the words used to explain how it works. I know he asked for a concept test, but I didn't think that would answer the question he came in with: 'Which one is the best concept?' Asking different people to assess each concept will result in scores that are all about the same for each of his new concepts. My test will show all the concepts to the same group of people and ask them to pick the one with the most convincing wording. It should be easier to find a winner, and much cheaper to execute."

"Excellent," said the research manager. Then she asked the third researcher to present his research plan.

"Actually, I don't have one," he said sheepishly.

"What? You've had an entire week. I thought you wanted this promotion as much as the others."

"Oh, I do," replied the third researcher. "I just don't believe this brand needs any more research."

"I'm listening," responded the very curious boss.

"Well, I understand the brand manager's question was which of his new concepts was the best. But after talking to him about his business, and looking at the research we already have on that brand, I realized that wasn't the right question to ask in the first place. The current concept scored very high when it was first tested last year. And the television commercials developed to advertise that concept are doing very well in market. Awareness is at an all-time high, and consumers are playing back exactly the concept we hoped they would. The problem with the brand isn't the concept. The problem is price. Our value ratings have been dropping all year because our competitors have been running more coupons and sale prices in the Sunday paper.

"So the right question to ask would have been 'What price do we need to have to be competitive?' But we already know the answer to that question, because we conducted a pricing study 18 months ago. We know exactly how much we need to reduce our price. We've never done it because we couldn't do that and afford the increase to our advertising budget that was already approved. So I checked our media schedules and found out we're now advertising well beyond the saturation point for our category. In fact, about 10 percent of our ad budget is completely wasted. If we cut that wasted ad spending, we'd have just enough to reduce our price back to competitive levels. And that's exactly what I recommend we do."

Researcher number three got the promotion.

The lesson, of course, is teaching the value of asking the right question. Researchers are sometimes treated like "test waiters." Business partners come in and attempt to order up a specific type of consumer test. "I'll take two product tests and a brand equity study to go, please." Even an average researcher can design, execute, and analyze the test asked for. A better researcher would first make sure it's the right test to answer the business question asked. The best researcher, however, will make sure the right business question is being asked in the first place. Telling a young researcher to make sure the right question is being asked isn't good enough. A story like this—real or imaginary—makes the point far better.

The benefit, of course, of creating a fictional story is that you can create it to meet all the criteria just discussed to use the two-roads stories. You can make the main character be relatable to the audience. You can make the situation similar to one they will encounter. And you can make the story lead to the conclusion you want them to draw. So, if you can't find true stories that teach the lesson you want, make one up. Just make sure to let your audience know you made it up.

* * *

The second story form that works well to teach lessons is a failure story. It's exactly what it sounds like—a story about someone who tried to accomplish something, but failed. As author and entrepreneur Craig Wortmann observed, "People are drawn to failure stories in the same way we are drawn to accidents. We have a desire to see what happened and to see how to make sure it doesn't happen to us."[2] But it's not simply the weaker half of a two-roads story. If you told the half of the Hans Christian Oersted story that involved the other physicists who noticed the jittery compass, it wouldn't seem like a failure. "Some scientists did experiments with electricity and magnets, and sometimes noticed something funny happening with the compass. The End." Not a very interesting story. And not necessarily a failure, either. It's only in comparison to the other half of a two-roads story that one path seems unsuccessful.

A failure story, however, is unambiguously bad. It clearly teaches what the wrong thing to do is, so your listener can avoid the same misstep. The story that follows is one man's personal example. The failure stories you tell don't have to be about you. Your audience will be happy to learn from anyone's mistakes. But telling a failure story about yourself offers two additional benefits. First, it earns you respect and appreciation from the audience unlike you can get any other way. It shows humility too rare in leaders today. People will recognize and appreciate that. They know it's much harder to share your own failures than it is sharing someone else's. To them, it shows you care enough to help them grow at the expense of exposing your own shortcomings. Second, it makes you vulnerable, similar to the way Jamie Johnson was in chapter 10. So it will help you build relationships with your audience the way Jamie did with his. Here's Kevin's story.

"I had just started a new assignment one month earlier when my boss called me into her office. The good news was that our business was great this year, and we were on track to overdeliver our objectives. The bad news was that next year was shaping up to be much tougher. To hit our numbers, we'd need to do some belt tightening. She asked me if there were any projects we planned to do next year that we could do now, since funding would be harder to come by next year. "Next year" started in six weeks.

"Eager to please my new boss, I told her I was sure we could. I quickly convened my team leaders and asked for ideas. They delivered plenty—about $1 million worth. I asked if we could execute that much work in only six weeks. (I was not so secretly hoping we could. It would be nice to deliver that big round number to the boss.) They assured me it would be no problem. I committed the number to my boss and my team swung into action.

"By the end of the month, it was clear I'd made a terrible mistake. My team was working around the clock. They were stressed out and tired. And in our haste to get the projects started, mistakes crept in. One was bad enough that we had to start the whole thing over. In the end, we only got about 75 percent of the work done we'd promised. In hindsight, I should have seen it coming. In addition to the million-dollar rush job, we were going through a corporate restructuring that put people into new and unfamiliar reporting relationships. And I'd just lost two of the department's most experienced leaders. It wasn't a good time to put the organization through this fire drill. I had shown poor judgment in committing my team to such a Herculean task.

"But why? I was normally a better manager than that. Why had I so foolishly accepted my team's assertion that we could get all that work done in the last six weeks of the year when there was so much evidence that it was a bad time to take on extra work? After some reflection, I concluded it was this: In my eagerness to please my new boss, I overlooked the fact that I wasn't the only one who had a new boss he wanted to bend over backward to please. The 25 people in my department also had a brand new boss—me! If I had been thinking about them and their best interests, instead of my own, I would have made a better choice. Part of being a good leader is thinking of others before yourself. As a leader, it's your job to help others succeed. You can't do that when you're only worried about your own success."

A few months after making that mistake, Kevin shared that story with his team. It was his way of admitting his mistake and apologizing, but also teaching them the lesson to learn from his failure when they find themselves in that position someday. A year later, he found himself in a similar business situation, with the same request from the same boss who had asked for the million dollars the first time. Here's where Kevin found a second use for this story. After sharing it with her, it was easier for him to respectfully push back and say, "So you can see how I screwed up last year. This year I'll shoot for half a million, okay?" She readily agreed.

* * *

As a last pitch for the value of sharing failure stories, let me tell you about one of my favorite books. As a market researcher by profession, I've read several dozen books on research methods and practice. The single most valuable one to me, without question, has been *Danger: Marketing Researcher at Work*,[3] by Terry Haller, published in 1983. The reason is simple. Every other research book I've read was about how to *do* market research, according to the author's area of expertise or pet theory. Terry Haller's book was about what *not* to do. It's essentially a list of the 111 worst mistakes he's either made personally, or seen made, in the name of market research—111 failure stories! You may have heard that in a team of 10 people—all of whom are in agreement—9 are unnecessary. Terry Haller is the odd man out, and therefore the most valuable voice in the room. To be clear, he is a cynic, claiming "90% of all marketing research is so seriously flawed as to be of questionable value." But that was almost 30 years ago. The industry has made much progress since then, largely by addressing the 111 shortcomings Terry pointed out in his book.

Tell your failure stories. People will listen.

SUMMARY AND EXERCISES

1. You can't tell people how to handle every situation that might confront them. Two-roads stories give them a picture of what success and failure look like so they can decide what path to take.

   a. If you have examples that involve real people your audience can relate to, with challenges your audience is likely to face, and one person succeeded and one failed, you've got the perfect makings for a real two-roads story, such as Barry's coffee vs. Mike's kitchen.

   b. If you don't have the perfect stories, find a two-roads story about a different situation and use it as an analogy for your situation (e.g., Oersted and the jittery compass).

   c. Can't think of one of those, either? Make one up! Use fictional characters and create the two-roads story from scratch, such as the one about the three researchers.

2. We learn more from our failures than our successes. Unfortunately, people are generally hesitant to talk about their failures. Don't be. Share your greatest failures so others can avoid them. They'll respect and appreciate you for it (e.g., million-dollar mistake).

Notes

1. This original story was inspired by the story of "The Three Guides" in Doug Lipman's book *The Storytelling Coach: How to Listen, Praise, and Bring Out People's Best* (Atlanta, GA: August House, 1995), p. 109.

2. Craig Wortmann, *What's Your Story: Using Stories to Ignite Performance and Be More Successful* (Riverside, NJ: Kaplan Publishing, 2006), p. 38.

3. Terry Haller, *Danger: Marketing Researcher at Work* (Westport, CT: Quorum Books, 1983).

CHAPTER 21

Provide coaching and feedback

"Feedback is the breakfast of champions."
—KENNETH BLANCHARD

I FIRST MET Mitch Weckop in 1997 when I moved to California, just as I received my first big promotion. It would be my first job managing other people. I quickly realized that if I wanted to learn how to lead a group of people effectively, Mitch was the guy I needed to learn from.

I watched in amazement at how he inspired, coached, and mentored over 100 people at that plant. Each time people came to him with a problem, he not only gave them exactly the right advice to navigate the situation, but also left them feeling better about themselves, their career, and the company.

I often talked to my wife, Lisa, about how impressed I was with his leadership. I didn't think I would ever know enough to have that kind of impact on people. But I knew I wanted to try. The day eventually came when I found myself in one of those situations with a direct report of my own, and finally felt like I had handled it exactly the way Mitch would have. I can't remember the details now. But I must have been very pleased with myself, because when I got home and Lisa asked me how my day went, I told her, "It was great! I was a 'Mitch-manager' today."

She knew exactly what I meant. Ever since, that phrase has been a simple code between Lisa and me that means I was the kind of leader (at least for a few minutes that day) whom I had aspired to be since working with Mitch in California. Although it doesn't happen often, there are usually at least a couple of days a year I get to come home and utter that phrase. Here is an example of one of those days.

187

I had a project review meeting with a junior manager in a corporate department that supported my team. He was an absolute top performer—the kind most managers dream of having work for them. Although he didn't report to me directly, I worked with him often enough that I took an interest in him. At the end of the meeting, as I always did, I asked him how he was doing personally.

"Not good," he replied. "My wife wants me to quit the company." I knew exactly what the problem was. He had been overworked for months. When his department reported directly to me, there were three managers doing his job. After a restructuring, a corporate function took over his department and eliminated two of the positions, leaving him to do all the work himself. Each month when I met with him, I asked how things were going, and he would admit that the hours were unbearable. I would offer to help him, but he would always say, "No thanks. After project 'ABC' things will get better." But then project ABC would come and go, and things still weren't any better. The next time, it was the same answer. "No thanks. As soon as project 'XYZ' is over, things will get better."

But here we were, six months later, and he was admitting to me that, in fact, this had been going on for almost a year. His wife had given birth to their second child two months earlier, and since then he could count on one hand the nights he'd gotten home before bedtime.

When I asked him what his manager was doing to remedy the situation, he said, "You know, I really don't think they care. They don't value what I do here. All they seem to care about is inventing new methods for us to use, and we don't even have time to use the tools we have today. They don't have the budget to hire any help for me because they're spending all their money on development."

After letting him vent a bit more, I reminded him of my monthly offers to help, and his monthly refusals. (I could tell he viewed asking for help as an admission of failure.) I said, "Can I get you to agree now that things aren't going to get any better, and that it's time to accept my help?" He agreed, and the first thing I did was spend several minutes telling him how valuable an employee he was to this company; how strong a performer I thought he was, and all the reasons why; how bright a future I saw ahead of him; how I would be honored to have him fill any position in my department, now or in the future; and how lucky any manager would be to have him in his group. He looked like he hadn't heard those words in a while.

Next I told him all the different ways I could help, starting by talking to his current boss to get her help. And if that didn't work, she might not have enough budget to afford to hire him an assistant, but I did. Or I could pay one of our suppliers to step in and pick up the slack. Or I could divide up some of his work across a handful of people in my department. Or I could help him prioritize his work and choose some things to simply not do anymore. Or all of the above!

We agreed on two of those solutions to start with the following Monday.

The last thing I did was give him some tough feedback. "As sorry as I am that this happened, this isn't entirely your boss's fault. Some of the responsibility lies with you. Seriously, shame on you as a manager, a husband, and a father for letting this go on for so long. You should have had the good sense to ask for help when you needed it, or at least have the humility to accept it when it was offered. You're far too valuable to this company and your family to put your physical and emotional health under this kind of stress. Don't let this happen again."

He shook my hand as he left, smiled at me, and thanked me in the most genuine way. I could tell by his words and the look on his face that he felt good knowing he was valued and cared for by someone at this company. He felt relieved to know that management was actually doing something to fix his problem. And he felt wiser having learned a valuable lesson that would make him a better employee, a better husband, and a better father.

As I turned back to my desk, I donned a smile of my own. Because in that instant, I knew that when I got home, I'd be able to tell my wife that I'd been a Mitch-manager today.

There are several lessons to be learned from that story. First, if you want to get better at something, find someone who does it exceptionally well, and watch what he does. For me, Mitch served that purpose. Second, take pride and celebrate when you succeed. Just telling my wife I'd been a Mitch-manager that day earned a special smile from her, and a warm feeling of pride for me. Third, when done right, even telling someone he made a mistake can be viewed as a gift, leaving him appreciative to you for giving it. Let's see how that was done in the story above.

First, it started with positive feedback. That opens your audience to listening to you. Starting with negative feedback shuts people down. The positive feedback also builds your credibility with the listener, so he's more likely to believe the negative feedback you give him. After all, if you're smart enough to see how brilliant he is in one area, just maybe you could be right about one of his deficiencies.

Second, I asked if he could agree that there was a problem, and that it wouldn't get better without being addressed. If your listener doesn't agree there's a problem, your advice for how to fix it will fall on deaf ears.

Third, I asked what was already being done about the problem. In this case, what his boss was doing about it. Even better would be to ask what the person is doing to address the problem himself. You don't want to duplicate any effort. Putting the responsibility of solving the issue with the person in the best position to solve it is always a good idea.

Fourth, it included an offer to help, not just advice. Advice is good. But tangible help is better. Moreover, there were many options offered for help, and the listener got to pick which ones he wanted to take advantage of.

Fifth, it made the assertion that this situation is unacceptable because he is too valuable to let this kind of thing happen. Most feedback feels like being told, "You're not smart enough to do this right." That kind of feedback tears down the receiver and becomes a self-fulfilling prophecy. Compare that to hearing, "You're too smart to keep performing like this." The latter is more likely to evoke the change in behavior you're after.

* * *

Giving feedback is a lot easier when the misstep is obvious once pointed out. Unfortunately, people sometimes have difficulty seeing even an obvious mistake when they're the ones committing it. That's why step number two is so important—making sure your audience agrees with the feedback. What can you do when others can't (or won't) see the error in their ways? Tell them a feedback story about someone else. One of the oldest examples of this is in the Old Testament of the Bible. Most Christians and Jews will recognize the story of King David and Bathsheba. But fewer are familiar with the powerful metaphorical story told by Nathan that follows it.

According to the Book of Samuel, one evening King David got up from his bed and walked around on the roof of his palace. From the roof he saw a woman in a nearby home—bathing! The woman was very beautiful, so the king sent one of his men to find out about her. Returning, the man identified her as Bathsheba, the wife of Uriah. Uriah was a soldier in the king's army and was away at war. Undaunted, the king called her to his palace and slept with her. (To refuse the king's request could be punishable by death.)

Later, King David sent word to the leader of his army instructing him to send Uriah to the front lines of the fighting, and then pull the other men back. His general did as the king commanded. As expected, Uriah died in the fight. King David then brought Bathsheba into his house and made her his wife.

A year later, the prophet Nathan went to see King David. One of the many job responsibilities of a prophet was to confront sin. Nathan reported to the king that there were two men who lived in town among them—one rich and one poor. The rich man had many sheep and cattle, but the poor man had only one lamb. The poor man raised that single lamb. It shared his food, drank from his cup, and even slept in his arms. It was like a daughter to him.

One day a traveler came to visit the rich man. But instead of slaughtering one of his own sheep or cattle, the rich man took the one lamb of the poor man to feed his visitor. When King David heard this he burned with anger. He said to Nathan, "As surely as the Lord lives, the man who did this deserves to die! He must pay for that lamb four times over, because he did such a thing and had no pity."

"You," Nathan told the king solemnly, "are that man." Nathan explained that the king had many wives. Uriah had but one. "You struck down Uriah with a sword, and took his wife to be your own."

Then King David said to Nathan, "I have sinned against the Lord."

There was nothing else King David could say. Not only had he been found out, but he had convicted himself by passing judgment on the metaphorical "rich man" in the story Nathan told him.

Sometimes it's difficult to understand the wrong we have done until we see it through someone else's eyes. The metaphorical story gives us that glimpse from another perspective. As you'll learn in chapter 24, metaphors and analogies are powerful story tools. In the previous example, the entire story is used as a metaphor. When used properly, this technique is one of the most effective methods to deliver coaching and feedback.

To use this technique in a business setting all you need to have is the equivalent of Nathan's rich man/poor man story. Fortunately, most leaders have seen several examples of the poor performance they're trying to correct with feedback. Select one of those examples sufficiently different from the situation you're dealing with that it won't be obvious. Tell the story of that situation, and ask your listener to identify the problem. Once he spots the problem you want him to see, it's time to tell the king that he is that man.

* * *

Another challenge leaders have with feedback is when they're asked for it and aren't prepared to give it. It typically happens right after an employee completes a big project or gives a big presentation, but before the boss has had a chance to think about it. The most common response is, "Oh, you did just fine. Good job!" Of course, the best thing to do in that situation is simply ask for a little time to consider it and get back to the person. When you do get back to him, two of the lessons from the last chapter will serve you well. First, make sure you're answering the right question. Second, if you can deliver the feedback with a two-roads story, do. The following example illustrates both.

Courtney Minor is a bright young manager with an exciting future ahead of her. She had recently been promoted and was now working with a new team on an important project. The day came when she, along with her teammates, had the opportunity to present their work to the leadership team and ask for approval to advance their project to the next stage of funding. Presenting to the directors and general manager for the first time can be both intimidating and rewarding for junior managers. Either way, it was a rite of passage everyone had to go through.

The day after the big meeting, Courtney approached her director and asked for some feedback. "Did I talk enough at the meeting yesterday?" she inquired.

Her director looked puzzled at first. Then after a brief pause responded, "That's not the right question." Her eyes widened in surprise. "The question you should be asking is, 'Did I accomplish my objectives?'" Then he asked her a few questions. "Did your team's progress get presented clearly?"

"Yes," she responded.

"Did the key risks you identified get surfaced fairly?" he asked.

"Yes," she said again.

"Were you able to answer all the questions in your area?"

"Yes," she nodded.

"And did the VP approve your project?"

"Yes!" she exclaimed.

"Sounds to me like you did great!" he concluded. "Congratulations."

Courtney was pleased with that conclusion. But she wasn't done learning. Her director went on to explain why she was asking the wrong question.

"There's no shortage of bad advice floating around. One of the worst pieces I've heard is, 'If you want to be seen as a leader, you need to say something in the first three minutes of a meeting.' While I'm sure there's some legitimacy to that statement, when it's followed as a guide to meeting behavior, it generally leads to the opposite outcome. I'm sure you've seen people who practice it. They sit impatiently on the edge of their seat, desperately vying for an opportunity to get a word into the conversation. It usually results in them blurting out some inane comment that only convinces the rest of the group that '*somebody* likes to hear themselves talk.' If your concern is whether you talked enough, you're at risk of falling into the same trap. There are enough eager young MBAs in the room to fill the quota of people racing to beat the three-minute clock. You don't need to be one of them. Consider this alternative.

"When Ashwini Porwal was the director of this department, the president and all the directors were planning a trip to one of the field sales offices. In preparation, one of them wrote an e-mail to the sales team. The purpose was to introduce each member of the leadership team and share a few key insights about each one prior to the visit.

"The author wrote a paragraph for each team member, starting with the president, Bob McDonald. 'Bob likes to talk the big picture . . . don't sugarcoat the issues, just tell it like it is . . . will probably ask about pricing,' etc. A few paragraphs into the e-mail, it got to Ashwini. Instead of the full paragraph used to describe the others, all it said about him was this: 'Ashwini Porwal, research director. Doesn't say much, but when he does, you'd better listen. Bob McDonald will be.'

"Which personal equity do you want to have? You can follow the three-minute rule and perhaps be seen as an arrogant person who likes the sound of her own voice. Or, you can follow Ashwini's example and when you talk, people will shut up and listen."

Courtney felt much better about her performance in the meeting. And she had a much better mental picture of what good meeting performance looked like. Worrying about whether she talked enough was no longer part of it.

* * *

All the preceding stories are about ways to effectively *give* coaching and feedback. But this chapter wouldn't be complete without at least one story on how to *receive* feedback well. One person who learned that lesson the hard way is Gail Hollander. Gail has been in the advertising business for over 20 years, and has worked in several of the most prestigious agencies in New York. She's helped grow successful brands in several industries, and delivered some of the most recognizable ads on television today.

Gail's role through most of her advertising career has been in account management. That means she's the one who meets with the clients, understands their needs, develops a communication strategy, and explains to her creative department what kind of ads to produce for them. So the people in the creative department have the good fortune of dealing with Gail most of the time. Gail, by contrast, has to deal with as many as a dozen demanding, quirky, and sometimes challenging clients at a time.

One client she recalls was more problematic than most. No matter how good her team's ideas were, they were never good enough for him. He would yell and scream and throw his hands up in the air during their meetings. And no matter how hard she tried to explain her point of view, he never seemed to understand, let alone agree with her. She described it as being like a chimp trying to talk to a lion. Both very capable people, but they just didn't speak the same language.

He wanted Gail off the account. And since he was the paying customer, he knew he would probably get his way. All he had to do was call the director of client services at the agency. That's the person whose job it is to assign agency personnel to client teams. The ironic thing was, at this agency, the director of client services was Gail Hollander. When the call finally came in, she wasn't surprised. It was inevitable. But it was her job to listen—patiently and empathetically—to the client as he detailed his list of reasons why he wanted her off the team. And to be sure, this guy was no more tactful and gracious in his description of her performance than he was in their meetings.

In any other setting, Gail would have respectfully disagreed with his assessment of her performance, and defended her positions. But he didn't call to complain to Gail Hollander, his account manager. He called to complain to Gail Hollander, the director of client services. That's who she was as she was listening. And when she honestly and objectively assessed the situation, she had to agree that she was not a good fit for this client. She removed herself from the account and placed another person in the job.

Most of us will never have to be in that awkward position of listening to someone complain about us right to our face as if we weren't even there. But that's unfortunate. Because it also means we don't have the opportunity to listen to that feedback, objectively, as if it were directed at someone else. The lesson is this: When you receive feedback—especially negative feedback—it's easy to become defensive and emotional and blame others for your own shortcomings. When the feedback is about someone else, however, it's easier to understand, accept, and determine what kind of changes are likely to make it better the next time. Of course, it's impossible to become completely detached and unbiased when receiving feedback about yourself. But try putting yourself in Gail's situation. In those situations, think of yourself as the director of client services for the agency of you. Assess the feedback as if it were for someone else—someone you work with and have an obligation to coach and mentor. How would you advise yourself to take the feedback and use it to change for the better?

If you took every piece of feedback that way, imagine how much you could improve. And you could do it without even having to fire yourself.

SUMMARY AND EXERCISES

1. If you want to get better at something, find someone who does it exceptionally well, and watch what he or she does.

2. Celebrate your successes, even if only in small ways (e.g., becoming a Mitch-manager).

3. Feedback is one of the few gifts often unwelcomed by the recipient. You can deliver feedback to others in a way that will be better received by (a) starting with positive feedback, (b) confirming they agree there is a problem, (c) asking what they're already doing about it, (d) including an offer to help, and (e) reassuring them they're too valuable to continue on this path. See the "Mitch-manager" story to see how.

4. Sometimes your audience can't or won't see the error in their ways, no matter how well you deliver the feedback. A person can be blinded by the fact that he or she is the one being corrected. If that's the case, tell a feedback story about someone else. The listener will likely agree there is a problem. Then ask how the situation is any different for that person. The story of Nathan and King David is a good example.

5. When you're asked for feedback, make sure you're answering the right question. "Did I talk enough?" isn't a question you should answer unless your questioner is a talk-show host. Think of Courtney's big meeting.

6. Being on the receiving end of tough feedback is, well, tough. Teach your leaders how to receive feedback graciously and objectively by sharing the story of Gail firing herself.

CHAPTER 22

Demonstrate problem solving

"We cannot solve our problems with the same thinking we used when we created them."
—ALBERT EINSTEIN

TIDE HAS BEEN the number one selling brand of laundry detergent in the United States since soon after its introduction in 1946. The main reason for that is that the chemists and engineers at P&G are committed to improving the cleaning formula year after year. In the late 1990s, one of the improvements they were working on proved to be more interesting than most. According to former Chief Technology Officer Gil Cloyd, the challenge that year was a certain type of soil that was unusually difficult to get out of a common fabric. The other unusual thing about this soil was that it would often come off of one garment in the washing machine and redeposit on another garment, instead of staying suspended in the wash water.

The typical challenge in strengthening laundry detergent is this: If the formula is too weak, it won't clean the dirt, but leaves the fabric safe. If the formula is too strong, it cleans well, but could harm the fabric. The trick is finding just the right formula to combat the particular soils and stains of interest without damaging the clothes. So that's exactly the journey the development team was on.

After months of unsuccessful effort, someone asked the question, "What if that soil never got to bond on the second garment to begin with? What if we could prevent the bonding reaction in the washing machine?" Instead of trying in vain to find chemicals that could remove the

196

dirt, the team switched its efforts to finding chemicals that prevented it from redepositing on the fabric in the first place. In a relatively short time, the team had accomplished exactly that. Soon thereafter, they launched the most effective Tide detergent ever produced, continuing to earn the loyalty of consumers across the country.

The lesson is this: Sometimes the best way to solve a problem is to avoid getting in it in the first place. The next time your team has a difficult problem, share this story. Then ask, "What if . . ."

Gil's tale is a classic think-outside-the-box story. It's useful for leading people to find creative solutions because you can't just tell people to think outside the box. That's a bit like telling them they need to start loving their job, as we discussed in chapter 17. Instead, you have to draw them a bigger box. Consider the classic nine-dot problem below:

The challenge is to connect all nine dots with four straight lines (or fewer) without lifting your pencil or retracing your path. Most people attempting this problem for the first time restrict themselves to the perimeter of the nine dots. And try as they might, there is no solution in that box. The only legitimate solutions are found once you give yourself license to extend your lines outside the imaginary box you're thinking within. Once you do that, several creative solutions present themselves quickly. Two of them are below:

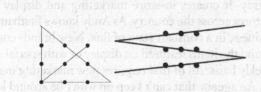

Humans need some frame of reference to think within. If you don't give them one, they'll construct one for themselves. So the way to get people to solve problems like this quicker isn't to tell them, "Think outside the box." It's to draw them a bigger box. For instance, give them the problem below and tell them to connect all nine dots with only four lines, without lifting your pencil, without retracing your path, *and keeping all your lines within the box shown.*

They will quickly come to a solution. By drawing a box around the nine dots—a box outside the box they would have naturally put themselves in—you force them to consider the space outside the smaller box. That's what outside-the-box stories do. Like the Tide story, they show people a solution space they might not have considered before. It draws them a bigger box. The Tide story, for example, can draw attention to all kinds of solutions that involve avoiding getting into a problem in the first place, when most people will naturally be searching for solutions to the problem they're already in. It certainly doesn't have to be a problem about laundry detergent, or chemistry even. It can serve that purpose for any problem.

* * *

Another way to build better problem solvers in your organization is to get them to look outside their own team, company, or even industry for solutions. Andy Murray's story illustrates that point well.

In 1997, Andy was one of the founding partners in a fledgling but rapidly growing shopper marketing agency in Springdale, Arkansas, called ThompsonMurray. It creates in-store marketing and display materials found in retail stores across the country. As Andy knows firsthand, retail is a fast-paced business, in a constant state of flux. New brands come in, old ones disappear, and the items featured on display or with special sale prices change on a weekly basis. All of that requires new marketing materials, so speed is critical. An agency that can't keep up won't be around long.

As a result, Andy was constantly on the lookout for ideas to help his company move faster without damaging quality. It turned out, some of his best ideas came from the unlikeliest of places. One of those unlikely places was the pediatrician who cared for his son—Dr. Jackson. Dr. Jackson was voted the best pediatrician in town, known for his great patient care and bedside manner. But that wasn't what impressed Andy. What impressed Andy was the fact that Dr. Jackson could have such a sterling reputation and still manage to see over 70 patients a day, at a time when most doctors would see only 40 or 50 a day.

Andy was so impressed, he asked Dr. Jackson to come visit ThompsonMurray and talk to his team about how he did it. On that visit, he learned Dr. Jackson's secret wasn't that he was willing to work more hours, and it wasn't that he cut his time with each patient shorter than other doctors. After all, you don't get voted the best doctor in town by spending less time with your patients. It turned out the secret to his success wasn't so much in the doctoring as it was in the nursing. For every 10 minutes a typical doctor spends with a patient, there are another 5 or 10 minutes she has to spend documenting the visit, writing prescriptions, and creating after-care instructions for the nursing staff. Dr. Jackson figured out a way to take those away-from-patient activities and either reduce or eliminate them, or turn them into time spent with the patient. When he arrived at each patient room, there was a folder on the door with the complete patient history, the reason for the visit, the nurse's preliminary assessment, and a Dictaphone. Dr. Jackson would perform his evaluation, consult the patient history, and determine the right course of action. Then, instead of leaving the patient and saving all the follow-up work for the end of the day, Dr. Jackson would do it right there in front of the patient. He used the Dictaphone to record the result of his evaluation, the prescription, and after-care instructions. Then he put the Dictaphone back in the folder. The nursing staff picked up the folder and Dictaphone and processed all the follow-up items while the doctor was with the next patient.

Handling all the follow-up items with the patient in the room had several benefits. First, it was more accurate than waiting until the end of the day, when his memory might be less than perfect. Second, it was faster. He dictated everything instead of writing it all out by hand. It was also faster because he didn't have to go back to his notes to remind himself of the facts and conclusions. Third, and most importantly, those three or four minutes were spent with the patient, instead of alone in a private office or with the nurses. The patients could hear exactly what the doctor was ordering for a prescription and after care, and could ask questions if they didn't understand. Instead of feeling like their time had been wasted, patients appreciated the opportunity to see and hear the typically behind-the-scenes work that went into their care. When dealing with personal health, it turns out patients value transparency more than time.

Andy took Dr. Jackson's process with patients and applied it to the shopper marketing business he was in. His team created job folders for each client assignment. Everything relevant was in there. As the project advanced from original consultation with Andy, to the shopper research department, to the creative department, to production of mockups and final materials, the folder went with the job. When the creative department got the folder for client A, they knew they could start work right away. They didn't have to wonder if the creative brief, or the brand images, or the shopper research was finished and ready to go. If any of it wasn't ready, they wouldn't have received the folder yet. This resulted in fewer restarts, faster turnaround, and more happy clients.

Andy learned something else from this experience. If you have a problem to solve, look outside your own industry for inspiration to solve it. Find an industry that has already solved that problem and use its solution to inspire your own creative answer. If you have a problem with speed, study how emergency ambulance service works, or visit the fire department or a NASCAR pit crew.

Andy solved the problem of speed at ThompsonMurray with a little help from his pediatrician. It became one of the competitive advantages that helped the firm continue its rapid growth. In 2004, global advertising giant Saatchi & Saatchi acquired ThompsonMurray and it became known as Saatchi & Saatchi-X. Today, it's one of the largest shopper marketing agencies in the world. It's also one of the most creative agencies in the world, largely because its employees are still willing to learn from the most unlikely of sources.

If you want your teams looking for solutions outside the four walls of their department, share Andy's story with them and see what happens.

* * *

Another barrier people run into with problems is that they can seem so complicated, it's difficult to know where to begin. That often means they don't begin at all, diverting their attention to less daunting tasks. As the leader, it's your job to remove that barrier and get them started. In situations like that, I find stories like this next one helpful. It comes from Margaret Parkin in her book *Tales for Trainers*, when she describes a personal experience she had at home in London.[1]

Margaret decided to knit herself a sweater with a sunflower on it. When she asked for some wool, her mother directed her to an old cloth bag under the stairs. That's where she kept the remaining yarn from old sweaters, scarves, and cardigans she'd worked on over the years. When Margaret opened the bag, all she found was a mess.

"It's hopeless!" she wailed to her mother. "All the wool is tangled up together. I can't possibly knit a sweater with that. How could I even start to untangle it all?"

"It's easier than you think," her mother replied. "All you do is look for the easiest knot. When you undo that, the next knot will be easier, too. Just keep going until all the wool is unraveled."

She did as her mother instructed and started to undo the first knot, then the second, and the third. Sooner than she imagined, the ball of wool started to loosen and different colors started to emerge. First she started working the red wool. Then she worked the yellow; then the green, and the gray. Very soon, instead of a huge knot, she had a number of neat balls of different colored wool in front of her. As she started to knit, the pattern began to form—a big, beautiful sunflower in the middle of her perfectly fitting sweater.

"Who would have thought," Margaret asked, "that such a beautiful sweater was hiding in that old bag of knotted wool?"

"But it was there all the time," her mother replied. "You just didn't know where to look."

The moral of the story is that people get overwhelmed when their problems get all knotted up together. It helps if we can begin to see each one as a separate issue and work on one problem at a time. Divide the work up into smaller chunks and work on one piece at a time. Once it's resolved, move on to the next.

* * *

All of these stories are designed to help your organization solve even the most difficult problems. But there is one kind of problem they won't help you solve—a problem you don't know you have. Before you can solve problems, you have to identify them. The last lesson in this chapter is about how to find problems in the first place. The next story illustrates one simple but highly effective way to do that. It comes from David Armstrong's book *How to Turn Your Company's Parables into Profit.*[2]

Sometime in the 1960s, the Everlasting Valve Corporation in New Jersey hired a new salesman. A few weeks into his training, he decided he was ready to visit customers, but not on a sales call. He wanted to see how they installed their Everlasting boiler valves, how they received them, serviced them, and inventoried them. He reasoned that if he understood how they used what he sold them, he would be better able to meet their needs in the future. So he arranged a visit at several customer facilities.

Arriving at the first one, his contact met him and they began their tour. When they reached the factory floor, he noticed a crane lifting a wooden box slowly into the air. Suddenly, the box fell to the ground with an enormous crash! The salesman yelled, "Look out!" and turned away as wooden splinters flew everywhere and the contents of the crate came to a rest on the cement floor.

"Is everyone okay?" the salesman asked.

His tour guide smiled and reassured him, "Everyone is fine. We do that on purpose. That shipping crate is so well built that it's easier to open by dropping it on the floor. It takes a lot less time than trying to pry open every plank."

The salesman looked down and saw the name on one of the broken wooden boards. It read, "Everlasting Valve Corporation."

The previous story is true, and is a classic example of what product designers call a *compensating behavior*. When your customers use your product in a way other than what you expect or intend, that's a compensating behavior. And it is a clear sign of a problem with your product. Everlasting Valve was spending about 10 percent of its sales on those sturdy wooden crates. Once this salesman realized they were too strong, the company replaced them with simple, inexpensive skids. That saved his company thousands of dollars in costs and spared his customers the time, hassle, and safety risk of opening them.

Have you ever used a hacksaw to open the plastic packaging around a small electronic toy? Ever added an ingredient to the cake mix not called for on the box? Ever placed a strip of black electrical tape over the flashing "12:00" light on your DVD player? Those are all compensating behaviors, and great indications that the product or packaging leaves something to be desired. Observing your customers using your product—the way the Everlasting Valve salesman did—is the best way to find compensating behaviors. If the only information you have on your customers is through impersonal online surveys or focus group interviews in a hotel conference room, you probably don't know what their compensating behaviors are. Get out of the office and visit your customers where they use your product, whether it's in a place of business or in their homes. You might not be lucky enough for someone to drop a crate at your feet. But if you watch carefully, you might find a compensating behavior just as telling.

SUMMARY AND EXERCISES

1. You can't just tell people to "think outside the box." You have to draw them a bigger box. Like the solution to the classic nine-dot problem, telling "outside-the-box" stories draws people a bigger box and forces them to think outside the confines they would naturally set.

2. Sometimes the best way to solve a problem is to avoid getting in it in the first place. The next time your team has a difficult problem, share the Tide story and ask, "What if . . . ."

3. Often the most productive places to look for outside-the-box solutions are outside your industry. Like Andy Murray, find an industry that's already solved a problem similar to yours, and learn from it. Share Andy's story with your team. Then send team members on a hunt for solutions (e.g., doctor with a Dictaphone).

4. Some problems appear so complicated and daunting that your team doesn't know where to start. Sharing Margaret Parkin's "ball of wool" story can inspire people to bite off small chunks of the problem at a time.

5. The most damaging problem is the one you don't know you have. Compensating behaviors are what customers do when your product or service isn't meeting their needs. As the Everlasting Valve salesman learned, finding compensating behaviors is a great way to find problems, and solutions. Share that story with your team. Then have them visit your customers and look for compensating behaviors.

Notes

1. Margaret Parkin, *Tales for Trainers: Using Stories and Metaphors to Facilitate Learning* (London: Kogan Page, 1998), pp. 129–130. Used with permission.

2. David Armstrong, *How to Turn Your Company's Parables into Profit* (Stuart, FL: Armstrong International, 1995), pp. 208–209. Used with permission.

CHAPTER 23

Help everyone understand the customer

"Storytelling has proven a powerful tool. It's removed the language barrier between the science of research and the language of business."[1]
—CHRISTOPHER J. FRANK, Microsoft researcher

IN 1993, ROHINI MIGLANI was a new brand manager for Whisper Feminine Pads in India. She was on her first of three sweltering days conducting in-home research with consumers in the southern Indian city of Chennai. Armed with a list of 15 names and addresses of middle- and lower-income women who had agreed to be interviewed, she was hoping to understand what had compelled them to recently depart from using simple cloth pads during their menstrual period and instead spend significantly more on Whisper. Rohini tells the story from here.

The day so far had been a disaster, with the morning completely taken up with wrong addresses, not-at-homes, and incomprehensible translation. After about six phone calls to the field agency, I was hoping for my first productive encounter with a consumer. I arrived on a dusty road in a distant, lower-middle-class suburb, hoping I could concentrate enough to block out my aching feet and the soaring mercury.

As if on cue, as I entered this particular consumer's home, the sluggishly whirling table fan shuddered to a stop, victim to an unscheduled brownout. The woman smiled apologetically and gestured me to sit on one of two metal folding chairs by the front door. I collapsed gratefully onto it.

As I slowly sipped from the metal tumbler of water she gave me, I took in my surroundings: a poorly lit dwelling of two small rooms with a kitchen alcove inadequately concealed by a curtain. Apart from the chairs we were sitting on, there was one other wooden chair and a metal table by way of furniture, and no TV or refrigerator. She turned off the radio when we began to talk. I noticed a jar of plastic flowers in the windowsill; on the wall, a garishly colored calendar with a picture of Lakshmi, the Hindu goddess of wealth. Behind the door, on two nails, hung a man's shirt, trousers, and a blue-checked linen towel. And on the table under the window, precisely stacked, were a pile of school exercise books, primly covered in the regulation brown paper.

The woman herself was serious in outlook, older than her years. Tiredness marked her in the droop of her limp sari, and the smudges under her eyes. I was intensely conscious that I was interrupting her quiet time of the day, when her children were away at school and her husband was at work. Why should she bother to talk to me, I wondered, as I made notes. I had nothing to offer her, except to be as good a listener as I could. Early on in the discussion, it became clear that she was not using Whisper herself. She was buying it for her eighth-grade daughter, who had earlier been using cloth. I asked her why she had started spending on Whisper if her daughter had already become used to cloth.

"It's because she has to go to school, you see," she replied.

"Well, what did your daughter used to do about school when she was using cloth?"

"She would go, all right, but she just felt uncomfortable . . . couldn't concentrate. With Whisper, she doesn't feel the wetness, so she feels more comfortable. And she doesn't have to worry about staining."

"But don't you think that Whisper is very expensive for you, just to give a comfortable feeling to your daughter once in a while?" I asked.

"Yes, it is expensive, but then she needs to be able to concentrate in school, to get good marks."

"Why is that important? After all, presumably you will want to get her married after school, so why are good marks important?" I pursued.

"I want her to study further after school. I don't want her to get married too early."

"But you yourself got married at the age of 16. What's wrong with that?"

She leaned forward and looked me in my eyes as she explained, her tiredness gone: "I don't want my daughter to be like me. I want my daughter to be financially independent; to be able to feel comfortable in the outside world. Whether she marries or not will be up to her. She has to study, get good marks, and go to college and then get a job. I don't want her to have two kids by the age of 20. I live my life through my children; I don't have many aspirations for my own life now. But my daughter must be different from me. And that's why Whisper makes sense to me."

No doubt when Rohini and the research team returned to the office, they wrote a proper, clinical summary of their conclusions and observations. It surely contained all the expected details, describing "the consumer" they met as an amalgam of the dozen women interviewed during the week. But the most effective vehicle she left for helping others understand the consumer was the intimate portrait contained in her personal meeting with one woman. It's been circulating for almost two decades now, and helps new Whisper employees understand their consumer to this day. The formal summary probably hasn't been seen in 15 years.

As observed by spy novelist John Le Carré, "A desk is a dangerous place from which to view the world." If the only customer information used in your organization resides in dry PowerPoint presentations and in reams of statistical data, the people you work with probably don't understand your customer any more than you understand your own medical charts. As advised at the end of the last chapter, get out of the office and meet your customer face-to-face. When you get back, write a story about your experience.

* * *

Don't be intimidated by the length of Rohini's story. As we've seen several times, stories don't have to be long to be effective. Jim Bangel (the corporate storyteller from chapter 1) still recalls a consumer interview in 1985 that made a deep impression on him. He was working on a brand of shortening and was talking to a woman about the differences between using shortening and using lard. She told him, "I know shortening is a lot healthier than lard. But it's better for my kids to buy lard."

That didn't make any sense to Jim. If shortening is healthier, how can it be better for her kids to buy lard? The woman explained, "If I buy shortening, I can't afford to buy milk. Lard and milk is healthier than shortening and water. So I buy lard . . . and milk."

The light went on in Jim's head. It was the first time he really understood at a gut level the trade-offs a mother on a tight budget had to make. Repeating his story ensured others on his team understood just as well.

That story is only nine sentences long. But it's powerful enough to change hearts and minds. Your customer stories don't need to be any longer.

* * *

The assumption so far in this book is that your stories are delivered either orally or in writing. But those aren't the only media fit for business stories. Some of the most powerful stories I've heard have been on video. The flexible work arrangements stories in chapter 8 came from a video on the company website. The one that follows was produced for a major U.S. retailer to help its employees understand their customer better.

The scene opens with an actress, portraying a shopper, speaking into the camera: "You know, they could make my life a whole lot easier if they'd just rearrange their store a little. Don't get me wrong, I love that store. But it's almost impossible to shop unless you have at least a couple of hours. Like the other day. I had a list of stuff I had to get—nothing major. So I ran by after I picked the kids up from school. We only had 30 minutes to shop, because my oldest son, John, was at soccer practice, and I had to pick him up. But I told the kids, if they were patient, we'd get stuff to make ice cream sundaes. They love ice cream sundaes!

"We had just pulled into the parking lot when my husband, Bill, called. He wasn't feeling well, and wanted me to pick up cold and headache medicine that would help him sleep. We got into the store, and it was packed, as usual. I started shopping on the grocery side of the store, because all the food is together. Well, almost all the food. I remembered the ice cream for the kids. But the dog food—I couldn't find the dog food anywhere! I kept checking the signs, but didn't see dog food. So I looked down the main aisle that's filled with all that stuff. I mean, seriously, there are so many displays down there I can't see what's in the aisles behind them. And they never have the brands I buy anyway. So I wasted five minutes just looking for dog food. And of course, I found it all the way on the other side of the store! I got the dog food, and I realized I wasn't even halfway done with my list.

"Then I remembered Bill's medicine. So I went over to the pharmacy. I knew I was in the right area, but I couldn't find the brand he likes. I mean, should it be with the pain relievers? Or maybe the cold medicine? Or could it be with the sleeping pills? I finally asked someone who works there for help, and he told me to look where I'd already been looking. Anyway, I finally found it, put it in the cart, and looked at my watch. I have 10 minutes left, and half of my list to go. I realized I could pick up the rest of my stuff from the drug store on the way home from the soccer field. Or I could get it tomorrow at another store that has a really nice dress I've wanted to get for Sarah.

"The checkout lines were full. We got in line and finally made it to the front. The cashier was almost done, when she scanned one final thing—the ice cream. Then it dawned on me. I forgot all the sundae stuff! The kids are going to kill me! I looked at the line behind me thinking I might have time to go back to get the whipped cream, cherries, and chocolate syrup. But it would just take too long to find everything. I checked my watch and realized there was just no time left. We have got to leave right now or we'll be late to get John from soccer practice."

In this short vignette, Mom is obviously disappointed in herself because she knows she'll be disappointing her kids. But she's also mad at the store for making it so hard to get her shopping done. She finishes her story, "We're almost to the car, when my daughter Sarah said, 'Don't forget, Mom. You promised we could make ice cream sundaes when we get home!'"

Mom shakes her head in remorse. The scene cuts to a still shot of a failed ice cream sundae attempt—a cup of plain vanilla ice cream—overlooked by a set of disappointed children's faces.

Fade to black.

The story you just read is the dialogue of a video created by Saatchi & Saatchi-X, the shopper marketing agency you learned about in chapter 22. Saatchi created the video to help illustrate the frustration customers have shopping a major U.S. retailer. None of the problems encountered by the shopper in the video were news to the client: the difficulty finding particular brands on the shelf, or the fact that the most popular departments are spread out all over the store, or the dozens of full-pallet displays of unfamiliar products that make walking the aisles like running an obstacle course. All of those frustrations were identified in countless research reports. So why the story and the video? Because senior leadership wasn't compelled by a bunch of statistics in a research report. But one woman's story—constructed to represent a typical experience from the hundreds of frustrated shoppers interviewed for the research—was much more successful.

A few months after this video circulated company headquarters, this retailer launched a national effort to test completely redesigned stores to address all of the issues identified in the video, and more. The statistics and research reports didn't change anyone's mind. This creative video story succeeded where the underlying logic failed.

SUMMARY AND EXERCISES

1. Get out from behind your desk and visit your customers. Take as many of your team members with you as you can. When you're done, write a story about the most insightful visit. Reports, charts, and memos are fine to share a dry, statistical profile. But a well-crafted story will create the intimate and personal understanding you want your whole organization to have. ("I don't want my daughter to be like me.")

2. Have an eye-opening moment with a consumer of your product recently? Write the story, even if it's only a few sentences long. Share your ah-ha moment with others. An example is the choice between shortening and milk.

3. Create a video that portrays a day in the life of your typical customer, or their interaction with your product or service, like Saatchi & Saatchi-X did. It's guaranteed to get played over and over again. Your research memo will still be stuck in a dusty file drawer. ("You promised ice cream sundaes!")

Note

1. Lori Silverman, *Wake Me Up When the Data Is Over* (San Francisco: Jossey-Bass, 2006), p. 187.

CHAPTER **24**

Metaphors and analogies

"If a picture is worth a thousand words, then a metaphor is worth a thousand pictures."

—GEORGE LAKOFF AND MARK JOHNSON, *Metaphors We Live By*

WHEN MY 10-YEAR-OLD SON, Matthew, came home from his first day of fifth grade, he announced, "I'm going to learn to play the euphonium!"

"That's great!" I said with the genuine excitement of a proud parent. Then I sheepishly added, "Uh, what's a euphonium?"

Very matter-of-factly, he responded, "It's like a small tuba that makes higher notes."

All I had left to say was, "Well I can't wait to hear you play!" I had no further questions about the instrument. Despite never having heard of a euphonium, I now knew exactly what it looked like, how it worked, how he would hold it, and how it sounded. I knew all that because I already knew what a tuba was. So it was easy to picture an instrument somewhat smaller and making higher notes.

Imagine, instead, if my son had answered my question by giving me the dictionary definition of a euphonium: "A musical instrument in the brass family with three valves, a conical bore, an upward-pointing bell, a cup-shaped mouthpiece projecting at a right angle, and that produces tenor tones." Granted, that's a very precise and accurate description. And if I were to ask him to repeat it two or three times slowly, I could probably get a rough image in my head of what it might look like and sound like. But that image wouldn't be nearly as accurate as the one I formed immediately after he gave me the tuba metaphor. And it would have taken a lot more time and mental energy to construct.

210

Why did the metaphor provide a more accurate and efficient description? Because most of the details of what a euphonium is already existed in my mind. Details like the upward-pointing bell, the cup-shaped mouthpiece, and brass family were already there. They were just attached in my brain to the word *tuba*. All my son had to do was help me access them and alter them slightly (smaller with higher notes). That's how metaphors work. They use words or phrases that already have entire stories attached to them inside our brain. In fact, a story is often defined as an extended metaphor, which is why metaphors deserve a place in a book on storytelling. You can use them to either improve your stories or replace your stories entirely by telling the whole story with a single metaphor. A great metaphor also serves as a catalyst to start conversations among employees, so many sets of stories can grow and surround the idea embodied in your metaphor.

Unfortunately, business leaders are often hesitant to use metaphors at work. Some think it will make them sound pedestrian instead of sophisticated and professional. It won't. You'll see several examples in this chapter to prove that point. Others are under the misperception that using metaphors is less precise than using more formal definitions and descriptions. Judge for yourself. Did you have a more accurate understanding of a euphonium after hearing the tuba metaphor or the dictionary definition? The tuba metaphor, right? Me too. It seems my son was wiser in this case than most adults.

* * *

You've already seen several examples of metaphors used in business stories in this book. In chapter 5 you saw how Scott Ford used the yellow cab metaphor at Alltel to make a highly effective recommendation. In chapter 15, Delaine Hampton used the metaphor of pioneers and settlers to keep her team inspired. In chapter 16, the metaphor of the shrinking giant representing fear helps people build courage. And in chapter 2, the entire story of the bricklayers building a cathedral was a metaphor for you understanding how your role fits into the organization's objectives.

This chapter will show you more effective ways to use metaphors at work. You'll also learn two methods to come up with just the right metaphor. Let's start by looking at a few more great examples of metaphors in business, starting with the happiest place on earth.

At most companies, employees are referred to simply as *employees*. At other companies, like Walmart, they're called *associates*. At Disney World, however, they're called *cast members*. And that's not just for the woman playing Cinderella, or the guy in the Goofy costume. All of the people working at Disney World are called cast members, even if they sell tickets, take pictures, or sweep the streets.

They do this because Disney isn't really selling a product. It's selling an experience. Every person working at the park can and does have an impact on the experience its guests have. It's a powerful metaphor because it helps people working there to understand how to behave in just about any situation without having to be uniquely trained for each possibility.

Let's see how that might play out. Imagine that you're the person who serves ice cream in a soda shop at Disney World. Little Johnny comes in, and his parents buy him an ice cream cone. You give Johnny his ice cream and as he turns around to leave, he accidentally drops it, spilling his ice cream all over the floor. He bursts into tears. Quick, what do you do?

You get him another one, of course! Do you make Johnny wait in line again? No. Do you make Johnny's parents pay for the second ice cream cone? No. Why not? Because that would ruin the experience. In fact, a bad experience is happening right now before your very eyes! And you, the ice cream dispenser, are the only person in the park who can fix it. Not Peter Pan. Not the Little Mermaid. Not even Mickey Mouse. You. You are the star of this show.

Did your boss have to tell you to get Johnny another ice cream cone? Did she have to tell you to not make Johnny wait in line, or to not charge his parents again? No. You knew what to do because you are a Disney cast member.

Now, imagine the same situation, but this time you're an "employee" at a fast-food restaurant. Little Johnny comes in and buys an ice cream cone. He turns to leave and spills it on the floor. What do you do? You probably won't do anything, since you're back behind the counter where you're supposed to be. You might think to yourself, "Gee, tough luck, kid," as Johnny and his parents get back in line to buy another ice cream cone.

And who's going to clean up that mess anyway? The guy in charge of cleaning up the floors, that's who! That's not your job. This problem is out of your hands. You're just an employee, and your job is dispensing ice cream and collecting money. That's it. Not cleaning floors, and certainly not managing little Johnny's so-called experience.

The "cast member" analogy is a powerful tool Disney uses to manage customer experience. Every time it's used, it reinforces that profound message: "Please complete the application to become a Disney cast member"; "Congratulations! You're now a Disney cast member"; "*All cast members, please report for duty. It's opening time, and the show is about to begin!*"

* * *

Consider these more recent examples from Procter & Gamble. Early in his tenure as CEO, A. G. Lafley used two simple metaphors to change the direction and focus of the entire company.

After a century and a half of developing and marketing some of the most ubiquitous consumer products in the world, it would be easy for an organization to think it knows just about all there is to know about consumers. It's also easy to get caught up in your own marketing and product development. Marketers at P&G were spending loads of time talking to themselves and their advertising agencies developing marketing campaigns. Engineers were spending even more time locked up in the lab developing the next great improvement, perhaps without enough regard for whether the consumer even wanted that improvement, or was willing to pay the extra cost to get it.

In several companywide speeches and memos, Mr. Lafley used three simple words to refocus the entire organization: "Consumer is boss." That short metaphor said so much with so little because everyone already knows what it means to be the boss. The boss is who tells you what to do, tells you if you've done a good job or not, and can fire you if you don't. He could have used the words "focus on consumers" instead. That directive is very clear. But it lacks the depth of meaning that the "consumer is boss" metaphor carries. We could "focus" on consumers the way a high school science class might focus on an army of ants to study them. But that's very different from the respectful attention one pays to the boss.

Just like the "cast member" metaphor used by Disney, the "consumer is boss" metaphor helped all 127,000 employees understand what to do without having to check with their manager. What they needed to do was check with "the boss," the consumer.

The second metaphor Mr. Lafley used was born out of his realization that the company's consumer research focused almost exclusively on what consumers think about products when they're at home using them. That's the point when they're forming an opinion about how well it worked versus their expectations, and whether they'll buy it next time. Mr. Lafley knew that was a critical moment for P&G—a moment of truth.[1] All the product development had been done and the advertising aired. With product in hand, the consumer would either like it or not.

But it wasn't the first such moment. And Mr. Lafley knew it. Before the consumer has the opportunity to try the product, she first has to buy the product. And that decision happens in the grocery store, when she's standing in front of the shelf. That's the first moment of truth. It was Mr. Lafley's belief that P&G was spending too much time researching the second moment of truth, the at-home moment when she's using the product, and not enough time researching the first moment of truth, at the store shelf.

He began to talk about the "first moment of truth," or FMOT, as it's referred to now. He asked business unit leaders how they were doing at the first moment of truth. Was their package noticeable? Did they have the right place on the shelf? The metaphor worked because everyone knew what a "moment of truth" was. It's that instant in time when a critical decision is made that will determine the ultimate success or failure of something important. Those three words raised the importance of our brands' retail presence up to, and even beyond, the importance of the at-home usage experience.

Again, he could have used other words, like "decision point at shelf" (DPAS). That would be just as transparent. But the metaphor "first moment of truth" adds so much more meaning without adding any more words.

As one example of the impact this had on the organization, prior to this, most of the packaging research at P&G was done by placing a new package prototype in the middle of a conference room table and asking consumers to react to it. But because of the company's new focus on FMOT, most package testing today is done on a real (or virtual) shelf, in context, alongside all the other packages. It's one thing to have a pretty package when it's all by itself on a table. But that same pretty package could be lost in a sea of me-too-looking products at the first moment of truth.

* * *

Do you have to be excessively creative, lucky, or have a degree in English lit to come up with great metaphors? Fortunately, no. Metaphors are so powerful in helping understand and explain human thoughts, emotions, and behaviors that consumer researchers developed techniques to generate them quickly and easily. The most popular of these methods was developed in the 1990s by Harvard researcher Gerald Zaltman, which he called the Zaltman Metaphor Elicitation Technique (ZMET).

In the most basic form, it works like this. Put a few people around a table covered with magazines: *Good Housekeeping, Popular Mechanics, Bride, Outdoor Living, People,* you name it. Ask the participants to think about the product or service your company sells. Then ask them to cut out pictures from the magazines that represent, for example, how your product or service makes them feel, and make a collage with them. Each participant explains to the group why he or she chose those pictures, and the researchers snap a digital picture of each collage. Presto! Dozens of metaphors and images straight from the minds of your chosen audience.

The collages can be amazingly creative, powerful, provocative, emotional, and telling. In one such exercise, I asked a group of women to create a collage that illustrated how they feel when they shop on a Saturday. The purpose of the exercise was to look for ways to improve the shopping experience on the most crowded shopping day. Collecting all the pictures that represented a bad experience, we found pictures of children throwing temper tantrums, people pulling their hair out, people screaming at the top of their lungs, cars in traffic jams, crowded football stadiums, even a pressure cooker blowing out its steam—all great metaphors for the frustration of a Saturday shopping trip. The subject of the metaphor, of course, can be anything you want: your brilliant new product idea, the vision statement you just wrote, or the solution you just proposed to your department's biggest challenge.

Another technique for generating metaphors is to simply ask for them. Here's how that might work. Let's say you're testing a new computer system at your company. It's supposed to help employees do their jobs faster. But it's rumored to be temperamental and prone to crashing. So your employees are apprehensive. The department that piloted the new software confirmed both that it was much faster and that the rumors about its reliability problems were true. But it found that with regular maintenance, almost all of those problems could be avoided.

To convince the rest of the company to adopt the new software without causing a revolt, you need them to easily understand the benefits and allay their fears of constant breakdowns. Yes, training classes will help, as will sharing the positive results of the pilot. But you need a short, simple way to win the support of the apprehensive masses. You ask some of the pilot department employees to answer this question: "If our old computer system were a car, what make and model of car would it be? Then answer the same question for the new system you tested." You ask other employees to describe each computer system as an animal; others, as a famous rock band.

The results? The old system is described as a 15-year-old Honda. The new one, a brand new Porsche 911. The old one is a bassett hound. The new one, a thoroughbred race horse. The old one is the Beatles. The new one is Metallica.

You like the car metaphor best. So in your memos and discussions with employees, you talk about trading in the 15-year-old Honda, and upgrading to the Porsche 911. "The good news," you tell everyone, "is that we bought a full-service maintenance plan for the Porsche. Every Saturday afternoon, it will go in for one hour of maintenance. When each of you comes to work on Monday morning, your new race car will be ready to go."

The technicalities and specifications of a computer system might as well be Greek to most people. Having your IT manager explain it to them will do little to win them over. Your simple metaphor can. And as with the first method, this one can be used with just about anything.

SUMMARY AND EXERCISES

1. Analogies and metaphors can have the same effect as a full story because they already have stories associated with them embedded in the mind of the audience. They can be used to turn a good story into a great story, or in place of a story altogether.

    a. Examples: the yellow cab in chapter 5; pioneers and settlers in chapter 15; the giant named fear in chapter 16; building a cathedral in chapter 2; and Disney's cast members, consumer is boss, and first moment of truth in this chapter.

2. To find appropriate metaphors, try these two methods:

    a. Use the magazine collage exercise.

    b. Ask for them! "If our old computer system were a car, what make and model would it be?"

Note

1. Mr. Lafley got the idea for defining key "moments of truth" from the book *Moments of Truth*, by Jan Carlzon (New York: Ballinger, 1987).

CHAPTER **25**

Delegate authority and give permission

"Never tell people how to do things. Tell them what to do and they will surprise you with their ingenuity."
—GENERAL GEORGE S. PATTON JR.

IN THE MID-1970S, Orville Sweet was CEO of the American Polled Hereford Association. As any CEO will tell you, one of his or her unenviable tasks is having to fire a close friend and colleague. Such was the case for Orville that year. For our purposes, details of the firing aren't nearly as important as what happened a few days after.

Orville got a distressing call from the wife of the man he'd let go. Apparently, he wasn't coping very well. In fact, she was concerned he was suicidal. Orville asked her to put him on the phone. The man admitted to Orville he was having a hard time, but claimed he'd pull it together. Orville could hear the stress in his voice. He knew both the man and his wife well enough to understand the gravity of the situation. Instinctively, Orville made a suggestion that surprised the man (and perhaps himself), "Well, why don't you come back?"

"Really? You're hiring me back?"

"Sure," Orville reassured him. "We haven't filled the position, and your office is still empty."

"Well, of course I will! Thanks, Orville. I'll be there first thing in the morning."

217

His return, of course, confused the others in the office. But out of respect, Orville told them only that he was coming back to his old job. He gave them no explanation, and no information about his emotional state or the suicidal suspicion his wife was harboring.

After three or four uneventful weeks, the man came to see Orville in his office. "Orville, I really want to thank you for letting me come back. I guess I really wasn't ready to go. Or maybe I just wanted to leave on my own terms. Either way, I'm ready now. I'll have my office cleared out by this afternoon." He shook Orville's hand, and walked out. True to his word, he packed up his things, and left the office for the second time—but this time with his head held high. Whatever reasons had led to him losing his job were certainly still valid. He knew that. The extra time Orville afforded him simply allowed him to accept it.

Orville's decision to bring a terminated employee back to the office must violate the good senses of every professional human resources manager today, and probably in the 1970s as well. Conventional wisdom would suggest keeping someone like that as far away from the office as possible. Or a compassionate boss might send him to counseling, but at least alert corporate security in case something happened.

Is it possible those more orthodox reactions could have worked out just as well? Perhaps. But what's certain is that Orville's unconventional solution saved the man's dignity, and quite possibly his life.

Orville's story circulated among his colleagues. To some it offered an interesting alternative for handling a tricky personnel issue. To others it was just a heartwarming story. But to Rodger Wasson, it meant much more.

Rodger was the executive vice president of the Indiana Beef Cattle Association at the time. He came to know Orville years later when they both worked at the National Pork Producers Council. Rodger and Orville were both recruited to interview for the CEO position at the Pork Council. Orville got the job. But in another unconventional move, he immediately offered a top position to Rodger and every other finalist who had interviewed for the CEO spot! What better way to quickly identify top talent for his leadership team? Rodger Wasson was the only one who accepted the offer.

So Rodger knew there was an unusual brilliance to Orville Sweet. When he heard Orville's firing and rehiring story, he knew there must be an underlying wisdom to it. And he found it. Ever since Rodger began his working career, he studied everything he could about management. He read all the great leadership books. He took all the right courses. He knew the "right answer" to just about every management challenge.

What Orville's story gave Rodger was permission to ignore all that. It gave him permission to follow his instincts—to do something unconventional when the situation warranted. It was a lesson he never forgot, and he put it to use on many occasions over the course of his career. Today he shares that story with others when he can tell they're wrestling between doing things by the book and doing what they believe in their heart is right.

In his book *Sources of Power*,[1] author Gary Klein refers to this kind of narrative as a "permission story." It gives the listener permission to behave a certain way, without explicitly listing out the acceptable behavior. Similar to the "two-roads" stories in chapter 20, a permission story lets listeners choose their behavior without telling them what to do. This one can be used exactly the way Rodger Wasson uses it—to help someone understand it's okay to trust your judgment instead of always following conventional wisdom.

* * *

The Orville Sweet story described how Orville had done something right in the way he handled his ex-employee's reaction to being fired. It showed Orville doing something unconventional, and the results turning out positive. It's a success story. Compare that to my million-dollar mistake in chapter 20. That story gives the listener permission to say "no" to the boss in order to avoid making a mistake they will both regret later. That's clearly a failure story. Permission stories can be of either variety. The final permission story below shows a third alternative. In its case, there's neither a success nor a failure. But it's every bit as effective.[2]

Early in her career at Eastman Kodak, Katherine Hudson had occasion to visit an important customer in Kyoto at the beginning of the Japanese economic crisis. This customer's father had worked very hard to build a successful family business from scratch. Over the years, they developed a strong and loyal relationship with Kodak.

At this particular meeting, Katherine was surprised when the customer handed her an order for an extremely expensive piece of equipment. "Given the difficult economic conditions in your country, are you sure you want to make this large investment now?" she asked.

He pointed to a large bamboo plant in his office and explained, "See how it grows? It has long spurts of growth and then stops for a while. It's during the times of slower growth that the bamboo plant builds the strong rings that serve as the foundation for its next growth spurt. Similarly for our business, it's wise to make whatever investments we need to ready our organization for the future."

Katherine never forgot that meeting, even after moving to the Brady Corporation as its CEO in 1994. She recounted the story often, especially when working with people struggling over making a necessary expenditure during tough economic times—times they now refer to as "the bamboo years."

Katherine's permission story relies on neither a success nor a failure. The power in it comes from the inherent wisdom in the bamboo tree metaphor. If you find yourself in a situation to give this advice, you could simply tell your listeners about bamboo tree rings. Even if they make the mental leap and understand the metaphor, it wouldn't be nearly as convincing as when the metaphor is couched in the context of a story. The story shows how at least three companies have relied on the wisdom contained in that metaphor, presumably with good business results—the Japanese company it came from; Eastman Kodak; and Brady Corporation, where Katherine later worked as CEO. That adds credibility to the advice, and makes it more likely the listener will follow it.

* * *

Now let's turn from permission to delegation. In a small company, with only a handful of employees, all the decisions might be made by one person—the owner. In larger companies that's not possible. They have to assign the authority to make different decisions to various leaders in the organization. Many even have a formal "Delegation of Authority" document that spells out exactly what decisions can be made by various levels of management. The next two stories illustrate the value of delegating that authority to the right level. In this first example, it shows the ramifications of getting it wrong.

Phil Renshaw is the London-based financial executive coach you met in chapter 12. Through his own personal work experience, and that of his clients, he's seen a lot of well-intentioned ideas do more harm than good. Failing to delegate responsibility and hold people accountable is one of the most common. He cites an example at a multibillion-dollar company he's dealt with in the past. It started innocently enough. Sometime during the year, senior management started believing that the individual sales managers weren't going to hit their targets. In an attempt to help, they arrange weekly calls with them to get updates and petition for ideas to do better. Of course, the managers able to come up with new sales leads in these calls are heralded by the executives. The executives, in turn, see direct evidence that their intervention is working. Thus, both the sales managers and executives have a positive feedback mechanism that encourages them to continue this practice. Soon the practice is repeated on an annual or quarterly basis, even when business is fine.

What do you think the smart sales managers do in preparation for this little game? They sandbag their forecast and hold out a few good ideas to deliver in the intervention meeting they know will happen. The result is that the executives think they are helping, when in fact all they're doing is creating unnecessary work. Worse, they're disempowering their sales leaders by usurping their delegated authority to deliver their own sales numbers. Taking back responsibility and accountability once delegated seldom results in a positive outcome. Don't fall into the same trap. Once you delegate authority, think long and hard before you take it back.

* * *

So how does it make your employees feel when you delegate authority properly? It feels great! Just ask Mike Tafuri.

In 1987, Mike was director of research and development for Olean, a brand of fat substitute that promised what seemed like a miracle. It added no fat, cholesterol, or calories to foods prepared with it. Of course, at the time the only people in the world who knew about that firsthand were Mike and the other engineers in the Olean lab. It was still years from being ready for market. For Mike, the single biggest challenge was manufacturing cost. His job was to figure out how to cut costs by 80 percent, or it would never get to market. They needed to do something amazing.

His team came up with a brilliant solution. Instead of making Olean in a batch process (cooking up one enormous pot at a time), what if they could make it in a continuous process, like a Detroit assembly line? With some effort and creativity, they actually made it work in the lab on a small scale. To work at full scale, however, they would need to do the same thing at 2,400 times more capacity.

Mike's boss, Peter Morris, reviewed the plan and said it looked like a real risk. "What makes you think we could scale this up to that level, Mike?" Mike told him he was using his judgment as a chemical engineer, along with the collective opinion of his team. They were using sound principles, so he was confident. Peter was not fully convinced, but agreed to let the team pitch the idea to the senior vice president who would make the decision.

At the first meeting with Senior VP Juergen Hintz, Mike's team planned to ask for $15 million to build a test market plant. Everyone knew Juergen could be a wild card in meetings like this. So they were all nervous. The engineering team prepared a 75-page booklet with the design details and cost estimates. It was a truly impressive work, but still they were nervous. They handed the book to Juergen and began their review with fingers crossed. Early in the presentation, Juergen held up his hand and said, "Stop. I'm not qualified to review this project." He turned to Mike—whom he'd worked with in the past—and said, "Mike, will this work?"

With 25 people in the room, including his boss, Mike was at center stage. He said, "Yes, Juergen, it will work." Juergen turned to Peter and asked what he thought. He responded, "If Mike says it will work, you should believe him."

Juergen then asked for a pen and where to sign.

Never before had Mike felt so much responsibility and authority. He was proud of his team, but also determined to do everything possible to show that Juergen's and Peter's confidence was well placed. By launch date, the continuous process they designed had met and exceeded every promise. And Mike's team went on to design several future improvements.

The lesson Mike learned was to seek to work with people you trust to deliver what they say they will deliver. And when you find people like that, give them the latitude and charge them with the responsibility to do something amazing.

SUMMARY AND EXERCISES

1. In business, as in life, sometimes you need to ignore what you've been taught and follow your instincts. Permission stories give people the freedom to follow their instincts. They let people know it's okay to trust their own judgment.

   a. Success story: Orville Sweet's story teaches that when it comes to something as serious as human safety, and as personal as firing someone you know well, it's better to trust your intuition than a corporate policy manual.

   b. Failure story: My million-dollar mistake shows that sometimes telling the boss "no" is the best thing for both of you.

   c. "The bamboo years" gives leaders permission to make necessary investments even in hard economic times.

2. Good leaders delegate authority to the level best equipped to make the decision. Poor leaders selfishly hoard that power, or foolishly reclaim it when times
are hard.

    a. Failure story: Phil Renshaw's "Self-fulfilling prophecy" story illustrates the
folly and unintended consequences of failing to delegate properly. Share
it when you see evidence of something similar happening in your organization.

    b. Success story: Mike Tafuri's experience in making Olean shows what it
feels like when delegation is done right. It's rewarding and empowering.
Use it to remind leaders how much their direct reports appreciate being
delegated authority.

Notes

1. Gary Klein, *Sources of Power* (Cambridge, MA: MIT Press, 1998).
2. Mary B. Wacker and Lori L. Silverman, *Stories Trainers Tell: 55 Ready-to-
Use Stories to Make Training Stick* (San Francisco: Jossey-Bass, 2003), p.
230. Used with permission by story author Katherine Hudson.

CHAPTER 26

Encourage innovation and creativity

"If people aren't laughing at your ideas, you aren't being creative enough."[1]
—DAVID ARMSTRONG

A MANUFACTURER OF window-unit air conditioners wanted to know how much more consumers would pay for a unit that was significantly quieter than traditional ones. Of course, it couldn't just ask, "How much more would you pay for a unit that only produced 35 decibels of sound? What about only 20?" Only an acoustical engineer would know how loud that was. What the company needed were several prototypes with different noise levels to put in front of consumers to listen to. The problem was, it hadn't actually invented any of these quieter units yet. Hence the challenge to the consumer research people.

What it decided to do was simple yet creative. Employees installed what looked like a regular air-conditioning unit in a window at a test facility. Only in this unit, they had taken the guts out, leaving only the outer shell. They ran a four-inch-diameter flexible duct out the back of the unit to a room down the hall, where it was connected to a real air conditioner (the loud kind). When consumers in the test lab turned on the window unit, crisp cold air came out, but almost without a sound! And by varying the distance to the real air conditioner, the loudness of the sound could be varied.

I heard this story years ago, from a source I can't remember. I've been unable to track it down to any published source. But it's a classic outside-the-box story, like the kind you read about in chapter 22. Such stories are worth an additional mention here because of their value in evoking creativity from an organization, not just problem solving. Use any of them when you're trying to encourage your team to think more creatively.

* * *

Sometimes getting your employees to be more creative isn't the problem. The problem is getting their less-than-imaginative boss to give them the space to invent. Innovation isn't a linear process. Inventors need the freedom to play with ideas to see what fruit they will bear. A well-meaning boss might think he's doing his job by keeping his team focused on the most productive areas to explore. But when you insist on knowing what the fruit will be before allowing the play, many of the most revolutionary discoveries might stay undiscovered. The following story illustrates that point in a way even the most controlling of bosses will understand.

One evening, young James was sitting with his aunt in the kitchen having tea. Frustrated with his apparent laziness, she barked out at him, "James, I never saw such an idle boy! Take a book or employ yourself usefully. For the last hour you have not spoken one word, but taken off the lid of that kettle and put it on again."[2] It seems he was fascinated with the steam coming from the kettle. He held a silver spoon over the jet of steam and watched as drops of water formed on the spoon and ran down the handle. Over and over again he studied this simple phenomenon. "Are you not ashamed of spending your time this way?" she scolded.

Fortunately, the boy was undaunted by her admonishment. Two decades later, in 1765, he was still fascinated with the phenomenon he discovered in his aunt's kitchen. It was that year the 29-year-old James Watt invented a new kind of steam engine that helped usher in the Industrial Revolution.

This story is helpful in coaching the manager of a group to give his or her inventors room to invent, to explore. It even works if that manager is you! What they're doing might seem like idle play, just like it did to James Watt's aunt. But it could start a revolution.

* * *

Another way you, as the boss, can foster creativity in your organization is illustrated in this next story. It can be very effective but is shockingly counterintuitive. Judge for yourself.

Many companies have a policy against moonlighting, even if it doesn't directly interfere with your main job. Most of these companies argue that holding down a second job drains you of energy and creativity that would otherwise accrue to the company. I once heard of an HR manager who explained why even having a temporary job while you're on vacation is bad for the company. "Vacation time is a benefit the company gives you so you can relax and recharge. That way you come back to work ready to be productive. If you spend your whole vacation time working somewhere else, the company isn't getting the return it deserves on that cost." I suppose that's one way to look at it.

Here's another. Blackbook EMG has a very different policy about outside jobs and interests. Every employee is strictly required to have one!

Blackbook helps companies retain good employees by getting them connected to the most relevant social and professional networks in town, even if that means they have to create them. Let's say you're a 32-year-old single female engineer from Saudi Arabia now living and working in a midwestern U.S. suburb. Let's face it. It's going to be hard for you to fit in. How are you going to find restaurants and grocery stores that have the kind of food you like; bars that play the kind of music you like; clothing stores that suit your taste; and social events where you can meet people who share your background, culture, beliefs, and values? Studies show if you don't, you're likely to quit your job and move back home. That's where Blackbook comes in. It finds all those things for you. And if it can't, sometimes it even creates them.

To be successful at this, Blackbook has to have creative, resourceful, and well-connected employees. And that's exactly why founder Chris Ostoich requires his employees to moonlight. "To be as creative as we need, everyone that works here must have something else in their life they are as passionate about as they are about working here." He believes outside interests increase creativity and energy, not diminish it. Chris saw this himself when he joined the board of directors of the local fine arts fund. During one of his first board meetings, he realized there were many similarities between running a fledgling business and running a volunteer organization. After debating solutions for the arts fund's challenges for three hours, he looked down at his notebook. He had filled up the left page with ideas for the arts fund, and the right page with ideas for Blackbook.

An even more telling example is what came of the moonlighting of one of his employees, Stephen. The local city council had recently approved construction of a casino downtown, not far from where Stephen lives. Several local civic groups came out against the idea. Stephen knew it was going to be built whether he joined the protests or not. So he decided to take a different approach. He started an organization to help turn the impact on the community into a positive one. For example, casinos are typically built with restaurants, bars, and retail shops in the center of the building. That way, shoppers have to walk by the gaming tables to get to them—which will hopefully lure some of them into the game. One of Stephen's ideas was to put the shops on the outside, facing the street. That would create foot traffic along the street, not hidden deep inside a windowless building, and contribute to a vibrant downtown atmosphere.

As Stephen's organization grew, the employees of many of his Blackbook clients joined the cause. Some even took on leadership responsibilities in the organization. The more committed they became, the more attached they became to the city. Before he realized what was happening, Stephen's outside interest started furthering Blackbook's business objectives. Remember, its mission is to connect its clients to the community. Stephen's moonlighting effort had suddenly become one of the connection points.

So, how much moonlighting are employees required to do at Blackbook? At least 25 percent of their time. And as long as they're getting their job done, it can be during their regular workday—which for most employees, it is. It's one of the first questions Chris asks in a job interview. If people don't already have that outside passion, they won't get the job offer. And if they lose it after they get hired, it could be grounds for termination.

The counterintuitive lesson is that if you want people to be more creative, tell them to spend less time at the office, not more. Tell them to get involved in something they're passionate about. They'll think you're crazy at first, and so might your boss. Start by telling them Chris's story. Then give it a try. My guess is, you'll be rewriting your company policy on moonlighting.

* * *

Being creative and innovative would seem, by definition, to involve coming up with something entirely new. Innovation is a forward-looking endeavor, is it not? Usually. But the last lesson in this chapter is that some very profitable creativity involves not creating something new but rethinking something old. The following story from David Armstrong's book *Once Told, They're Gold*[3] illustrates how.

In 1979, Armstrong International acquired Hunt Moscrop, Ltd., a manufacturer of heavy-duty unit heaters. Picture in your mind an electrical space heater that you might have under your desk at work. Then imagine it much larger, and working with steam or glycol instead of electricity. Now you've got a good mental image of these unit heaters that are used to heat a much larger space like a factory. A key component of these enormous heaters are the baffles. These strips of metal look like the blinds on your home windows and are used to direct the flow of hot steam or glycol in the core of the heater.

Thirteen years after the acquisition, two Armstrong engineers named Carl Looney and Chuck Rockwell were reassigned to the Armstrong-Hunt division that still made these unit heaters. As most Armstrong employees do at least once a year, Carl and Chuck set out to find cost-savings opportunities. With their fresh set of eyes, they began to question things others took for granted. "Why do we do it this way?" And "Why is this part needed?" Soon they discovered the baffles were only necessary on the heaters that used glycol. They served no purpose on the steam units. When Armstrong acquired Hunt, it assumed the baffles were required on both kinds of heaters. Ironically, only 10 percent of the unit heaters sold were the glycol kind that really needed the baffles. So for 13 years, the company had been unnecessarily installing baffles on 90 percent of the unit heaters it produced.

Of course, it immediately stopped installing baffles on steam heaters and saved a considerable sum. But there was no way to recover the past 13 years' worth of wasted expense. Importantly, can you imagine how many times a new production worker at Armstrong-Hunt might have been taught to put baffles on the steam unit heaters because "that's the way it's always been done"? Sometimes being creative doesn't mean thinking of something new. It means thinking of something old, and asking why. If "What if . . . ?" is the most powerful question you can use to encourage creativity and innovation, "Why?" is a close second.

SUMMARY AND EXERCISES

1. As with problem solving, outside-the-box stories help people be more creative. Use the story about window units and the others in chapter 22 to spark creativity whenever needed.

2. Innovators require time and space to play with ideas. A boss who thinks she's keeping the staff focused might be squelching the creativity of the entire team. If you think that's happening in your department, share the story of James and the teakettle with your boss.

3. Passion fuels creativity and innovation. How can you increase passion in your people? Try moonlighting. Chris Ostoich at Blackbook EMG found outside interests increased the creativity and energy of his team, not diminished them. Is moonlighting not allowed at your company? Share Chris's story with the boss and ask for a change.

4. Innovation doesn't always involve creating something new. Sometimes it means rethinking something old. As "baffled for 13 years" shows, asking why in long-established practices can sometimes bear profitable fruit. The next time you're looking for hidden opportunities, tell the baffles story and see what creative ideas come up in your organization.

Notes

1. David Armstrong, *Managing by Storying Around: A New Method of Leadership* (New York: Doubleday Currency, 1992), p. 150.
2. Andrew Carnegie, *James Watt* (New York: Doubleday, Page & Co., 1905).
3. David Armstrong, *Once Told, They're Gold: Stories to Enliven and Enrich the Workplace* (Stuart, FL: Armstrong International, 1998), p. 187. Used with permission.

CHAPTER 27

Sales is everyone's job

"The real selling doesn't start until the buyer says no."
—UNKNOWN

GREG HAS BEEN IN SALES for 25 years. He tells war stories of buying agents at major retailers who react in an odd fashion when presented a slick sales binder during a sales call. "They open the binder, pull out the price list and product spec sheets, and throw everything else in the trash can, right there in front of the salesperson—the sales materials, marketing presentation, even the three-ring binder it came in. They'll say something like, 'We don't want you to waste money on all this sales stuff.'" Can you imagine how lost the poor rookie salesperson would be who's experiencing this for the first time?

Here's the lesson: If your sales presentation is in the trash can, you'd better have a good story. And the unfortunate truth is, whether literally or only mentally and emotionally, your sales material often ends up in the trash can. You're better off with a good story. It doesn't matter if you're trying to sell something to a multibillion-dollar retailer or to a single client of a small business. The following is a situation where an average business leader might recommend whipping out the fancy sales binder to answer the would-be buyer's objection. Fortunately for Melissa Moody's company, she's not your average business leader.

"If you have to pay for anything up front in this industry, it's a rip-off!" So goes a familiar but unfortunate saying in the modeling and talent

230

business. It's familiar because it's been floating around for decades. It's unfortunate because it isn't true—at least it's not if you want the best odds of success. Many an aspiring model naively thinks she can land a lucrative contract with no training, experience, or understanding of the business. "All I need," she might think, "is an agent to represent me." Not surprisingly, that rarely works. As in any industry, those with relevant skills and experience are in a better position to succeed. And one of the best places for that aspiring model to get that skill and experience is Excel Models & Talent, which you read about in chapter 18. For 25 years, owner Melissa Moody has been placing models in women's magazines like *Vogue*, *Elle*, and *Cosmopolitan*, and on runways in New York, Paris, and Milan. The singers and dancers she represents have claimed prestigious awards, including a Grammy, an American Music, and a Teen Music award.

Unlike a traditional talent agency, Excel doesn't just match clients with models and collect a commission for brokering the deal. It trains its students in modeling, acting, professional etiquette, and the business side of the industry. And Melissa personally takes them to shows in New York, Los Angeles, and Paris every year to get experience. Of course, she sometimes books them directly with clients. But she can also find them engagements all over the world through a network of international agents she works with.

So it's understandable that she needs to charge her students for these services. But still, she often gets the objection from a potential client that she doesn't think she should have to pay anything up front. Melissa has three responses for such people. First, she asks them to look around the office. "What do you see? How do you think I pay for the classrooms, the furniture, the lights?" Next she asks the prospective student, or her parents, what they do for a living. "Oh, good, you're an accountant. Because I really need my taxes done. But I don't want to pay for it unless I get a refund. Will you do them for me?" Of course not.

If those two responses don't resolve the objection, Melissa pulls out her biggest gun—a story. This story is about Kristine, a 17-year-old, brown-haired, long-legged beauty with high cheekbones. She had the makings of a world-class model and was one of Melissa's best students. During one of the annual New York competitions, Kristine came in first runner-up out of 1,200 girls! She got an unprecedented 42 callbacks from agents and clients the next week. Melissa helped her pick the best opportunities, and Kristine and her parents were off to New York to sign a deal with their top prospect.

The day of the big meeting, Melissa got a call from Kristine. She was calling from her cell phone in the backseat of a cab heading to the client's office to sign the contract. Kristine was in tears. "What's wrong?" Melissa asked.

Kristine was having second thoughts. Being a model was never really her idea. It was her mom's. She wanted to be successful. Just not in this business. "Melissa, I graduated at the top of my class. I don't want to make my living off my looks." She wanted to go to business school and run a company. "What should I do, Melissa?"

At this point in the story, Melissa pauses and explains to the potential student how she would have answered the question if Kristine hadn't paid for the training and experience she'd gotten from Excel. "I would have told her, 'Kristine, I've got $15,000 invested in you and a contract. Get your butt in that office and sign those papers so I can get my money back!' But because I don't work that way, what I actually told her was this: 'Kristine, follow your heart. Come home and pursue *your* dream.'" And that's exactly what Kristine did. Today she is a sophomore in college, studying business, and no doubt has a successful career in front of her— a career of her choosing.

There are two lessons in Melissa's method to resolving this objection. First, she knows her biggest and best weapon is a story, not a fact or an argument. Second, this particular story allows her to highlight the benefit of her pricing policy for the customer, not for her. That's very different from her first two attempts. The need to pay for lights and furniture is a reason *Melissa* needs to charge a fee. The analogy of the free tax service again explains why *Melissa* needs to charge up front. The story of Kristine shows a benefit to the student. Paying up front gets you an agent who has *your* best interests in mind and keeps you out of a commitment you might not want to have later on. As far as Melissa's concerned, anything less would be a rip-off.

If you find yourself defending your pricing, sharing Melissa's story might help you. Even better, it might inspire you to think of your own similar story that would be more relevant to your industry. If so, remember to highlight the benefit to the customer, not to explain the internal reasons why you have to charge the price you do. You can extrapolate that to any objection, really. Whatever it is, find a story to illustrate the benefit to the customer.

* * *

Sales stories aren't just helpful when talking to the buyer. They're also helpful to you as the leader to turn your entire organization into a formidable sales force—whether they're in the sales department or not. The next two stories offer lessons to do exactly that.

One way to develop an effective sales team is to conduct formal sales training. Many companies do this on an annual basis, either by bringing in a professional trainer or by sending the group to a sales seminar. But there's an amazing sales training resource already in most companies that's rarely leveraged. Bob Smith's story explains.

Before retiring in 1998, Bob spent 41 years in purchasing for companies making products from commercial building material, to school furniture, to fertilizers. Early in his career, when he was first promoted to purchasing manager, he found that his predecessor had been buying steel almost exclusively from one supplier. When he met the salesperson representing that steelmaker, he understood part of the reason why. He was exactly the kind of person buyers love to deal with. He was honest, fair, and wasn't afraid to go to bat for his customers back at headquarters when they really needed something special. But Bob believed having a single source of supply for a key material was too risky. So he started purchasing from additional suppliers, but still kept buying most of the steel from the same supplier.

Soon thereafter, his ideal salesperson got promoted. Unfortunately for Bob, his replacement was nothing like him. He had no sales experience. In fact, he had been a scientist in the metallurgy department. He was a cordial but very sober character. During his first sales call with Bob, he made quite a show of the fact that he represented one of the biggest steel producers in the country and was Bob's biggest steel supplier. Skipping all the normal pleasantries, and before even getting to know Bob personally, he reached into his briefcase and pulled out a detailed report. "I see here that during the last quarter, you only bought 450 tons of steel from us. What's the problem?"

"Excuse me?" Bob replied.

The salesman restated, "It looks like you were buying significantly more in prior quarters. What happened?" Bob explained his philosophy about single suppliers. But the new salesman was unsympathetic to that answer. He concluded by saying to Bob, "I certainly hope the next time I call on you we'll have seen a change in these numbers."

As the buyer, Bob wasn't used to such direct language from salespeople. He was taken aback, and responded simply, "I'll bet you will."

True to his word, over the next three months, Bob changed the orders from this particular steel company. By the time that salesman came to see him next, his orders had dropped 200 tons! He entered Bob's office with an entirely different air about him. His first words were, "I guess you can tell I'm new at this." He wasn't throwing his company's name around like it meant something special. And he certainly didn't presume to tell Bob he needed to change his orders again. It was never clear to Bob why the salesman's first call was so caustic and arrogant. Was it just inexperience? Or was it some new "power sales" technique that resembled a Jedi mind trick? Either way, the salesman learned that it didn't work. He took the time on this sales call to get to know Bob a little better. More importantly, he took the time to learn about his customer's needs. Orders picked up over the next quarter and continued to grow as the salesman's skills grew.

Raw material salespeople weren't the only ones who called on Bob Smith. The salespeople who worked at his own company did also. When the field sales reps came into headquarters, they would always stop by the purchasing department and see Bob for 15 minutes, sometimes before going to see the sales manager. Why? Because Bob's office is where they got to hear stories like the one above. It's one of the stories Bob liked to tell new salespeople so they wouldn't make the same mistake when they were out making sales calls.

The lesson to be learned from this story isn't just how a salesperson should treat the buyer. There's a much more important idea. Every company that manufactures a product has a purchasing department and a sales department. The buyers in the purchasing department, like Bob Smith, spend every day dealing with salespeople. Some are good, some are bad. Some they award enormous sales contracts to. Some they send away disappointed. Who better to teach the sales department how to do its job successfully than the buyers? That's exactly what Bob was doing when he told stories to his sales department. But at most companies, the purchasing and sales department personnel don't even know each other. They are as far from each other on the company organization chart—and in the building—as possible. What a wasted opportunity. If you want to create master salespeople, have your buyers tell them stories of the best and worst salespeople they deal with. You might even see a change in your sales numbers next quarter—for the better.

* * *

At many companies, everybody (even those not in the sales department) at some point gets involved in a sales call. It could be the engineer going to explain the details of the new product upgrade, or the consumer researcher going to explain who the target consumer is, or the marketing manager going to explain the new ad campaign that will double revenues. As a result, creating master salespeople sometimes involves making good salespeople out of people who aren't salespeople at all. The last story in this chapter is a case in point.

In 1995, I was starting a new assignment in one of P&G's West Coast sales offices. The sales team there met with retail executives on a weekly basis. But occasionally one of P&G's vice presidents from Cincinnati would fly out to join on a particularly important sales call. Early in my assignment there was one such day.

The buyer was upset about some changes we'd made to one of our brands and wanted the VP to hear about it. Our objective was damage control. Our VP flew in for the meeting. It was a tough call. Tempers were high. But during the hour, the buyer got to speak her peace. We listened and committed to remedy the situation. The meeting ended with our brand lineup intact and our sales protected.

As we left the meeting room, our VP—in a final attempt to repair the strained relationship with the buyer—shook her hand, gave her a business card, and said, "Your business is very important to me. Here's my number. Sometimes things can get lost in the translation back to Cincinnati, so feel free to call me directly anytime." It was a very genuine offer. The buyer thanked him, and we left.

Back at our offices, we debriefed the call for a few minutes. Then we all walked out front to put the VP into a cab to the airport for his flight home. As the cab pulled away, I turned around to the rest of the team with a smile on my face, and said, "Well that went a lot better than I expected!"

But to my surprise, they all looked at me like I was from Mars. "Are you insane?" one of them quipped. Obviously I missed something. But what was it? I didn't have to wait long to find out, as one of my new coworkers explained.

"You're right, Paul. It was going pretty well, right up until the end when the VP gave the buyer his business card and told her that we were basically a bunch of idiots who can't even pass along messages to headquarters without something 'getting lost in the translation.' It'll probably take us six to nine months to rebuild the trust he just lost us in 10 seconds."

And he was right. That buyer went straight to the VP with all her questions for several months. She didn't need us. It was a powerful lesson for me. Sales is a relationship game. Without a relationship, not much

sales happen. That VP was honestly trying to repair the strained relationship between our companies. What he didn't realize was that he did
so at the expense of the relationship with the P&G sales team.

What the VP should have said was, "Your business is important to us.
So we've put one of our best sales teams right here. If there's ever anything
you need, just let these folks know. They know how to get things done,
even if that means getting me, the president, or the CEO involved."

Today, having worked on several sales teams with P&G, I'm often
asked for advice when young research managers are about to make their
first trip to a customer. I used to give them a long list of dos and don'ts.
But I eventually realized I could never give them advice for all the possible
scenarios they could encounter. Instead, I just started telling them the
story of the unwelcome business card. Every young manager from headquarters wants to make a good impression on the buyer, just like that VP
wanted to. But he needs to understand that after he flies home the next
day, the sales team has to stay and work with that buyer day in and day
out.

The role of the visitor should not be to impress the buyer and be the
hero but to make the sales team's job easier. Offering help is fine. But if it's
done in a way that disempowers the sales team, it does more harm than good.

SUMMARY AND EXERCISES

1. If your sales presentation is in the trash can, you'd better have a good story.
    And sales presentations have a way of ending up in the trash can. A story will
    stick with the buyer far longer.

2. You should be able to explain every aspect of your business model in terms
    of the benefit it provides the customer. Even if it's why you have to charge the
    price that you do, explain why that price benefits the *customer*, not why *you*
    need to charge that much. ("Paying in this industry is a rip off.")

3. Training budget a little tight? Tap into the best source of advice on successful
    sales techniques in your company—the purchasing department. Share Bob
    Smith's story of the new steel salesman with the heads of your sales and pur-
    chasing departments. Make arrangements for sellers and buyers to spend
    more time together. They both have much to learn from each other.

4. At some point, just about everyone gets involved in a sales call, even if you're
    not a salesperson. Before you send people out to the field for the first time,
    tell them the story of the unwelcome business card. They'll be much less likely
    to make a similar mistake. And your sales team will thank you for it.

CHAPTER **28**

Earn respect on day one

"People are going to tell stories about you whether you want them to or not. Choose which ones they tell."
—BOB MCDONALD, CEO, Procter & Gamble

IMAGINE YOU'RE A midlevel manager at a technology company in Dusseldorf, Germany.[1] You've worked there for 20 years, since the company was founded by one of your best friends. Ten years ago, it was acquired by an American competitor. Every few years since then, the new owner sends one of its American VPs to Dusseldorf to run the "German operations." Each time, it's a disaster. The Americans don't understand how business is done in Europe, and German customer expectations are as foreign to them as the language. The 15 to 20 percent annual growth rates you'd become accustomed to in the first decade dropped to 2 to 3 percent since the takeover. The last vice president actually went so far as to say he would consider implementing some of the strategies advocated by local employees. But of course he never did.

Now imagine it's the first day on the job for Burt, the next American VP. He's never lived or worked outside the United States in his life, speaks only one language (English), and his uncle is the retired CEO of the company. You've never met him, but you already don't like him. And neither does anyone else in the Dusseldorf office.

You go to the big meet-and-greet event to welcome the new boss. Between the hors d'œuvres and the handshake lineup, he takes the opportunity to make a short speech. After the obligatory "I'm happy to be here" comments, he tells the following story.

237

"I grew up in the Texas panhandle—cattle country. After high school I spent a few years working for my father on the family ranch. So by the time I started college at Texas Tech University in Lubbock, I was several years older than the other freshmen. That made it easy to get a job bartending. By the time I was a senior, I was one of the best bartenders in town. Patrons would drive past several other bars just to come to mine. I knew everyone's favorite drink by heart, and served them with a smile. But my secret was that I was the best listener in the business. I could have 30 customers in a six-hour shift and they would all swear I spent a whole hour just listening to them personally.

"A year later, I moved to Chicago for graduate school. With my experience, I got the first bartending job I applied for. I was excited and confident my first night—eager to show those big-city boys how to tend bar.

"It was a catastrophe! I was behind my orders all night. I was used to selling Scotch on the rocks and Bourbon Whiskey, straight. These customers were ordering drinks I'd never heard of like Red Hot Lover and Illinois Cocktail. Plus, I was running through 30 customers every 30 minutes! I tried, but I couldn't possibly listen to them all. And when I did ask customers how their day was going, they looked at me like I was a stalker. At the end of my shift, the owner pulled me aside and told me to come in the next night, but not clock in. Just sit at the bar, and watch. Todd was the head bartender that night, and he was the best.

"I showed up on time and sat at the end of the bar. I learned more in the next two hours about tending bar in Chicago than four years in North Texas could teach me. Todd was amazing. He didn't need to memorize his customers' favorite drinks because he had new customers every hour. Despite being slammed with customers, he made eye contact with everyone who walked anywhere near the bar and yelled out at them, asking what they wanted to drink. In Texas, that would be considered rude and pushy. In Chicago it was good business. And he knew exactly when to ask them if they wanted another one and when to call them a cab. It took me a few months to perfect the new techniques. But it only took me two hours to realize what new techniques I needed.

"I learned two important lessons that night. First, I learned that what makes you successful in one place won't necessarily make you successful in another. Second, I learned that if I want to get better at something, I should learn from the best.

"I'm looking forward to getting to know each and every one of you over the next few months. I'll be the one sitting at the end of the bar, watching you, and learning."

Now how do you feel about your new boss? Relieved? Hopeful? Excited? And you're probably feeling a bit guilty for judging him too early, aren't you? In this imaginary tale, telling that story is probably the only thing Burt could have done to ingratiate himself to that audience of people who were already determined not to like him. It probably would have taken him six to nine months to earn that kind of respect on the job.

This story illustrates one way to earn respect on day one—introducing yourself with a story that lets people know "I'm not who you think I am." These stories anticipate a preconceived notion and prevent it from ever taking hold. It's one of the best ways to earn respect on day one.

* * *

That example was particularly powerful because it helped the hypothetical audience overcome a specific preconceived notion it had about the storyteller. But telling a story about who you are doesn't have to be that intentional to be effective. How can that be? Consider the results of a July 1999 *New York Times*/CBS survey. It asked, "Of people in general, how many do you think are trustworthy?" The average answer was 30 percent. Then it asked, "Of people *you know*, how many do you think are trustworthy?" The average answer shot up to 70 percent! Why would that be? The answer is that if people don't know you, they default to not trusting you. "I don't know him. He might not be honest." But if they know you, personally, they default to trusting you. "I know her, and she's never done anything to make me not trust her. She's probably trustworthy." That human proclivity for trusting people you know creates a powerful role for stories that let people get to know you a little.

A great example of this happened in January of 2005 when Procter & Gamble bought the Gillette Company in the largest consumer packaged goods acquisition in history. As you might expect, Gillette employees were naturally concerned about what would happen to their jobs, pay, and benefits.

A few days after the deal closed, the CEO of P&G, A. G. Lafley, and several senior Gillette officials, held a huge meeting at Gillette headquarters in Boston's Prudential Tower. The purpose of the meeting was to put employees at ease over the change in ownership. They invited as many Gillette employees as could fit in the auditorium. One of them was Mike Berry.

The Gillette officials spoke first. In their prepared remarks, they covered a number of reasons why this was a great deal for Gillette employees.

"P&G is a market leader in almost every category they compete in . . . they have a 160-year history of treating their employees well . . . they have a very generous profit sharing plan," etc. When it was A. G.'s turn to speak, he also had his list of reasons why this would be a good thing for Gillette employees. But before he got to those details, he told the audience a little about himself personally. How he started his career in the military, a little about his family, his hobbies, where he likes to go on vacation, and so on.

When the meeting was over, Mike's reaction reflected the sentiment of many in the room. "Wow. I know A. G. better after five minutes than I know my leaders after five years!" And that's exactly what they needed to know—a little about A. G. personally. After all, what those Gillette employees needed most at that moment was to trust the man in charge of the company that just bought them. A. G. could have told them, "Trust me. We'll take care of you." But that wouldn't have been nearly as effective as letting them get to know him a little. A. G.'s "a little about me" story moved him in the minds of his audience from the 30 percent to the 70 percent.

* * *

Another way to earn respect on day one is to tell stories about why you chose to be where you are. What made you choose the particular job, career, company, industry, or department you just joined? What made you start this journey? As long as the answer isn't "Because I needed the money," it will probably help jump-start your road to respect.

These "why I work here" stories don't need to be long. I learned that lesson from Jeff Strong, one of the most inspirational leaders I've ever had the privilege to work with. We met when I was working in a New Business Development group at P&G. Our job was to create new products in categories P&G had never competed in before, perhaps ones that had never been invented before! His first day on the job as our marketing director, he introduced himself with these words. "I'm a practical guy. That's why I work at this company. I have a wife and kids to support and a college fund to build. Taking a lot of risk with my career and income doesn't fit well into that equation. But I also love the thrill of creating something new, and doing something nobody has ever done before. That's why I'm so excited about working in this department. It's the only place in the company where I can help run an entrepreneurial business, and still sleep well at night knowing my family is secure. I can't wait to get started."

Who wouldn't be excited to work with a guy who was so excited to be there? And that's the point. People want to work with, and work for, a leader with passion. Figure out why you chose the path you did. Then tell people your "why I work here" story.

* * *

A final word of advice—when selecting a story to tell about yourself, make sure it supports the image you want your colleagues to have of you. If you choose poorly, you may do more damage than good. For example, a few days after attending one of my training sessions on storytelling, one young manager came to me excited to share his story. I knew him prior to the class. He was incredibly bright and rapidly moving up. But fairly or not, he had a reputation for putting his own self-interest ahead of others. So I was a bit surprised when he told me his story. It was a poignant account of growing up in poverty in a small town. He was among the poorest in his school and suffered the social stigma that came with it. Weary of his predicament, he made a commitment to better himself and earn a more respectable and comfortable life. He worked hard in school, graduated at the top of his class, was the first in his family to go to college, and continued on to a prestigious graduate school. "I swore to myself I wouldn't raise my kids in that squalor! And I won't stop until I can have the best life has to offer and give my kids the same."

It was a lovely story . . . for someone else.

For him, all that story accomplishes is to support the already unfortunate reputation he had for being self-centered. Only now his colleagues would understand why he was so. He needed a different story. I asked him what he liked best about his current job. It turned out this was the first time he'd managed other people. The role he was filling had been vacant for some time, and the junior managers who now reported to him were thirsty for leadership. Despite his inexperience as a leader, after only a few weeks on the job his direct reports began to thrive. After a few months, they were telling him he was the best manager they'd ever had. And the department's results showed it. I asked him how it felt to see other people succeed and know that he had something to do with it. "It felt amazing! I had no idea. Plus, I realized the whole department gets much more accomplished when I spend my time coaching them instead of focusing on me."

"Now that," I told him, "is your story!"

His story should tell about that *ah-ha* moment when he realized helping others succeed is more rewarding than managing his career. That's what people need to hear about him, especially those who report to him now, or anyone who might consider doing so in the future. Instead of supporting his bad reputation, that story will replace it with a positive one.

SUMMARY AND EXERCISES

1. Your reputation is nothing more than the stories people tell about you. Choose what stories people tell by telling them first.

2. You never get a second chance to make a first impression. The best way to introduce yourself to a new team is with a story—*your* story. Three kinds of stories will help you earn respect on the first day.

    a. "I'm not who you think I am" stories to fend off whatever preconceived notion your new team has about you. (For example, Burt's story of bartending in Chicago.)

    b. "A little about me" stories let your new group know you personally. Even a short story will put you in the 70 percent of trustworthy people your new team knows personally, and get you out of the untrustworthy 30 percent, as A. G. Lafley did at Gillette.

    c. "Why I work here" stories inspire people because almost everyone wants to work for a leader with passion. Figure out why you chose this path, and tell people about it (e.g., "I'm a practical guy").

3. Make sure your stories support the image you want people to have of you. A bad story can do more damage than no story at all (e.g., "I won't stop until I have the best!").

Note

1. This original story was inspired by the story of Skip in Annette Simmons's *The Story Factor* (San Francisco: Jossey-Bass, 2001), p. 1.

CHAPTER **29**

Recast your audience into the story

"Tell me, I'll forget. Show me, I'll remember. Involve me, I'll understand."
—CHINESE PROVERB

IN 1997, I WAS THE finance manager of one of P&G's West Coast manufacturing plants. Halfway through my assignment, my boss (the plant manager) moved to a new role, which meant I got a new boss. His name was Joe Lovato.

One day during his second month as the new plant manager, right before quitting time, Joe sent his leadership team a memo, with a note attached. The note read, "Tomorrow morning at our leadership team meeting, I'll be telling you about a new pay and promotion policy I'll be implementing for all the managers at this plant. But I wanted to give each of you a chance to think about it overnight first. Talk to you in the morning. Joe."

We all read the memo before going home. Essentially, what it said was this: Unless you work in one of the three most important departments in the plant—production, packing, or shipping—you will not be eligible for any promotions or pay raises. There were probably three managers on the leadership team who didn't mind this new policy—the heads of the production, packing, and shipping departments. But the rest of us were livid! We went home that night in a rightfully foul mood, grumbled to our spouses, yelled at our kids, and didn't get much sleep because we were busy thinking of all the nasty things we were going to say to Joe Lovato the next morning.

243

When the morning came, and the meeting started, we lit into Joe Lovato like you wouldn't believe. We belched out all the reasons why his idea was foolish—"This isn't fair! We hire people from all over the world to come here . . . we benchmark salaries nationally . . . this will make it impossible to get good managers to work at this plant . . . who do you think you are to go against the corporate policy! And besides," we told him, "You don't even have the *authority* to make such a decision!"

He let us vent for about 20 minutes. And then he said, "Okay, you can stop worrying now. I never intended to implement that policy anyway. I just wanted you to know what it feels like, for one night, to live under the same pay and promotion policy you implemented for the non-management personnel at this plant before I arrived." Awkward silence.

He was right. We had. We did so because working in production, packing, and shipping was the hardest work in the plant. The other jobs were cushy in comparison. Desk jobs. Air-conditioned jobs. Since company policy didn't allow for significantly higher pay for the hard jobs, we resorted to this tactic to encourage people to want to stay in the hard jobs. And if they did go take one of the desk jobs, this would incentivize them to come back to the hard-on-your-feet work in a couple of years. It made sense at the time.

Joe could have simply brought up the promotion policy in the staff meeting and told us he didn't understand it, or didn't think it was fair, or wanted to change it. But then we would have just calmly told him all the very good reasons why we put that policy in place to begin with. But after making us live with that policy for one night—as if it applied to us—and then letting us argue with him about why it was a bad idea for *us*, it was much harder to justify that it was okay for the rest of the employees.

Joe didn't just tell us a good story. He made us part of it. He let us, his audience, play an active role as the story unfolded around us. That's what made it amazingly effective. Any time you can actually bring your audience into the story, instead of just telling them a story, it magnifies the effectiveness of your message many times over. It takes the power of storytelling to an entirely new level.

Of all the elements of storytelling discussed in this book, this is by far the most powerful. But you have to wield that power carefully. Used unwisely it can be dangerous, and even counterproductive. For example, in the case of Joe Lovato, there may be a few of those leadership team members today who are still upset with him for pulling that little ruse on us, even though it only lasted for about 15 hours.

This is an admittedly extreme example. Executed this way, it's probably the kind of tactic you can get away with only two or three times in a career. But if there's something that's vitally important to you or your audience, it might warrant going to this length. Joe is passionate about people and making sure they're treated fairly. To him, this was one of those times it was warranted.

* * *

So is there a way to use this tactic without upsetting anyone? Yes. Consider the story of the first day of Jim Owen's history class in chapter 19. There are two main differences between that story and the Joe Lovato story: First, in the history class story, the ruse only lasted about 15 seconds, not 15 hours. Second, the audience wasn't threatened by the pretend criminals—only the teacher was. In Joe's story, the bad news about the new pay and promotion policy was directed at the listening audience, not Joe. It was the audience themselves who had to suffer in the drama of the story, not the storyteller. So, limit the time your audience is under some kind of pretense. Also, construct your story so that the drama is directed at you, the storyteller, or any accomplices you've recruited, instead of your audience.

What if that's not possible? How do you know if your lesson is worthy of the stronger measure, as it was in the Joe Lovato story? Here's the acid test: Imagine you were the audience and it was happening to you. After it was over, would you thank your instructor for teaching you such a valuable lesson? Or would you resent him for it? If the lesson is important enough to your audience, they'll thank you for it. If it's only important to you, they certainly won't.

Not every message you have will pass the test. And you may not be able to construct the alternative like Jim Owen did. So, is there a way to put the audience into the story with this same impact, but without any false pretense? Fortunately there is. Here are a few examples.

About once a month, one U.S. company's regional sales office holds a meeting. Everyone gathers in the largest conference room to listen to leadership team members comment on the state of the business, celebrate key milestones, and recognize great work. It's generally a great pep rally.

One month, the human resources manager took the microphone. With a celebratory tone in her voice, she said, "Did you know next month our West Coast team will be launching the biggest initiative in 10 years? It's a new technology that boosts product performance by 10 percent! A huge breakthrough in the category." Cheers and applause followed.

She continued, "Did you know we got extra money from the corporate office, and in three weeks we'll be doubling our price discounts to help deliver our sales forecast?" More cheers and applause.

"Did you know we've canceled some of our advertising scheduled for the fall, and are using the money instead to send samples of the new and improved product to customers all over the country?" Again, cheers and applause.

Several more such rhetorical questions followed, along with the expected hurrahs from the team. After the applause died down, the HR manager answered her own rhetorical questions as follows: "Well I didn't know any of that until last night at 10 o'clock when I walked around our open office space and read some of the memos left out on people's desks, printers, and fax machines." The celebratory mood in the room immediately vanished into an awkward silence. She continued, "What would happen if those memos fell into the hands of our competitors? Do you think they would do something to ensure our efforts failed?" Sheepish, guilty nods from the audience. "We have a 'clean desk' policy for a reason. Please do your part to keep our competitive secrets just that—secret."

The HR manager could have just gotten up and reminded everyone (for the umpteenth time) about the company's "clean desk" policy. But what she did was far more effective. She wrote the audience into the story. And she did so without calling out anyone in particular.

Violations of the clean desk policy dropped dramatically the next day.

In addition to avoiding false pretenses, how did that story deliver the impact without offending the audience? Answer: There is safety in numbers. Nobody got singled out. In the Joe Lovato story, three leadership team members weren't affected by the "new" policy. The remaining five were. That lack of equal treatment can lead to resentment. Unless you're trying to make a point about how it feels to be treated unfairly, it's better to avoid the situation entirely.

* * *

In the previous example, technically there was no false pretense perpetrated by the HR manager. But she did lead them on a bit with her rhetorical questions. Can you put your audience into a story without even this forgivable sleight of hand? Yes, again. Here's one way: Create a scientific experiment, and make the audience your subjects.

In 2007, I attended a two-day company seminar on private-label products. Most of the two days consisted of speeches and presentations on the growing success of private label and what we could do to better compete. The most memorable part for me was a 30-minute exercise where we actually tried using the products. In groups of 15 to 20, we were escorted into a separate room where tables were set up with sample products on them. One table was filled with glasses of milk. All the glasses on one side of the table were labeled A and on the other side B. No other information about the milk was shown—not the store it came from, not the brand name, not the price.

The instruction was to try one glass of A and one of B, and note on a piece of paper which one was the expensive national brand and which one was the cheap private label. At the other tables were similar arrangements with other products—chocolate chip cookies, hand lotion, and orange juice. One table actually had diapers on it, where we were instructed to pour in the orange juice left over from the previous table to see how well it absorbed.

After trying all the products and making our selections, participants returned to the main room. We were immediately told which products at each table were the national brands, and which were the private labels. I was shocked to find out that four out of the five products I had chosen as the national brands turned out to be private labels. Four out of five! It didn't matter that three of them were in categories that Procter & Gamble didn't even make. The point was that if private-label products were that good in those categories, what made me think they weren't that good in the categories my company did compete in?

Later that afternoon we found out what percentage of the audience correctly identified the national brands at each table. We were also told the result of extensive consumer research on how consumers rate the performance of national brands versus private-label products in these categories and in all the categories P&G competes in.

But I don't remember any of that. What I do remember is that four out of five times I personally picked the private-label brand as being the "better" national brand. I became part of the story—part of the experiment. That had a bigger influence on my opinion of the private-label threat than any research or statistics ever could. The next time you want to convince an audience of something, you can share all the academic and professional research on the topic you can find. Or, you can think of a way to demonstrate it. The second method will almost always be more effective.

* * *

Despite your best efforts, sometimes it's just not possible to put the audience into the story. In those cases, the next best alternative is to make them a part of the story*telling*, as this final story shows.

A few years ago, I was preparing for a full-day meeting with several senior executives at one of our retail customers. At one point during the meeting my role was to discuss how one of their key competitors was out-advertising them three-to-one on some of the most recognizable brands on their shelves—ours!

I had all the advertising data researched, and could clearly document the three-to-one rate of advertising on these key brands between the two retailers. I created a fancy chart that illustrated the pattern very clearly. Even the colors of the bars in the charts corresponded to each company's brand logos. I really liked my chart.

But a few days prior to the event, my boss, Jeff Schomburger, told us the entire meeting had to be a discussion. "No slides, no charts, no graphs." Did I mention that I really liked my chart? I suppose I could have simply stated the fact that their rival was out-advertising them three-to-one on these brands. But we all know from freshman psychology class that humans remember only 20 percent of what they hear, but 30 percent of what they see, and 50 percent of what they see *and* hear, which is why I really wanted to use the chart.

But if you look back in that old college textbook you'll be reminded that even more than what they hear or see, humans remember 70 percent of what they say, and 90 percent of what they actually *do*. There was my opportunity—getting them to say or do something would be even more memorable than having them see even my fabulous chart. So I grabbed last Sunday's paper out of the trash and got both retailers' advertising circulars. I counted the ads for the brands in question in the first circular—three. In the second one—nine. Bingo!

I got some little yellow star stickers like the ones I used to reward my three-year-old with when he went pee-pee in the big potty. I stuck them on the circulars next to the brands in question, to make them easy to spot. Then I went to the meeting.

When it got to the right point in the discussion, I pulled out the circulars. I held them up for the audience to see, and placed them on the table in front of the most senior executive in the room. I asked him if he would kindly count up the number of ads with the little yellow stars on them in his company's circular. "One, two, three," he said.

"Thanks. Now could you please count up the stars in your competitor's circular?"

"One, two, three, four . . . nine," he concluded.

I finished with "We've looked back over the past six months and found that exact same ratio in advertising frequency for these brands. Week in and week out, you're getting out-advertised three-to-one."

If Jeff had let me use my beautiful chart, as I'd wanted to, I'm sure the meeting would have gone fine. But the odds of that executive internalizing and remembering this one little fact out of that full-day meeting would have been much lower. In fact, about 40 percent lower, according to your college textbook.

SUMMARY AND EXERCISES

1. Stage a teachable moment. Arrange a scene or an event for your audience to participate in, so they can learn the lesson themselves instead of being told.

   a. Springboard story: the new promotion policy.

   b. Make sure it's worth the risk. *Does it pass the acid test?* After it's over, will your audience thank you for teaching them such a valuable lesson? Or will they resent you for it?

2. Limit the risk of offending someone:

   a. Avoid a false pretense entirely (e.g., clean desk policy).

   b. Treat all members of your audience equally in the story. Don't create any "winners" and "losers" (e.g., clean desk policy).

   c. Direct the drama toward yourself, or some other actor in your story, not toward your audience. (Refer back to Jim Owen's first day of history class.)

   d. Let the audience in on the surprise quickly—within a few seconds or minutes, not hours.

3. Create an experiment or demonstration with your audience as subjects. Let them prove it to themselves, as in the private-label test.

4. People remember only 20 to 30 percent of what they see or hear. But they remember 90 percent of what they actually *do*. If you can't make the audience part of the action of the story, make them part of the story*telling*. (Count the stars.)

* * *

Now that you've completed all the "how-to" chapters, use the story elements checklist in the appendix to make sure you're using the power of each in your stories. In addition to chapter 7, "Structure of a Story," the six other "how-to" chapters are Metaphors and analogies, Appeal to emotion, Keep it real, the Element of surprise, Recast your audience into the story, and Stylistic elements. MAKERS. Add this to the mnemonic you learned in chapter 7 and you have the complete mnemonic for the structure of a great story: CAR = STORY MAKERS. If you follow the advice in this book, that's exactly what you'll be. Story makers.

Context, Action, Result

=

Subject, Treasure, Obstacle, Right lesson, whY

+

Metaphors and analogies, Appeal to emotion, Keep it real, the Element of surprise, Recast your audience into the story, Stylistic elements

Similar to the story structure template, feel free to copy this template and use it each time you draft a new story.

CHAPTER 30

Getting started

> "*I taught my dog to whistle!*"
> "*I can't hear him whistling.*"
> "*I said I taught him. I didn't say he learned it.*"
> —**1991** CARTOON

THIS QUOTE APPEARED in a cartoon featuring two boys and a dog in David Minton's book, *Teaching Skills in Further and Adult Education.*[1] The lesson is that just because you've been taught something doesn't mean you've learned it. You've come to the end of a book on storytelling as a tool for leadership. But that doesn't necessarily mean you've learned the skill. To master the art of storytelling, mostly what you need to do is practice. Practice using the stories you've read so far. And start crafting stories of your own, using the tools in this book.

To help get you started, this chapter outlines the most common barriers that keep leaders from using storytelling, and offers solutions to each.

Barrier 1: I don't know where to find good stories

This is the single biggest barrier most leaders have to using stories. They just don't have any stories to tell. The solution is to not wait until you need a story to look for one. Start collecting them now. Recall that this is one of the main purposes of this book—to give you a set of stories for the most common leadership challenges. So you're off to a good start. You now have over 100 stories at your disposal, and they're in your hands

251

right now. But you'll want more. Fortunately, there are many places to look and ways to find them. Following are a few of the most productive. Each fits into one of three groups: those you recall from your own past, those you see happen around you, and those you hear from other people. Let's start with you.

Stories from your past. Most people think good stories are born from interesting things that happened to other people—presumably the kind of people interesting things happen to. Surely an ordinary person like me couldn't have interesting stories, could I? Yes, you can. And you do. People with great stories don't necessarily lead more colorful lives. They're just in the habit of sharing their everyday challenges in an engaging way. You can do the same now that you've learned how. So, let's do some digging into your own past to recall good stories, then fashion them into great ones.

Think about the times in your professional life when you had your greatest successes. These are the handful of times over your career where you were the most proud of your accomplishments. Undoubtedly, these were times when you had a great obstacle to overcome, and for which you received enough of a professional or emotional reward to count it among your greatest moments. These times have all the beginnings of a great story—a relatable subject (you), a worthy treasure, and a formidable obstacle. Flesh out these stories using the story structure template and the story elements checklist in the appendix and store them away for future use.

Next, think about the times in your career when you've suffered your greatest failures. As you learned in chapter 20, failure stories are one of the best ways to teach lessons. They're how you help keep the people in your organization from making the same mistakes you did. Again, pick the handful of most costly mistakes you've ever made. They're certain to be the subject of your most useful and often-told stories. Develop them with the tools you now have. When the time comes to use them, you'll have them ready.

Here are a few questions to help with your historical story hunt. Make a list of the events in your life for each, and craft out the beginnings of each story. Even if you only do this mentally, you'll be surprised at how many stories are lurking in your past:

- Think of the people you admire most. What did you learn from them that made you admire them so much?

- What are the moments in your career from which you learned the most important lessons?

- What are the times in your life you felt the most inspired?

- When did you have the greatest sense of belonging and team spirit?

- What's the most difficult experience you've ever been through at work?

- What's the most creative thing you've ever done?

- When were you given the toughest feedback that made the biggest difference in your performance?

- What's the best working relationship you've ever had?

- What was the most surprising thing that's ever happened in your professional life?

- What's the toughest problem you've ever solved?

- What was the job you loved the most, and why?

Stories you see happen around you. Great stories happen all around you every day. At the time they're happening, you don't think of them as stories. You probably don't *think* about them at all. You experience them. You enjoy them. You learn from them. You're inspired by them. They only become stories if someone is wise enough to share them. That's when a story is born.

So how do you spot these great moments when they happen? You've already taken the first step. Just having read this book, you now have a greater sense of awareness of what a good story looks like. It's got a relatable hero, a worthy objective, and a formidable villain. But before I get to that level of analysis of a situation to determine if I'm witnessing a good story, I employ a simpler test: Did someone learn an unexpected lesson, or learn it in an unexpected way? If so, that's my first clue that a good story might be in the making.

For example, learning how to present to senior managers in a class on presenting to senior managers probably wouldn't make for a good story. It's a lesson you'd expect to learn in that class. And it would probably be taught the way most courses are taught—the teacher explains how and you take notes. It's an expected lesson, taught in an expected fashion. Compare that to the lesson I learned in that round room about how to present to the CEO (chapter 1). You could argue that I should have expected to learn a thing or two about presenting to senior managers by presenting to one. But I certainly wasn't expecting to learn that lesson because the CEO sat underneath the projection screen and refused to look at my slides the entire time. That was unexpected. When Jeff Brooks told me his conversation about toilet paper on his train ride in Budapest (chapter 17), I certainly wasn't expecting to learn how to love my job. When Martin Hettich told me his story about the printer codes that prevented confidential documents from being left out all night (chapter 4), I was expecting to learn how to enforce the clean desk policy. But I certainly wasn't expecting to learn about it from a cost-saving project involving personal printer codes.

If there's a single best predictor of the story value of a narrative, it is the existence of an unexpected lesson or an unexpected way it is taught. When you see one of those two things happen—whether it's happening to you or to someone else—take note. A great story is about to be born.

Stories that other people tell you. The richest source of stories you'll ever have are the stories you hear other people tell. There's only one of you, but about 7 billion other people in the world. Even if you never create a single personal story of your own, you can have an endless supply of great stories by just paying attention to the stories you hear from others. If you simply pick and choose the very best, you'll have your own "greatest hits" collection of stories to use.

Taking mental note when you hear a good story is the first step to collecting other people's stories. As you just learned, you're listening for unexpected lessons or unexpected ways of learning it. Fortunately, you don't have to wait for people to tell you stories. Here are more proactive ways to find other people's stories.

Ask them. In his book *Leadership*, management guru Tom Peters noted, "As I see it, an effective leader, as she makes the rounds at her organization, must ask one—and only one—question: 'Got any good stories?'"[2] Not everyone will have stories top of mind to share. But as they come to expect this question from you, you'll be surprised how many will squirrel away good stories and save them for the next time you ask. At Mary Kay Cosmetics, the staff goes one step further and solicits stories from sales reps by sending them e-mails with questions like, "How has your Mary Kay business enriched your life?"[3] Their responses provide a never-ending supply of great stories.

Hold a contest. In June 2011, the Global Business Services division at Procter & Gamble held a storytelling competition. To celebrate diversity and inclusion in their organization, they issued a challenge to all 7,000 employees to share their stories of how diversity is touching their lives. They provided videotaping and editing support, and encouraged anyone who was interested to come record his or her story. Over 200 people participated in the competition from every region around the world. The videos were posted on the company intranet for all to see. Over 2,600 votes were cast and the winners selected. Among the winners were the three ladies from Costa Rica you read about in chapter 8: Silvia, Annette, and Maria.

Everyone has a story to tell. All people need is a little encouragement. A competition like this gives it to them. Hold a contest for the best stories about whatever topic serves your needs best at the time: great customer service, problem solving, model coaching, or creativity. Celebrate the winners and add them to your collection of stories.

Hold storytelling sessions. At global advertising giant Saatchi & Saatchi, every quarter they gather 20 employees from around the world who've never met or worked together. Half of them are asked to share a story about how they inspired someone at work. The other half tell stories about how they were inspired by someone else.[4] Each Container Store retail outlet holds daily cheerleading sessions where employees share stories. The best are written up and sent to corporate headquarters to send out broadly.[5] It turns out many companies hold employee meetings expressly for the purpose of telling and collecting stories. Yours can, too.

Conduct formal interviews. The Environmental Protection Agency videotaped professionally facilitated interviews with executives on topics like leading change, driving results, and building coalitions. The result was an 18-minute video featuring 10 powerful stories.[6] Procter & Gamble hired a pair of professional journalists and authors to interview dozens of current and former executives and capture stories to inspire and train the next generation of leaders.

Don't think people are willing to be interviewed for stories? They are. Most people would love to tell their stories if they could just get someone to listen. In conducting the research for this book, I requested interviews with over 80 people. Only seven declined. Ask.

Ask inspiring questions. Here's a final word of advice about asking for stories in any of the previous scenarios. Have you ever seen an interview for a church or civic group where the interviewee is asked to comment about the importance of the organization? Most are vague and uninspiring ramblings. I suspect that's because they're asked to respond to vague and uninspiring questions such as, "What does this organization mean to you?" You need to ask more specific questions. For example, in preparing for chapter 28, on earning respect on day one, I asked my interviewees questions like these:

- Have you ever heard someone introduce himself and gain immediate respect? What did he say?

- Has anyone ever told you a personal story about herself that completely changed the way you thought about her? What was the story?

- Have you ever seen someone completely blow any chance of acceptance on the first day? What did that person do?

What if you're just hunting for great stories and don't have a specific topic in mind? That's fine, too. But saying, "Tell me your best stories," is not specific enough to get a good response. Would that be my most-effective stories? My favorite ones to tell? The ones my audiences seem to like the most? It's not clear. I found the single most productive question to ask executives as I was researching this book was, "What are the stories you find yourself telling over and over again during the course of your career?" Any stories they tell that often must be their most effective, engaging stories. And the question is specific enough that people can actually answer it.

The second problem with those bad civic group interviews is that the interviewees probably had a camera shoved in their face and were asked to respond to that question without having time to think of a good answer. Don't make that mistake, either. I gave my interviewees the questions several days in advance of the interview so they'd have time to think of good stories. It worked amazingly well. Only 1 out of about 75 interviewees showed up without a story to tell.

Stories from strangers. Sometimes our own resources are inadequate to provide a story to meet a specific need. Here are two ways to collect stories from people you don't even know.

Search the Internet. I recently found myself in a situation where I needed a good story but had nothing quite right. I needed a story to motivate a small brand team to succeed despite the fact that they were significantly outmatched by their competitor's market share and advertising budget. I needed a modern-day David versus Goliath story—one that had a relevant lesson to teach about how my David could beat their giant.

Having exhausted all my other sources, I went to Google's search page and typed in "how underdogs win." I was sure I'd get dozens of links to lists of bullet points and other mundane advice. But I was hoping I'd get at least one good story. And I did. One of the first links returned was to a *New Yorker* magazine article written by Malcolm Gladwell in May 2009.[7] It told the story of a basketball coach who led a team of inexperienced 12-year-old girls to the national championships by using unconventional strategies like a full-court press. The story was intriguing, and the lessons were easy to extrapolate to my underdog's situation. It was the perfect story to share with my team. No matter what kind of story you're looking for, chances are it's already been written. Find it.

Search the media. Books, magazines, movies, newspapers, and television shows offer a rich source of stories to use. I especially like folktales because they often illustrate a wisdom that transcends time or culture. You've seen several examples in this book already. Just be sure to credit the source where you found it.

Barrier 2: I have trouble remembering the stories when I need them

Modern businesses database everything from sales and purchases, to personnel information, market shares, production schedules, accounts receivable, and inventory levels. Just about anything that can be measured is saved in a computer somewhere. Everything, that is, except for the richest source of wisdom in any company—its stories. Those are left to the frailties of human memory and the inevitability of attrition.

It's time we start databasing our stories!

Write down your stories and save them in a place you can access them easily. Mine are all written in a single word-processing document where I can search for them by title, subject, or names of the people in them.

A simpler option is to list out your stories by name and indicate what situations they can be used for. I've provided such a matrix in the appendix to help you find any story in this book you need quickly and easily. Most stories can be used for more than one purpose. For example, take the story of my learning how not to present to the CEO in chapter 1. You can use that to illustrate to other people:

1. Why they should be using storytelling

2. How to make recommendations stick

3. How to teach important lessons

The story of Pledger's competition at Merrill Lynch in chapter 3 can be useful in four of the tough leadership challenges:

1. Setting goals and building commitment

2. Encouraging collaboration

3. Inspiring and motivating the team

4. Helping people find passion for their work

Just find the tough challenge you're in across the top of the page, and scan down the column to see all the relevant stories.

But those are just my stories. Wouldn't it be better if companies maintained a corporate database of stories? Imagine your employees all having access to a single database of stories from around the company. They can add to the database and search it for exactly the right story whenever they need it. If someone needed a story about creativity, she would search the database for the word *creative* or *creativity* or *innovation* and come up with a list of potential stories. Everyone will be better able to pick just the right story for the occasion rather than relying on his or her own limited inventory.

Another way is to print them in book form. Many companies do this and distribute them to their employees. Armstrong International, P&G, General Electric, and Medtronic are among them.

Do you think you don't need to write down your stories to save the wisdom they contain? Consider what happens to a good story if it's not written down and retold. It could be forgotten entirely. But if it's important enough, it will quickly be distilled down to a few bullet points in a memo or presentation, thereby killing any real chance it had of making a difference ever again. The person who writes the bullet points will still understand the true meaning. But unless the author is there to retell the story each time the bullet points are trotted out, the real impact will be forever gone. For example, imagine if Jayson Zoller's story of the jury room tables in the introduction was reduced to bullet points. It would look something like this:

- Study revealed shape of table in jury rooms affects quality and speed of deliberations.
  - Round tables lead to fair and accurate, but lengthy, deliberations.
  - Square or rectangular tables lead to faster, but less-thorough, deliberations.
- Findings were delivered to sponsoring judge.
- Team of researchers shocked when judge ordered jury rooms outfitted with square tables to quicken the pace of court proceedings.
- Lesson: It's important to be clear on your objectives before you start your project.

Jayson's powerful story has now been rendered completely impotent. The odds of these bullet points being shared broadly—or impacting anyone's behavior if they were shared—are now a tiny fraction of what they would be if maintained and retold as a story. Don't let this happen to your stories. Write them down and save them.

Barrier 3: I'm not sure where to tell my stories

First of all, storytelling doesn't need a special time or place to happen. It's best executed where and when leadership normally happens: in formal meetings or informal hallway conversations, in big speeches in front of hundreds of people or one-on-one discussions, in e-mails or memos or during PowerPoint presentations, in the corner office or in the lunch room. Anytime you would normally tell someone what to do, give advice, or teach a lesson, a story can be inserted without worry.

Second, you can tell your stories where and when stories are already being told around your office: in training sessions, on the company website, in corporate newsletters, in client meetings, at company social events, in the annual report, and in team meetings.

Third, many company leaders create venues specifically as an outlet to tell even more stories. David Armstrong, former CEO of Armstrong

International, posted them on bulletin boards around the office, stuffed them in paycheck envelopes, framed them on office walls, recorded them on CDs for the field salespeople, and broadcast them on factory floor TV sets. He bound books full of company stories and left them around working areas and reception areas and sent copies to every employee. Other companies create storytelling events to allow employees to share stories live. Some even have storytelling clubs that meet regularly to swap stories.

In short, it's hard to think of a place you shouldn't be telling stories.

Barrier 4: I don't think stories belong in a formal memo or e-mail

This is one of the most common misperceptions I hear. Usually it's articulated this way: "I can see the value of *telling* stories—when I'm giving a speech, or making a presentation, or in a meeting, or just over the water cooler. But I can't see myself actually *writing* a story in a company memo or e-mail. Stories are too informal, aren't they?"

Nonsense! As you learned in chapter 14, you should be writing like you speak, anyway. If you're comfortable telling a story, you should be comfortable writing one. Especially when addressing the leadership challenges highlighted in this book, your e-mails and memos will be even more effective if they include a story. To prove the point, consider the following tale of two e-mails. The first version is written in standard corporate form (i.e., no story). The second includes a story. Both address the same business topic and are written to Marc Pritchard, chief marketing officer of P&G.

[*Note:* The brand, category, and consumer insights have been altered to protect the confidentiality of the ideas.]

From: Smith, Paul
Sent: Tuesday, January 05, 2010 5:09 PM
To: Pritchard, Marc
Subject: Results from Crest Big Idea Session

Marc,
Per your direction, today we held a "Big Idea" session to generate new ideas for the Crest brand. This summarizes the result of that session.

Objective
To generate "Big Ideas" to grow Crest sales and market share faster

---

Background/Business Issue

- Company experience suggests that time constraints of daily business prevent most managers from spending enough time ideating new product, concept, or communication strategies to grow our business.
- Big Idea sessions were started to address that limitation.

Success Criteria

At least one, but ideally multiple, big ideas that have the potential to meaningfully grow the brand's sales or market share by (1) delivering on known but unmet consumer needs and (2) identifying previously unarticulated consumer needs.

Conclusions

Over 100 new product, concept, packaging, and communication ideas were generated during the day. Each was ranked according to its estimated breadth of appeal, size of prize, and complexity of execution. The top 25 ranked ideas will be moved forward to a concept screening in February.

Next Steps

- Modify January qualitative research agenda to assess consumer interest in top 25 ideas and better develop concept statements.
- Conduct concept screener to determine breadth of appeal of top ideas among our target consumers.
- Develop new panel of respondents ages 7 to 12 to assess ideas developed to address needs specific to that age group.

Most readers would conclude this is a well-written corporate e-mail, following standard business memo protocol. The objective, conclusions, and next steps are all clearly outlined. It's brief and to the point. But what kind of response do you think a memo like this would get from the very busy chief marketing officer, if it got a response at all? My guess: "Thanks for sharing, Paul. Good luck with your ideas. —Marc." And that's probably more than it deserves.

Now have a look at the second version.

From: Smith, Paul
Sent: Tuesday, January 05, 2010 5:09 PM
To: Pritchard, Marc
Subject: Results from Crest Big Idea Session

Marc,

We just completed a very productive Big Idea Session today. While we generated over 100 creative ideas, I thought you might appreciate hearing about one area that I think you'll agree is truly inspired.

As you might imagine, most of the innovation on Crest is aimed at delivering better cleaning, cavity prevention, or whitening. But during our Big Idea session, one of the insights generated was what might be the most frustrating problem surrounding brushing teeth a parent ever has, and it has nothing to do with cleaning, whitening, or preventing cavities.

That problem is this: the fighting, bribing, yelling, cajoling, coaxing, and begging that parents do with their kids just to get them to brush their teeth!

Despite all those fights and strained relationships, nobody's working to solve that problem.

That insight resonated with me personally because I'm having exactly that problem with my nine-year-old, Matthew. So that led me to ask this question: "What if we could make brushing your teeth so much fun, kids would actually want to do it—the way Flintstones vitamins did to get kids to want to take their vitamins? What if when you brushed your teeth, the toothpaste turned bright purple! Or what if the tube lit up like a Christmas tree when you squeezed it?"

I went home that night and talked to Matthew about the idea. I asked him what would it take for him to enjoy brushing his teeth. Within a matter of minutes, he rattled off a half-dozen ideas. What if we put a prize at the end of the tube like in a Cracker Jack box? What if the toothbrush talked to you when you used it and said, "Good job!" or sang you a song. What if each tube came with a few droppers of food coloring and you could make each dose whatever color you wanted?

As you can tell, we're excited about this idea. We see this as an opportunity to solve a real problem parents have with their kids that can bring them closer together as a family, and truly improve the lives of the world's consumers far beyond the brand promise we typically offer.

As next steps, we're planning to include questions in our next round of research to find out how many parents have this problem, what age their kids are when they have it, what tactics they typically use to get them to brush their teeth, which ones work best, etc. But my conversation with Matthew makes me want to add a round of research with kids! Why don't they want to brush their teeth? And what other creative ideas do they have to make it more fun?

> I'll let you know as we learn more. But so far, it appears the Big Idea session really delivered for Crest this year! Thanks for encouraging us to spend this valuable time away from our desks.

What's different about this version? First, it doesn't discuss the 100+ ideas generated that day. It discusses only one. The entire memo focuses on just one interesting, insightful, emotion-filled idea. Second, it discusses that one idea through story—in fact, two or three short stories depending on how you count them. It starts with the story of how parents fight with their kids just to get them to brush their teeth. Then it talks about how our team brainstormed ideas to solve the problem that nobody is working on. The last story is about what happened when I got home and talked to my son, Matthew, and all the good ideas he came up with. Whether that's one complex story or three short simple ones is unimportant. The point is, the entire memo is a story.

Fortunately, the second e-mail is closer to the one I actually sent. And it did get a response, less than two hours later. It began, "Paul, This is an inspiring story! I'm thrilled that the Big Ideas session produced a great insight—especially one filled with great tension. And you are so right—getting kids to brush their teeth is a huge issue!" It went on to offer several suggestions on how to move forward with the idea, and an offer to help however needed. It concluded with, "Have fun and keep me posted on the Big Ideas! —Marc."

One minute later, he forwarded his e-mail to the CEO complimenting us on our great insights. Before bedtime, I'd received a note from the CEO with his personal thanks and praise.

If you'd prefer to get this kind of response to your e-mails and memos, don't be afraid to include a story—or two.

* * *

Let me close by answering the last question I usually get from my students on storytelling: "How will I know if I'm doing it right?"

Of course the most direct sign you've become an effective storyteller is that you're accomplishing whatever you'd hoped to accomplish by telling the stories in the first place. If your stories about collaboration get your team to work together better, you're a good storyteller. If your team is inspired, and learning the lessons you're attempting to teach, you're a good storyteller. But there are other signs you've become a good storyteller. One of the more enjoyable ones is described next.

In November 2001, I left my career as a finance and accounting professional at P&G to join the consumer research department. I left everyone I knew and had worked with for eight years for an entirely new set of colleagues, none of whom I'd ever met. About three months into my new role, my boss was explaining to the department about a new business model she'd recently heard about. She didn't know who started it, but described what she'd heard about its origin in the diaper business unit. Apparently, someone had taken the president and leadership team through a discussion about the four-decade relationship he'd discovered between sales and profits. Oddly, he made them guess at the reasons why that relationship had changed in the early 1980s until someone finally figured it out.

It slowly dawned on me that the person she was talking about was me! And the story she was describing was my discovery journey that I shared with the diaper leadership team less than a year earlier, and that you read about in chapter 5. It was a surreal but proud and awkward moment for me all at the same time. I listened to the story with the smile of a proud parent. I nodded with the others at the main points. And I found amusement in the many new and altered parts my story had picked up through its intermediate tellings.

Great stories spread virally. With enough tellings, the unimportant details disappear, like the exact dates, or places, or even the names of the people involved. What remains is the essence of the story that each teller finds meaningful. When that happens, it's not unusual for the story to make its way back to the originator in altered form, like my diaper story. It might even be better than when you originally told it. Having a story circle back to you anonymously like this is a sure sign you're becoming an effective storyteller. When it does, just smile and say, "That's a great story."

* * *

The most important first step to becoming a great storyteller, of course, is to become a storyteller. Stammering out your first one or two awkward stories is a necessary start, but doesn't make one a storyteller. Being a true storyteller requires a respect for the story and a passion for its telling that the newcomer may take time to develop. Writer and poet Maya Angelou once observed, "There is no agony like bearing an untold story inside of you." So how do you know you're becoming a real storyteller? You'll have the agony. A compelling story will strike you; but instead of simply enjoying it and then dismissing it from your memory, you'll feel an uncontrollable urge to tell it to someone. That's when you'll know. From that moment on, you can be certain that when you lead, you'll lead with a story.

SUMMARY AND EXERCISES

Barrier 1: I don't know where to find good stories.

- *In this book:* There are over 100 stories in this book, arranged by situation. Refer to them by chapter when you experience a challenge. Use the story matrix in the appendix to find the right one.

- *Stories from your past:* Recall your greatest successes and failures for great story content. See the 11 other questions at the beginning of this chapter for more ideas.

- *Stories you see happen:* When someone learns an unexpected lesson, or learns it in an unexpected way, a great story is about to be born. Write it. (Think of the train ride in Budapest, chapter 17.)

- *Stories that other people tell you:*
  - As you're walking around the office, ask people, "Got any good stories?"
  - Hold a contest (Think of the diversity video contest that produced the "FWA Policy" story in chapter 8.)
  - Hold storytelling sessions (the Container Store and the EPA).
  - Conduct formal interviews for stories.

- *Stories from strangers:*
  - Search the Internet (e.g., article on how David beat Goliath).
  - Use books, magazines, movies.

Barrier 2: I have trouble remembering the stories when I need them.

- *Database your stories:* Write them down and save them. Index them so they can be easily searched by topic or characters.

- *Write a book* with all your company stories, like Armstrong International, or P&G, or General Electric, or Medtronic.

- *Create a story matrix,* like the one in the appendix.

Barrier 3: I'm not sure where to tell my stories.

- *Where leadership normally happens:* Whenever and wherever you would normally tell someone what to do, give advice, or teach a lesson, you can use a story.

- *Where stories are told at your company today:* Companies use storytelling in training sessions, company websites, newsletters, bulletin boards, client meetings, social events, the annual report, and team meetings.
- *Create your own storytelling venues:* Use storytelling clubs and meetings, frame stories on the wall, or stuff them in paycheck envelopes.

Barrier 4: I don't think stories belong in a formal memo or e-mail.

Yes, they do. See the "Tale of two e-mails" to Marc Pritchard as an example.

How will you know you're doing it right?

- Your leadership will improve. Your team will have a better grasp on your vision, be more inspired, work together more collaboratively, and be more creative than before you started telling stories.
- You'll hear your own stories told back to you by people who don't know it was your story.
- You'll have the agony—an uncontrollable urge—to share a story. Give in to it. Tell your story.

An Invitation

You've taken your first step to being a storyteller, but there is much more to explore. If you'd like to learn more, discover more stories, share some of your own, and get connected to the large and growing community of organizational storytellers, visit me at www.leadwithastory.com and continue the journey.

Notes

1. David Minton, *Teaching Skills in Further and Adult Education* (Florence, KY: Cengage Learning, 1991), p. 3.
2. Tom Peters, *Leadership* (New York: DK Adult Publishers, 2005).
3. Evelyn Clark, *Around the Corporate Campfire* (Sevierville, TN: Insight Publishing, 2004), p. 81.

4. Lori Silverman, *Wake Me Up When the Data Is Over* (San Francisco: Jossey-Bass, 2006), p. 118.
5. Clark, p. 164.
6. Silverman, p. 135.
7. Malcolm Gladwell, "How David Beats Goliath," *New Yorker* (May 11, 2009), www.newyorker.com/reporting/2009/05/11/090511fa_fact _gladwell.

Appendix

STORY STRUCTURE TEMPLATE

(CAR = STORY)		
	Questions	Answers for YOUR Story
Pre-story	• What main idea are you trying to communicate?	
	• What do you want your audience to DO as a result of your story?	
Context	• When and where?	
Subject	• Who is the **Subject**?	
	• Hero is real/fictional/you?	
	• Audience: "Hey! That could be me!"	
Treasure	• What does the character want?	
	• Identify his/her passion or **Treasure**.	
Obstacle	• Who or what is getting in his/her way?	
	• Identify the villain or **Obstacle**.	
Action	• What happened to the hero? Conflict? Temporary setbacks? Ups and downs along the way? Research done? Conclusions drawn?	
Result	• What happened to the hero in the end? Did he/she win or lose?	
Right lesson	• **Right lesson**: This is the moral of the story.	
	• Conclusion should link back to the reason	
whY	**whY** you told the story (the main idea) and compel the audience to DO what you wanted it to do.	

© 2012 Paul Smith. From Paul Smith, *Lead with a Story* (New York: AMACOM, 2012).

STORY ELEMENTS CHECKLIST

(MAKERS)

	Questions	Ideas for YOUR Story
Chapter 24 **M**etaphors and Analogies	*Use metaphors:* • In your stories (The yellow cab in Ch. 5). • As an entire story in itself (pioneers and settlers in Ch. 15; giant steps in Ch. 16; building a cathedral in Ch. 2). • Instead of telling a complete story (Disney cast members, consumer is boss, FMOT, all in Ch. 24). *Generate great metaphors:* • Use the magazine picture collage exercise. • Ask your audience what kind of animal/car/ book/movie, etc. their idea would be.	_____ _____ _____ _____ _____ _____ _____ _____ _____ _____
Chapter 18 **A**ppeal to Emotion	• Are you trying to influence a decision that was made on purely emotional grounds? If so, you need a highly emotional story, not a rational one (Special Olympics in Ch. 18). • If your audience doesn't naturally care about your topic, what does it care about? Connect your idea to those things (don't mess with Texas, "I've never been to Japan" in Ch. 18). • Generate empathy: Identify the people affected by the decision you're trying to influence. Tell their stories. • Use consumer research verbatims and qualitative discussions as sources for emotional content.	_____ _____ _____ _____ _____ _____ _____ _____ _____ _____ _____ _____ _____ _____
Chapter 13 **K**eep It Real	• Take your abstract idea and explain it with a concrete story about a single example. (Examples are on the banks of the Tammerkoski River in Ch. 2; *Business-Week* on Bounty in Ch. 4; "Lisa" the high-potential shopper and Julie Walker, achiever mom in Ch. 13). • Avoid technical jargon your audience might not understand.	_____ _____ _____ _____ _____ _____ _____ _____

(continued on next page)

American Management Association • www.amanet.org

	(MAKERS)	
	Questions	Ideas for YOUR Story
	• Make the facts, numbers, or events relevant to your audience—something they can relate to in their everyday lives (snowstorm in the courtroom in Ch. 13). • Be brutally open and honest about difficult subjects. Avoid waffling or weasel words typical of management speak today (making payroll in Ch. 13).	_____ _____ _____ _____ _____ _____ _____ _____
Chapter 19 The Element of Surprise	*Grab your audience's attention with a surprise at the beginning:* • What's unusual or unexpected about your story? (Examples are stories on moonlighting required in Ch. 26, canceling your retainer in Ch. 10, the sharecropper's daughter in Ch. 11.) • Does it involve a newsworthy event? (Consider revolution in Egypt in Ch. 8, earthquake in Japan in Ch. 8.) *End your story with a surprise to seal it in memory:* • Make use of surprises that occur naturally in your story (first day of history class in Ch. 19, jury room tables in the introduction, giant steps in Ch. 16). • No natural surprise at the end of your story? Create one. Hold back a key piece of information till the very end (after a lifetime of failure in Ch. 16, on the banks of the Tammerkoski River in Ch. 2, James and the teakettle in Ch. 26). *Ah-ha moment stories:* The next time you have a surprising, eye-opening moment, write a story about it (breakfast in Mexico in Ch.19).	_____ _____ _____ _____ _____ _____ _____ _____ _____ _____ _____ _____ _____ _____ _____ _____
Chapter 29 Recast Your Audience into the Story	• Arrange a scene or an event for your audience to participate in (new promotion policy and clean desk policy from Ch. 29). • Does it pass the acid test? After it's over, will your audience thank you for teaching them such a valuable lesson? If not:	_____ _____ _____ _____ _____ _____

	• Keep the suspense brief—minutes or hours, not days (first day of history class in Ch. 19, clean desk policy in Ch. 29).	_____ _____ _____
	• Direct the drama toward yourself (first day of history class).	_____ _____
	• Treat all audience members equally (clean desk policy in Ch. 29).	_____ _____
	• Stage an experiment or a demonstration your audience can take part in (private-label test in Ch. 29).	_____ _____ _____
	• Get the audience involved in *telling* the story (count the stars in Ch. 29).	_____ _____
Chapter 14 **S**tylistic Elements	*Great beginnings—Start your stories with one (or more) of the following devices:*	
	• A surprise (see Ch. 19).	_____
	• A mystery (1983 discovery journey in Ch. 5; building a cathedral in Ch. 2; three researchers in Ch. 20).	_____ _____ _____
	• A challenge—quickly introduce a relatable main character facing a difficult challenge (how *not* to present to the CEO in Ch. 1; Gail firing herself in Ch. 21)	_____ _____ _____ _____
	Writing style: Write the way you speak:	
	• Use short sentences (15–17 words per sentence).	_____ _____
	• Use small words (15 percent or fewer words over two syllables).	_____ _____
	• Write in the active voice (15 percent or fewer passive voice sentences).	_____ _____
	• Get to the verb quickly (place the verb at the beginning of sentences).	_____ _____
	• Omit needless words (fresh fish story in Ch. 14). Stories should be 250–750 words, or 2 to 4 minutes when told orally.	_____ _____ _____
	Literary devices to use often:	
	• Dialogue	_____
	• Include real names of characters.	_____
	• Repetition (building a cathedral story in Ch. 2, the three researchers in Ch. 20).	_____ _____
	• Don't announce or apologize in advance of a story. Just tell it.	_____ _____

STORY MATRIX

Source: *Lead with a Story: A Guide to Crafting Business Narratives That Captivate, Convince, and Inspire*, by Paul Smith (AMACOM Books, 2012) Paul@leadwithstory.com

STORY MATRIX (continued)

Chapter	Story name	Page	ENVISION: Set a vision	Goals & commitment	Lead change	Recommendations	Customer service	ENVIRONMENT: Culture	Values	Collaboration	Diversity	Policy	ENERGIZE: Inspire & motivate	Courage	Passion for work	EDUCATE: Teach lessons	Coaching & feedback	Problem solving	Understand the customer	EMPOWER: Delegate & give permission	Creativity	Sales	Earn respect
8 Culture	FWA Policy	70						•		•	•	•	•	•	•								•
8 Culture	Earthquake in Japan	71						•	•		•	•				•							
9 Values	Caught in the rain	74						•	•			•				•			•			•	
9 Values	Train wreck in Wisconsin	76							•			•			•	•					•		
9 Values	Sam Walton's ironing board covers	77							•						•		•						
9 Values	A dog at the Met	78			•				•						•								•
10 Collaboration	New boss from the big city	82								•	•				•								•
10 Collaboration	Jamie has depth!	83								•					•								
10 Collaboration	Cancelling your retainer	86								•	•				•								•
10 Collaboration	One night on the company plane	88								•			•		•			•		•	•		•
11 Diversity	The sharecropper's daughter	91						•		•	•	•			•								•
11 Diversity	"You don't see what I see."	94						•		•	•												
11 Diversity	"I hate the EEOC!"	95						•	•	•	•						•						
11 Diversity	The Traveler	96						•		•	•	•	•		•								
12 Policy Without Rules	Five monkeys in a cage	100						•				•											
12 Policy Without Rules	Getting "Polked"	101						•				•											
12 Policy Without Rules	Financial restatement at D&B	103						•				•				•				•		•	
12 Policy Without Rules	Unintended consequences	105						•		•		•										•	
13 Keep It Real	Lisa, the high potential shopper	108				•												•	•	•			
13 Keep It Real	Julie Walker, achiever mom	110				•										•							
13 Keep It Real	Snowstorm in the courtroom	113				•										•							
13 Keep It Real	Making payroll	114				•										•				•			•
14 Stylistic Elements	Fresh fish	124				•										•							
14 Stylistic Elements	15 minutes with the CEO	125				•																•	•
14 Stylistic Elements	Learning leader	126								•													
15 Inspire and Motivate	Finishing the race	131		•									•	•	•		•						
15 Inspire and Motivate	Pioneers and settlers	133		•	•								•	•	•		•						
15 Inspire and Motivate	Cal-Almond v. The Dept. of Agriculture	134			•								•	•	•								

(continues on next page)

Source: *Lead with a Story: A Guide to Crafting Business Narratives That Captivate, Convince, and Inspire*, by Paul Smith (AMACOM Books, 2012) Paul@leadwithstory.com

STORY MATRIX *(continued)*

Chapter	Story name	Page	ENVISION — Set a vision	ENVISION — Goals & commitment	ENVISION — Lead change	ENVISION — Recommendations	ENVISION — Customer service	ENVIRONMENT — Culture	ENVIRONMENT — Values	ENVIRONMENT — Collaboration	ENVIRONMENT — Diversity	ENVIRONMENT — Policy	ENERGIZE — Inspire & motivate	ENERGIZE — Courage	ENERGIZE — Passion for work	EDUCATE — Teach lessons	EDUCATE — Coaching & feedback	EDUCATE — Problem solving	EDUCATE — Understand the customer	EMPOWER — Delegate & give permission	EMPOWER — Creativity	EMPOWER — Sales	EMPOWER — Earn respect
15 Inspire and Motivate	There isn't always a next time	137											•	•		•							
16 Build Courage	After a lifetime of failure	140		•	•								•	•						•			
16 Build Courage	Pringles turnaround	142		•	•									•									
16 Build Courage	Giant steps	143							•					•									
16 Build Courage	What do you care what other people think?	146					•	•							•				•				
17 Passion for Work	Train ride in Budapest	148					•	•							•		•		•				
17 Passion for Work	This is my Dollar General	150		•						•					•								
17 Passion for Work	The staff meeting	152													•								
18 Emotion	Special Olympics	154					•			•					•								
18 Emotion	"I've never been to Japan"	157						•				•		•	•					•			
18 Emotion	Don't Mess with Texas	158				•			•					•								•	
18 Emotion	Teenaged mutant ninja turtle	160							•						•								
19 Surprise	First day of History class	167		•												•						•	
19 Surprise	Gary Cofer's arresting comments	169		•																			
19 Surprise	Breakfast in Mexico	173																					
20 Teach Lessons	Barry's coffee vs. Mike's kitchen	176						•			•	•				•	•		•				•
20 Teach Lessons	Oersted and the jittery compass	179								•			•			•	•		•				
20 Teach Lessons	The Three Researchers	180														•	•						
20 Teach Lessons	My million-dollar mistake	183			•											•	•						•
21 Coaching and Feedback	Becoming a "Mitch manager"	187				•						•			•		•		•	•			•
21 Coaching and Feedback	Nathan and King David	190				•							•				•						•
21 Coaching and Feedback	Courtney's big meeting	192								•							•			•			
21 Coaching and Feedback	Firing yourself	193															•						
22 Problem Solving	"What if . . ."	196				•							•										•
22 Problem Solving	Doctor with a Dictaphone	198				•								•				•					
22 Problem Solving	Ball of wool	200														•		•			•		
22 Problem Solving	Compensating behavior	201														•		•	•		•		
23 Understand the Customer	I don't want my daughter to be like me	204																•	•				

Source: *Lead with a Story: A Guide to Crafting Business Narratives That Captivate, Convince, and Inspire*, by Paul Smith (AMACOM Books, 2012) Paul@leadwithstory.com

STORY MATRIX (continued)

Chapter	Story name	Page	Earn respect	Sales	Creativity	Delegate & give permission	Understand the customer	Problem solving	Coaching & feedback	Teach lessons	Passion for work	Courage	Inspire & motivate	Policy	Diversity	Collaboration	Values	Culture	Customer service	Recommendations	Lead change	Goals & commitment	Set a vision
23 Understand the Customer	Shortening and milk	206					•				•								•	•			
23 Understand the Customer	"You promised ice cream sundaes!"	207					•			•													
24 Metaphors	"What's a euphonium?"	210								•				•					•				
24 Metaphors	Disney's cast members	211		•		•	•			•								•	•	•			
24 Metaphors	Consumer is boss	213					•					•		•				•	•				
24 Metaphors	First moment of truth	213		•								•											
25 Delegate	Orville Sweet and the empty office	217				•						•		•									
25 Delegate	The Bamboo Years	219				•																	
25 Delegate	Self-fulfilling prophecy	220				•										•							
25 Delegate	Making Olean	221				•																	
26 Creativity	Window unit air conditioners	224			•			•					•										
26 Creativity	James and the tea kettle	225			•																		
26 Creativity	Moonlighting required	226			•			•						•									
26 Creativity	Baffled for 13 years	227			•													•					
27 Sales	"If your sales binder is in the trash . . ."	230																•		•			
27 Sales	"Paying in this industry is a rip off!"	230																		•			
27 Sales	The new steel salesman	233					•																
27 Sales	The unwelcome business card	235							•	•													
28 Earn Respect	Bartending in Chicago	237	•										•										
28 Earn Respect	A. G. Lafley at Gillette	239	•										•										
28 Earn Respect	"I'm a practical guy."	240	•										•										
28 Earn Respect	"I won't stop till I have the best."	241	•													•							
29 Into the Story	New promotion policy	243							•											•	•		
29 Into the Story	Clean desk policy	245								•				•							•		
29 Into the Story	Private-label taste test	246								•				•						•	•		
29 Into the Story	Count the stars	248								•										•	•		
30 Getting Started	Tale of two e-mails	260								•										•			
30 Getting Started	"Hey, that's my story!"	264			•		•			•	•												

Source: *Lead with a Story: A Guide to Crafting Business Narratives That Captivate, Convince, and Inspire,* by Paul Smith (AMACOM Books, 2012) Paul@leadwithstory.com

Index

276